THE GENTILE ZIONISTS

By the Same Author

Baffy: The Diaries of Blanche Dugdale, 1936–47
(Vallentine, Mitchell, 1973)

The Gentile Zionists

A Study in Anglo-Zionist Diplomacy, 1929–1939

N. A. ROSE, B.Sc.(Econ.), Ph.D.

Lecturer in International Relations,
The Hebrew University, Jerusalem

FRANK CASS : LONDON

First published 1973 in Great Britain by
FRANK CASS AND COMPANY LIMITED
67 Great Russell Street, London WC1B 3BT, England

and in United States of America by
FRANK CASS AND COMPANY LIMITED
c/o International Scholarly Book Services, Inc.
P.O. Box 4347, Portland, Oregon 97208

Library of Congress Catalog Card No. 72–92977

ISBN 0 7146 2940 5

Printed in Great Britain by
The Anchor Press Ltd., Tiptree, Essex

For
My Parents

Contents

Preface   ix
Acknowledgments   xi
Abbreviations   xiii

1   The Crisis of 1929–31   1
2   A Note on the Whitechapel By-Election   37
3   The Question of Self-Government   41
4   The Seventh Dominion   71
5   Some Strategic Aspects   97
6   The Debate on Partition
    I. The Proposal   123
7   The Debate on Partition
    II. The Withdrawal   151
8   The Conference at St. James's Palace   179
9   The May White Paper   201
10   Some Conclusions   221

Bibliography   229
Index   235

Illustrations

Between pages

Baffy
The Webbs

Col. J. C. Wedgwood
Malcolm MacDonald

82–83

A. J. Balfour
Arthur Wauchope

Walter Elliot
L. S. Amery

98–99

Preface

This is an account of the political activities of Gentile Zionists. It is not an examination of the roots of Gentile Zionism, or even of the motivations of Gentile Zionists, though, naturally enough, these questions are touched upon from time to time.[1] Rather, this is a portrait of how the Zionist movement reacted to the crises that emerged with persistent regularity in its relations with the government throughout the 1930s. It will tell how the Zionists tried to overcome them; how they attempted to mobilise government, parliamentary, and public circles through their Gentile supporters in an attempt to attain solutions more amenable to the Zionist idea. It will relate how the Gentile Zionists, prompted by the Zionist leadership, sought to shift successive British governments from their established position on the Palestine question.

The 1930s were among the most dramatic years in the history of Zionist diplomacy; they began with a crisis over the Passfield white paper of 1931; and ended with an even greater crisis, the May white paper of 1939, an event which even today can hardly be discussed in dispassionate terms. The intervening years saw the first mass Jewish immigration to Palestine; the first armed Arab revolt against the British administration and Zionist aims; and the first whisper, however faint and ambiguous it then sounded, of a Jewish state.

But this volume is not a formal history of Anglo-Zionist relations. Broadly speaking, that particular story is well known. The milestones are familiar: the white papers, the memoranda, the periodic crises. Rather, this study seeks to examine Anglo-Zionist relations not only on the official level but also, perhaps mainly, on the more personal plane. Owing to the specific character of this work, it has been necessary to rely heavily upon the personal correspondence of

[1] The interested reader may be referred to an early essay by C. Sykes, *Two Studies in Virtue* (London, 1953); and to more recent work being done on this subject by Professor M. Verité, 'The Idea of the Restoration of the Jews in English Protestant Thought, 1790–1840', *Zion*, No. 3-4 (Jerusalem 1968).

Dr. Chaim Weizmann, who, during the period under consideration, constituted the main link between the Zionist movement and the British government.

Inevitably other problems intrude. At the time Great Britain was struggling to maintain a precarious world position. Beset by many problems, the Palestine issue had to be reconciled to the wider spectrum of British political, military and strategic considerations. This is particularly evident for the period 1935–9 when it becomes impossible to isolate the Palestine question from general problems on British policy in the Near East. These aspects too are the subject for some discussion.

The Hebrew University   N. A. ROSE
Jerusalem, 1973

Acknowledgments

I would like to express my gratitude to all those too numerous to mention by name who facilitated my research and aided me in the preparation of this study.

Particularly to the officers of the Central Research Fund of the University of London and the Memorial Foundation for Jewish Culture, New York. Their generosity enabled me to collect source material both in Israel and England and made certain the completion of this volume.

I am also grateful to the directors and staff of the Public Record Office, London; the Central Zionist Archives, Jerusalem; the Israel State Archives, Jerusalem; the Weizmann Archives, Rechovoth; the British Library of Political and Economic Science at the London School of Economics; and the Press Cuttings Library at Chatham House. Their patience and assistance ensured for me the most favourable conditions for the writing of this book.

I would also like to express my thanks to the editors of *Middle Eastern Studies; The Historical Journal,* Cambridge; *The Journal of Modern History;* and *The Wiener Library Bulletin,* for permission to use material which first appeared in their journals. Since then I have added and changed much, but it remains substantially the same.

Finally, I am especially indebted to Mr. D. C. Watt of the London School of Economics. From the moment I began this study, his advice and encouragement were placed at my disposal. His critical eye and intimate knowledge of the period saved me many faulty judgments and added greatly to whatever of value may be found in this volume.

Acknowledgments are due to the Radio Times Hulton Picture Library for the photographs of the Webbs, Wedgwood, MacDonald, Balfour, Wauchope, Elliot and Amery.

Abbreviations

W.A.	Weizmann Archives, Rechovoth
W.D.	Weizmann's Diaries, Rechovoth
D.D.	Dugdale Diaries, Rechovoth
C.Z.A.	Central Zionist Archives, Jerusalem
P.R.O.	Public Record Office, London. All Premier, F.[oreign] O.[ffice], C.[olonial] O.[ffice], CAB.23. [cabinet minutes], and CAB.24. [cabinet papers] files are located at the P.R.O.
P.D.	Parliamentary Debates. *Hansard*, 5th series, Commons and Lords
P.P.	Passfield Papers, The London School of Economics
G.D.	Documents on German Foreign Policy, 1919–1945, Series D, v
B.D.	Documents on British Foreign Policy, 1919–1939
F.R.U.S.	Foreign Relations of the United States

1

The Crisis of 1929-31

From 23 until 29 August 1929 serious communal disorders erupted throughout Palestine. In all, some 472 Jews and 268 Arabs were either killed or wounded.[1] These events came as a climax to eleven months of mounting communal tension.[2] But the ferocity and general nature of the outbreak came as a rude shock to the Zionists. Dr. Chaim Weizmann, the Zionist leader, received the first news of the riots on the morning of 25 August while on holiday in Switzerland. He was, as he recalls, "struck as by a thunderbolt".[3]

He did not wait upon events. The same day he contacted London, pressing the government for speedy action.[4] By 28 August he had already conferred with Lord Passfield, the colonial secretary.[5] Passfield proved most responsive to Weizmann's admonitions, assuring him that the *Yishuv* (the Jewish community resident in Palestine) would not be disarmed and that an instruction had already been sent to Jerusalem to that effect. In fact, on the previous day forty-one Jewish constables had been disarmed in Jerusalem, a pertinent reminder that communications between Palestine and the government were not as efficient as might be imagined.

Passfield also concurred in Weizmann's strongly worded complaints about the behaviour of the Palestine administration, and even agreed to suspend two senior officials, Mr. Luke and Mr. Cust,[6] on the grounds of incompetence. Weizmann emphasised the need for "a complete restatement of policy . . . The Jewish people must know how the government will react!"[7] Passfield promised to be in constant communication and invited Weizmann to approach him directly whenever he felt so inclined.

Two days later Passfield's initial sympathy had evaporated. In a letter to Weizmann he expressed agreement only on the need to settle the Wailing Wall question, for the rest there was merely prevarication or total disagreement.[8] This was particularly evident over the central issues of a favourable government statement which

Passfield described as "premature", and an increase in the immigration quota.

Was this change due to the influence of his officials who had meanwhile reinforced his feelings of *esprit de corps*? It seems more than likely. The Palestine administration had come under extremely heavy fire and this was bound to reflect upon the efficiency and good name of the colonial office. Passfield's letter was clearly his attempt to defend his officials' reputation; but his swiftly changing opinions did not augur well for the future.

Meanwhile, the Gentile Zionists had also been active. Colonel J. C. Wedgwood[9] suggested that a parliamentary commission be sent to Palestine to investigate the working of the mandate; he volunteered his services as "something must be done to put the matter right".[10] Colonel R. Meinertzhagen[11] wrote to his uncle, Lord Passfield, castigating the Palestine administration and pleading for a full and impartial enquiry into their responsibility [*sic*] for the riots. The most eminent Gentile Zionist of the day, Lord Balfour, although bedridden, was "waiting for the signal when he can be of some use".[12] Blanche Dugdale[13] forwarded Balfour's message of support to the Zionists : "[the National Home] is in harmony with the best opinion of Western civilisation . . . to its fulfillment is promised the support of the British Empire. That pledge has been given. Depend upon it, it is not going to be withdrawn."[14]

It was generally acknowledged that a commission of enquiry would be sent to Palestine. The question of its composition and its terms of reference now became crucial. The Zionists wished for an investigation unlimited in scope and conducted by persons who commanded world-wide respect. And they did not want the mandate *per se* to be investigated, only the manner in which it had been administered.[15]

Such a position had an inherent weakness in that the appointment of an eminent body might mislead public opinion into believing that the government was considering radical changes in the mandate. The government, fully alive to this danger,[16] issued a communiqué to the effect that a commission under the chairmanship of Sir Walter Shaw, a former chief justice of the Straits Settlement, had been appointed to investigate the immediate causes of the outbreak, not questions of major policy.[17] Thus, initially, the Zionists failed to attain the kind of commission they wanted to investigate the issues they considered most important.

Whether the Shaw commission exceeded its terms of reference or not aroused great controversy. The Zionists later complained that this had occurred. However, this was no simple matter of black or white. From the outset the commission had been placed in a false position by its limiting terms of reference. Where do immediate causes end and fundamental ones begin? It is possible to investigate the former without considering the latter and still produce a balanced report? Equally, and this was the Zionists' main complaint, to allow the investigation of the mandate by unqualified and inexperienced persons would be clearly irresponsible. This dilemma, played up by the Zionists, went undetected by the government.[18] Consequently, the Zionists entered this crucial period with profound suspicions of government intentions and, as events unfolded, these suspicions grew in intensity.

The prime minister's assurances of the government's good intentions did little to allay Weizmann's fears.[19] On the contrary, he was more concerned than ever before, hinting at resignation unless definite proof were given that the mandate would be enacted in the letter and spirit of its conception. The notion that the commission was intended as "a whitewashing affair" haunted him, and he promised his friends that this would never happen.[20]

For this reason Weizmann wanted the commission to hear counsel and permit the calling of witnesses.[21] This issue assumed such significance that Balfour tentatively suggested that Weizmann bypass the government and appeal directly to a League commission of enquiry. This might "have the advantage of frightening the C.O. . . . and be looked on with favour by a large body of public opinion".[22] No such action was taken.

Weizmann was due to leave for the Continent on 27 September; he had been ordered by his doctors to rest for a week or two and was bound for the Italian resort of Meran.[23] Before his departure he formulated certain demands for the benefit of Passfield and MacDonald. These included the implementation of the mandate; a liberal immigration policy—a figure of 15,000–20,000 a year was mentioned; a progressive economic policy with regard to land settlement, public works, and taxation; and adequate security measures, including fuller Jewish participation in the police and frontier defence forces. Weizmann dealt also with the Arab problem, asking the government to convene a round table conference, but only after the Arabs had been informed that the Jewish position in Palestine was inviolable. The prime minister listened attentively and agreed to forward a minute incorporating these proposals to the colonial office.[24] The interview with Passfield followed the same lines. Weizmann taking the initiative, Passfield expressing sympathy but hinting that he might have to square his conscience with the opinion of the cabinet.[25]

Weizmann's return to England coincided with the arrival of another staunch Gentile Zionist, J. C. Smuts.[26] They met on 25 November.[27] Later, Weizmann summarised the discussion.[28] He gave vent to his growing feeling of apprehension.

> We feel an atmosphere of hostility . . . at present it seems practice to explain away our rights and whittle down our claims on immigration, security or compensation . . . it would be a terrible blow to us if Great Britain gave up the Mandate, but both as a British subject and a Zionist, I would prefer her to give it up than she should continue the methods of the past ten years.

These words were written by a dedicated Anglophile, a man who had spent his political life in furthering Anglo-Zionist relations. Clearly Weizmann intended exploiting the present crisis to effect a radical change in the government's attitude towards the National Home; and the intensity of his feelings had their effect upon Smuts.

Smuts spent the weekend of 29 November in the company of Passfield and A. Henderson, the foreign secretary.[29] As one of those statesmen responsible for the Balfour declaration, he explained to his companions its meaning. It was not merely a platonic declaration but implied active assistance to facilitate the development of the National Home. There were two essential requirements : adequate security and increased immigration. Later, Smuts told Weizmann that Passfield is "a rather tired man . . . he thinks the Jews are well represented . . . [Passfield said] 'they have their Weizmanns and Melchetts and Readings . . . Weizmann is rather formidable and the Arabs are not represented, they are nowhere'."[30] Smuts believed that Passfield saw it as his duty to protect the Arabs. But he was warned not to tamper with history; no Empire could afford to be unjust to the Jews, Smuts claimed, invoking the terrible example of Russia.

The discussion then turned on the question of the Palestine administration. Smuts admitted that he had received an invitation from Amery[31] requesting him to take the post of high commissioner, but, owing to his many other commitments, he had refused. As they parted company, he told Weizmann, "I shall always be your friend and help you, because I am honour bound to help and I believe in it."[32]

Weizmann attached a great deal of importance to gaining the active support of Smuts and repeatedly turned to him in times of crisis. Whether the South African possessed any real influence over a British cabinet is highly questionable. There was, however, a certain mystique attached to his name. He was regarded as a world statesman and not as a party hack. It was assumed that he had the best interests of the Empire at heart and would not lend his name to any scheme detrimental to British imperial policy. Widely esteemed by the general public, respected by most politicians, Smuts could always be relied upon to drop the right words in the right ears at the right time.

In parliament there was no great flurry of activity on behalf of the Zionists. Ormsby Gore[33] explained why : "Questions," he contended, "merely provoke counter-questions by those who are hard at work against us."[34] But the parliamentary scene was not quite barren. On 12 November a parliamentary pro-Palestine group was formed.[35] An executive was elected with Wedgwood as chairman, Dr. Spero as secretary, and Amery, Sir H. Samuel,[36] Sir H. Hamilton, Sir M. Conway and James de Rothschild as serving members. The prime purpose of the group was to act as a watch-dog for Zionist interests; and in the delicate political balance of forces that had emerged since the formation of a minority (some would say captive) Labour government in May 1929 this factor took on an added significance.

Meanwhile reports from Palestine indicated that the commission was overstepping its terms of reference; it was touching on questions of high policy : land settlement and immigration. It was neither equipped nor instructed to deal with such matters. Weizmann was positive that its conclusions would be both superficial and harmful. The remedy appeared to lie in jerking the government out of its present mood of complacency with a sharp reminder of its previous promises. How to achieve this?

On the evening of 17 December Weizmann met a number of his friends at the House.[37] Elliot[38] reminded the company that in less than a week the House would rise and when they next met the commission's draft report would be in the hands of the government and nothing could then be changed. The agreed they must prevent the commission from further transgressing its terms of reference. The concept of a new commission to deal with major policy questions was approved, and it was suggested that a letter to *The Times* signed by Balfour, Lloyd George, and Smuts to that effect would create the greatest attention. A deadline was set for 20 December.

John Buchan was delegated to draft the letter. On the 18th Weizmann approved the draft, and Lloyd George gave his consent. On the 19th Weizmann motored down to Fisher's Hill, Woking, and obtained Balfour's signature. The same day Smuts telegraphed his approval. On the 20th *The Times* published the letter.[39] By any reckoning this was a remarkable exercise in public relations. It was a vivid demonstration of the scope of Zionism's contacts, and the ability of the movement to conscript the most powerful support on its behalf during periods of government hesitation.

Prior to the publication of the letter it had been shown to the prime minister.[40] MacDonald reiterated that the commission must not report on major policy issues, but expressed doubt in the usefulness of appointing another commission. Elliot remarked that "Ramsay is at present averse to a [new] commission on the ground that it might report against the mandate as well as for it".[41]

But the letter did force the government's hand. MacDonald reminded the House that major issues are "clearly outside the terms of reference of the Shaw commission and cannot be made a part of its report".[42] Elliot was also satisfied with the effect the letter had had and drew some general conclusions for the coming year : "It is practically impossible that 1930 will pass without a general election . . . the Palestine situation, therefore, will be reviewed not by the Labour party, but by the three parties."[43] This idea was well in line with Weizmann's own conception that Zionism should rise above the narrow confines of party politics and be subject to a general consensus of political opinion.

Events had turned in a favourable direction. Weizmann contended that relations with the government had never been better : ". . . for a time the relationship was strained, but the British are sportsmen; they know how to accept defeat if necessary . . . the whole spirit is somewhat changed".[44] His one fear was that the natural tendency for every commission to inflate its own importance might prevail and hence it might not follow the prime minister's lead.[45]

The Shaw Commission was due to report in March. By this time Weizmann's feelings, no doubt reinforced by information from Palestine, had turned almost a full circle. Dr. Drummond Shiels, under-secretary of state for colonies, was warned that the Zionists would launch a determined attack against the report if it dealt with major policy questions.[46] By 15 March the "situation had become critical",[47] and Weizmann invited some of his parliamentary friends to lunch in order to discuss the changed situation. In consequence it was decided to seek a renewal of the prime minister's assurance of 23 December.[48] This was duly organised, and MacDonald reaffirmed his previous statement.[49]

Two days later, on 26 March, the report was received by the Zionists. It confirmed all of their worst expectations.[50] By way of quietening the impending storm the Zionists were invited to lunch with the prime minister and Passfield at the House.[51] The prime minister admitted that the report was "very bad, it will depress the Jews and elate the Arabs; it contains a great many *obiter dicta* for which there is no evidence . . . The effect of it will be very bad on the public in general." He continued about the difficulties in finding suitable officials for Palestine. "It needs big men . . . and the ordinary civil servant's mind is . . . *borné.*" He foresaw two alternatives : either to send out another commission with all the disadvantages that would follow; or, to send out "one big man who carried great weight in international circles, who would . . . wash out this report. Imagine my position. Here is a report and I have got to say it all means nothing." MacDonald undertook to persuade Smuts to take on this task. "He would only have to go to Palestine for a month, to look over the situation."[52]

Weizmann remained unimpressed with these frank admissions. No longer could he go on defending the administration with tongue in cheek. Once again he hinted at resignation. Then the government could deal with the mandate without his aid. He was particularly incensed over the report's allegations on land settlement :

> . . . it's a fight between a Jew and a goat. If you want to graze goats in places where you can have flourishing orange plantations, then there is not room in Palestine, but if you want to have progressive development of the country it requires no investigation . . ., only a certain amount of good will; no experts either. There is at least room for 50,000 families, to say nothing of industrial and urban development.

He lambasted the administration :

> . . . the administration didn't want the National Home to succeed, and we know that if the administration doesn't want a pogrom, that pogrom doesn't happen . . . I am going to say the

fundamental thesis of the report is false . . . I shall attack the administration; I shall appeal to the Jews to remain loyal. We believe in Palestine and justice.

MacDonald attempted to excuse away the present misunderstanding by the government's preoccupation with other problems.[53] Weizmann understood. But he reminded MacDonald that he was dealing with "an eternal problem" which no nation could afford to ignore with impunity.

Despite MacDonald's personal sympathy,[54] Weizmann remained extremely wary of actual government intentions. He was wavering between an all-out attack upon the government which would inevitably disrupt Anglo-Zionist relations; or limiting himself for the present to diplomatic niceties. After much consideration he opted for the latter.[55] Thus his initial reaction to the report would be confined to a brief press comment in the form of a letter to *The Times*.[56]

By the beginning of April the Zionist position was fairly satisfactory in spite of the adverse nature of the Shaw report. The leaders of all parties were agreed that the report was unsatisfactory and embarrassingly anti-Zionist. The cabinet had accepted that a more authoritative examination of land settlement, immigration and development was required, "and to such an extent as might be deemed desirable, on the political questions in the background!"[57] Smuts—a committed Zionist—had been earmarked to conduct the investigation. If he was unable to go, a real statesman "with Palestine in his bones"[58] would replace him. Weizmann had also made his case before the political parties. On 7 April he addressed the Conservative 1922 committee and on the 9th the Labour advisory committee.[59] Both bodies received his statements favourably.

The first setback occurred on 11 April. Passfield informed Weizmann that Smuts had been discarded because of his pro-Zionist views.[60] The assumption follows that opinions in the colonial office and at the prime minister's side were seeking to re-establish a more balanced view between the conflicting sides. About this there was very little the Zionists could do. Sir J. Hope Simpson,[61] the new commissioner, was presented to them as a *fait accompli*. His background did not augur well for an investigation that would "wash out" the Shaw report. MacDonald's previous pledges faded into the distance. Weizmann, feeling that the most he could achieve at the moment was to gain Hope Simpson's acquaintance, requested that he be given the opportunity of meeting him before he set out for Palestine. Passfield agreed, and on this note they terminated their interview.[62]

On 2 May *The Times* announced that Hope Simpson was leaving for Palestine early the following week. No meeting had yet been arranged with Weizmann. As the matter seemed urgent, Lewis Namier[63] cabled Weizmann informing him of the situation. Weizmann hurried back to London [he had been on holiday at Meran], telegraphing from Paris that he was prepared to see Hope Simpson any time on 6 May.[64] Meanwhile, Namier had been informed by Passfield's secretary that Hope Simpson was leaving on the morning of the 6th, and that he had already taken leave of Passfield who had given no undertaking to arrange any interview.[65] In fact, Hope Simpson did not leave London until the night of the 7th and then he left for Geneva, not Palestine. As Weizmann was already on the Continent, a meeting could easily have been arranged.

It is not clear why Passfield broke his word. The logical explanation is that he was anxious to scotch the rumours put about by the Palestine Arab delegation, then in London for conversations with the government, and their friends that the government was in the back pocket of the Zionists. Perhaps Passfield was over-eager to emphasise Great Britain's role as an independent umpire in the dispute. At any rate, the incident had unfortunate consequences.

Weizmann was very indignant over this clear breach of a previous agreement. There were additional causes for annoyance. The permanent mandates commission was due to meet in Geneva on 3 June. The government was to be represented by Dr. Drummond Shiels and two officials, Mr. Luke, and a Mr. Lloyd, who had acted as secretary to the Shaw commission. These last appointments were interpreted by Weizmann as a "studied insult",[66] particularly in view of MacDonald's opinion of the report and his plain intimation to promote Luke out of Palestinian affairs.[67] Furthermore, their presence at Geneva indicated to Weizmann that the government intended to endorse, not shelve, the report.[68]

Government negotiations with the Arabs were another cause for concern. Namier was convinced that the Arabs were making headway and that the government was deliberately holding back relevant information from the Zionists.[69] When Namier wrote this there may have been some cause for concern. But by 14 May the communiqué had already been published proclaiming a deadlock in the talks, and the Arabs left England under the impression that their "case will not be justly solved by the British government with whom the Jews have such great influence".[70] Hence there was little reason for Weizmann to labour the point when he wrote to Warburg on the 15th.[71] No doubt there was a cumulative effect in all these events. Weizmann felt badly treated. Passfield's broken promise weighed heavily upon him; he was not used to such treatment from ministers of the crown.

In these circumstances Weizmann felt that the situation had become untenable and that decisive action was required. He told his friends that the present policy of drift was bringing Zionist affairs to obvious ruin. If the government continued to ignore Zionist interests, he would break with the government, summon a congress of the Jewish Agency, and resign. His friends counselled caution. They agreed that the colonial office officials, acting in collusion with the Palestine administration, were unravelling the work of the politicians. Weizmann accepted this explanation, describing the effect as "devastating . . . literally hitting our heads against a blank wall. The officials seem to be utterly impervious to reason and certainly haven't a spark of sympathy."[72]

It was decided that Weizmann should interview the leaders of the opposition. Sir Archibald Sinclair arranged a meeting with Lloyd George while Buchan promised to press the Zionist case with Baldwin the coming weekend. They also wished to put the Zionist case before parliament. But in fact no full-scale debate took place until after the publication of the Passfield white paper in October 1930. A hint was given that the government considered a debate undesirable because of the Indian Moslems and the influence they might exert on the debate. The Zionists were inclined to belittle this factor on the grounds that either it was bluff, and if so it should be called; or, if there was any substance in the argument, it was just as well to face the problem now.[73] Nevertheless, they judiciously avoided pressing the issue. And it was just as well, for there is little doubt that in the uncertain atmosphere then prevailing in Indian affairs the government might easily have succumbed to Indian Moslem opinion, and the Zionists, by unnecessarily forcing the pace, would have worsened, not bettered, their position.

The government, keen to reassure the Zionists, arranged a meeting for 12 May.[74] The meeting served little purpose except to allow Weizmann another opportunity to let off steam. He unleashed his broadside against the Luke–Lloyd affair, the Hope Simpson affair, the Palestine administration, and the general indifference of the

government. MacDonald voiced particular concern over the effects
of the government's policy in America : ". . . that the Jews there are
becoming very bitter and because of Palestine are trying to hurt
British interests in general". Weizmann replied : "Palestine influences Jewish public opinion . . . [and] that American Jews are
. . . very critical, but they trust the word of a British prime minister,
and are anxious to see these words confirmed by deeds."[75]

However, there was no respite in the assault launched against
the Zionist position. On 15 May the high commissioner, Sir J.
Chancellor, suspended 2,350 immigration certificates pending Hope
Simpson's investigation.[76] This seems an extraordinary act of folly in
view of the round of meetings and assurances that had recently
taken place. Immigration was fundamental to the Zionist case, and
Chancellor's last step seemed deliberately to flout the principle of
economic absorptive capacity, hitherto the guiding line in immigration policy.[77] It must have confirmed Weizmann's impressions of
a conspiracy between the permanent officials and the Palestine
administration. The evidence for this thesis may only be circum-
stantial. But what clearly merges is the lack of effective communication between the cabinet and its subsidiary bodies almost
amounting to dereliction of duty.[78] Passfield, in particular, was
thought not to be in sufficient control of his officials.[79]

Throughout this period Weizmann strengthened his contacts with
Ramsay MacDonald's son, Malcolm,[80] who was now acting as a
liaison between his father and Weizmann. Weizmann wrote that
he could hold back no longer. The pressures were such that he felt
compelled to issue a communiqué convening Congress and laying
his resignation before it. The situation was "grotesque" and
"intolerable" in that the fate of the National Home, the fruit of
some fifty years' labour, now depended upon the report of one
man.[81] MacDonald replied the same day :

> When the interregnum [i.e. the period until the publication of
> the Hope Simpson report] is over they intend to act in every way
> to carry out the mandate . . . I can assure you most sincerely that
> my father and the rest of us who are your friends appreciate the
> difficulties of your position fully. But the government also has a
> delicate task . . . let us keep the spirit of co-operation alive at any
> rate until hopes of co-operation are more dashed than they are
> today.[82]

This assurance had its effect. Two days later Weizmann replied :

. . . in deference to your father's wishes, and out of respect for you and in deep appreciation of your genuine efforts to help in this critical time, I have decided firstly to modify my communiqué and not to mention my resignation in it. Secondly to postpone its publication until I have had a further opportunity of seeing you . . . we shall wait patiently and try to do our best in the interregnum.

On Anglo-Zionist relations he was more specific.

If there were any real co-operation between the government and ourselves, difficulties such as the present would not arise; or if they did arise, could be put right before they got out of hand. In the past I have often defended acts of the British government before my own people, or have had to face many a storm for things which I could hardly have been expected to assume responsibility. I did so for the sake of policy and co-operation. But the spirit of co-operation of which you speak so well . . . does not exist in the Colonial Office at present. They not only place us before *faits accomplis,* but they do so, if you will allow me to say so, to your own father . . . the whole situation need not have arisen had this co-operation been sincerely and truly adhered to.[83]

On May 28 the government published a statement of policy explaining that specific proposals on land settlement, immigration and development would await the Hope Simpson report.[84] But temporary measures were already under consideration. Suspension of immigration, already in effect, and land legislation "to prevent the dispossession of the indigenous agricultural population".[85] *The Times* warned against encouraging Arab extremism, and continued that Jewish alarm should not be disregarded, for the closing of Palestine to immigration would have widespread political and financial consequences, with the British taxpayer bearing the brunt of the burden.[86] For the Zionists the position was less involved; the government had endorsed the Shaw report.[87]

By now protests from world Jewry against the government's policy, particularly the suspension of immigration, were taking effect. This concerted attack had undesired, although perhaps foreseeable, results. Instead of persuading members of the government, it alienated them. Even the prime minister was affected :

I do not want to lose my patience with the Zionists but they try it greatly. They have gone very near to destroying any influence they have by their policy. They know perfectly well what we are trying to do in the face of great difficulty much of which they have created . . . friend after friend is being alienated, and I have had reports from Geneva which are anything but encouraging regarding their conduct there . . .[88]

It was not only the official Zionist leadership that made its voice heard. Far more strident, and less diplomatic, sounds were uttered by the opposition groups, particularly the right-wing Revisionists. Shiels, when he saw Weizmann, waxed indignant over their activities "[which] are impressing the members of parliament by pointing out all the iniquities of the government".[89]

This points to a standing deficiency in Zionist diplomacy. And, paradoxically, it stemmed from the democratic nature of the movement. For behind Weizmann, a diplomat in the British mould, stood the Zionist opposition, unversed in British diplomatic tradition and more adept at scoring ideological debating points than at patient negotiation. The shrillness of their protests must have grated sharply on British nerves and often appeared more than hysterical.

Weizmann's repeated threats of resignation throw some light on the pressure under which he was working, the same pressures, in fact, of which the prime minister also complained. The essential difference being that Weizmann realised that the protests, however shrill or hysterical, had their basis in a genuine grievance which could not be wished away with words but only rectified by concrete action.

. . . one word about the protests. I think they are the spontaneous expression of the indignation of the Jewish people. Whether it's politically expedient or not, I am not going to discuss, but you could no more stop them than you could stop Niagara . . . I verily believe we are rendering a service to the honour and prestige of Great Britain by warning them that even an Empire of its magnitude cannot afford either to break or even whittle down an obligation which was solemnly given.[90]

Zionist activity now turned on reversing the suspension on immigration and delaying the proposed land legislation. Again Malcolm MacDonald proved invaluable. He promised Namier he would spare no effort to reverse the government's decision.[91] Within a few days the situation had improved.[92] By 19 June Weizmann received definite, although unofficial, information from M. MacDonald that the land proposals had been deferred, a fact he reported to a meeting of his executive the same day.[93]

Weizmann's personal contact with Passfield had, in effect, ended with the Hope Simpson incident. On 4 July Passfield broke the deadlock and invited Weizmann to a meeting.[94] When they met he proved most accommodating. There was no intention "to hamper Jewish immigration or to restrict land purchases", or of "encouraging any policy which was inimical to agricultural . . . development". Quite the contrary, the government wished to encourage these aspects of the National Home. But they had "to make an authoritative reply" to Arab assertions, hence the Hope Simpson investigation.

Weizmann replied that,

> The Government ought to be clear on the point that we were not interested in building up a country for the Arabs, and to play a role similar to that, say, played by the Germans in Czechoslovakia . . . our conception of the Jewish National Home was that of a great Jewish settlement. To that end we should seek to pack as many Jews into Palestine as was at all possible.[95]

Passfield did not wish to "discuss figures", but promised that he would see about releasing the suspended immigration certificates. In fact the certificates were not released until early November, and then only 1,500 and in entirely different circumstances.

With Passfield apparently once more sympathetic the Zionists wished to press their advantage in parliament. However, they recognised the necessity of differentiating between immediate problems and those connected with major policy questions. Weizmann was distinctly perturbed that the debate would develop into an inter-party squabble. It was this fear that strengthened his belief in a big debate based on great principles rather than on raising administrative problems, however important. Moreover, he was anxious to achieve real progress before the House rose for the summer recess. To continue in the present state of tension and uncertainty would, he believed, be disastrous. He suggested coming to an initial arrangement based on the so-called Rutenberg proposals.[96]

Rutenberg had raised these suggestions during the meeting with the prime minister on 12 May, and in fact they constituted a ten-point scheme for a comprehensive settlement of the Palestine question. Among the more important points were : constitutional measures involving the election of separate, communal Jewish and Arab councils to function under government guidance; a joint advisory committee to the Palestine administration based on political parity between the two communities; government grants for development schemes; the preservation of the rights and functions of the Jewish Agency as stipulated under the mandate; a development project for TransJordan, provided that country undertakes to absorb Arabs whose lands have been acquired by Jews; and the reorganisation of the Palestine administration in order to make it more responsive to the ideals of the Jewish National Home—this would have meant the replacement of the chief secretary and the chief of police ![97]

None of these plans materialised. The government was not prepared to take any initiative; and the opposition decided against a full-scale debate on the grounds that as Hope Simpson and the mandates commission had not yet reported, the essential material for a constructive debate was lacking. In this situation, argued Amery, the government would give evasive, non-committal replies and an ineffective debate would result, satisfying no one.[98] Everything now seemed to depend upon the report of Hope Simpson. This was obviously not to Weizmann's pleasure. "Hope Simpson could not do justice to the Jewish cause however honourable and just he might be . . . he has not the background of the political and historical values inherent in the whole business."[99]

Hope Simpson would not have disappointed Weizmann. He was seriously perturbed at the way the Jews were buying up land, dispossessing Arab cultivators and pursuing a policy of economic exclusiveness.[100]

His report was submitted towards the end of August. By 10 September a draft statement had been ratified by a cabinet committee, though not before considerable amendments designed to severely limit Jewish land purchases and immigration had been incorporated.[101] At a further meeting Snowden, chancellor of the exchequer, agreed to recommend a guaranteed loan of two to two and a half million pounds for agricultural and other developments.[102] On 24 September Passfield noted : "The whole Palestine proposals were approved today; and I am to have the troublesome task of importing them confidentially to Lord Reading . . . and to

Dr. Weizmann . . . Whether we can anyhow avoid a shriek of anguish from all Jewry I don't know."[103]

Lord Reading was informed of the contents of the report and the government statement on 25 September, and came away very disquietened at what he had learned.[104] On 1 October Weizmann met Passfield at the latter's request. Passfield conveyed to his listeners—Namier was also present—the main lines of the intended statement. He also disclosed some of Hope Simpson's findings upon which the government had based its policy. Weizmann refused to commit himself until he had seen and examined the papers in detail. Namier was more forthright.

> . . . the general character of the discussion showed a certain *empressement* on the part of Lord Passfield as if to soften things and put a sugar coating on the very bitter pill. Our attitude was one of extreme restraint . . .[105]

Passfield interpreted the Zionists' attitude as "very reasonable and amicable".[106]

It has since been argued that the government statement passed through the cabinet without adequate discussion. (See H. Laski, *Reflections on the Constitution*, Manchester 1951, pp. 122–3.) However, it is perfectly clear that the main recommendations were known and approved of by leading members of the cabinet in committee. No objections, it seems, were voiced there. Moreover, the Palestine proposals came before two meetings of the full cabinet, on 19 and 24 September. If there was no adequate discussion of the statement then it could only have been because the cabinet was satisfied with the proposals, not because the opportunity for discussion was lacking.[107]

On 13 October Weizmann notified Passfield of Zionist objections and emphasised that he would be left with no option but to resign if the statement were issued.[108] This veiled ultimatum resulted in yet another interview to find some way out of the *impasse*. Namier wrote : "This will be the crucial interview; I am afraid if nothing comes of it, it will have to be Weizmann's 'farewell visit'."[109] The visit solved nothing. The impression the Zionists brought away was, "that Lord Passfield tried to say everything he could to prevent any kind of unpleasantness or difficulties and was playing for time".[110]

On Friday, 17 October, at 5 p.m., the government statement and the Hope Simpson report were delivered to the Zionists. The contents of the documents surpassed their worst expectations,[111] and it is abundantly clear that in general they were damaging, often extremely so, to the Zionist case. In particular the Passfield white paper was considered to be formulated in a manner calculated to cause offence. That, at any rate, is how the Jews reacted. And Beatrice Webb, who could by no standard be considered sympathetic towards Zionism and often revealed glimpses of undisguised hostility, confirmed this when she recorded that "The statement . . . is a badly drafted, a tactless document."[112]

There were some last-minute attempts to persuade the government to reconsider its decision and postpone publication of the white paper (it was due to be released on 21 October). They all proved equally unrewarding.[113]

On the evening of 20 October Weizmann called a press conference and announced, before an audience of some sixty to seventy journalists, his resignation from office as president of the Jewish Agency and of the Zionist Organisation. He explained that the government had showed a complete misunderstanding of the whole purpose and meaning of the National Home. In taking this step he would save the Zionist movement from complete demoralisation.[114] Weizmann's resignation was followed immediately by that of Lord Melchett, joint chairman of the Council of the Jewish Agency, and F. Warburg, chairman of the administrative committee of the Agency. At one blow the whole framework of Anglo-Zionist relations had been shattered.

The "Jewish hurricane" of which the Webbs spoke[115] now blew at gale force. Anti-British demonstrations occurred throughout the Jewish world, in London, Warsaw, New York, South Africa and Palestine. In New York plans to bring economic and political pressure to bear on the government were reported to be under discussion.[116] MacDonald must have been extremely sensitive to any such rumours.

Kenworthy[117] wrote : "Please assure your friends that they have many friends and sympathisers in this crisis amongst non-Jewish M.P.'s and that, speaking for myself, and I have no doubt for my friends, we shall do all we can to repair this blunder by the C.O."[118] Mrs. Dugdale canvassed the support of the Conservative leadership. She drafted a letter, attained the signatures of Amery, Baldwin, and Sir Austin Chamberlain, and had *The Times* publish it on 23 October.[119] The letter contended that the new policy was of so "definitely negative a character that it appears to conflict with the intention of the mandate, and the whole spirit of the Balfour declaration and of statements made by successive governments". Churchill associated himself with this protest.[120] Two legal experts, Lord Hailsham and Sir J. Simon, questioned the validity of the white paper, and suggested obtaining "from The Hague Court an advisory opinion on the questions involved . . . the British Government should not enforce those paragraphs which are challenged unless and until the Court has pronounced in their favour".[121]

Weizmann was anxious to get similar action from the Liberals. He saw Lloyd George on the morning of the 23rd, only to discover that Smuts had already cabled him to take action.[122] Speaking at Cowbridge, Glamorganshire, Lloyd George squared Liberal support with that of the Conservatives. He claimed the white paper was a breach of national faith, a revocation of a solemn pledge; that British honour was tarnished and we were now held up before the world as Perfidious Albion. He warned the government that the majority of the British people were not "scuttlers" whether in India or Palestine.[123]

Sections of the Labour party also revolted publicly against the white paper. Kenworthy recorded that the Labour party, no less than the two other parties, was committed to fulfilment of the Balfour declaration. He reminded the Labour leaders of the resolution in favour of the National Home which was passed, without dissent, at the last annual conference, and recalled no parallel case of the flouting of party and parliamentary opinion.[124] In the evening of 27 October Major Marcus, M.P., was invited to Downing Street to put Jewish objections to the white paper before MacDonald and Passfield. He informed the ministers that many Labour members saw little alternative but to go into the opposition lobby when the House divided on the new policy.[125]

This violent reaction to the white paper showed no signs of abatement. The Palestine question, hitherto relatively free from inter-party strife, had now become the centre of a political storm. There is little doubt that the opposition's militancy did not spring from purely altruistic motives but was also generated by a desire to belabour a minority government and make political capital out of the government's inadequate handling of the crisis. This was in the interests neither of the Zionists, who wanted the Palestine issue to remain above party loyalties, nor the government, who wished to avoid unnecessary complications and continue with the tradition of a national policy towards Palestine. Hence the conditions existed for compromise. But of the two sides the Zionists were unquestionably in the stronger position. The white paper had been roundly condemned. Sections of the Labour party and the opposition were up in arms, and the Jewish world was in uproar. It was obvious that the government would have to act to calm the storm.

Passfield commented : ". . . the Jewish hurricane continues to trouble us, though some people—e.g. Bennet, p.m. of Canada—expresses approval of our statement. I have offered to meet the Labour M.P.'s who are disgruntled. J. R. [MacDonald] is very vexed, but not unpleasant."[126] At the meeting, which was convened for the 28th, Passfield informed the "disgruntled" members that "there is no question whatsoever on the part of the government to diverge from the policy carried out by successive governments . . . the agitation which has been created must be due entirely to misconception".[127]

The prime minister expanded in characteristic fashion :

> I am more convinced than ever that the substance of our difficulties are of the most minor character . . . [the] great bulk of divisions between us are words, interpretations upon words, assumptions of what is or is not inevitable . . . together with a great deal of misunderstanding. I am more certain than ever that the bad weather in which we find ourselves is really in the nature of a storm in a tea cup, and that a thorough exploration would remove practically everything and reduce the real difficulties between us to such small proportions and importance as to enable co-operation to continue.[128]

A meeting was arranged for the following week.

Pressure was not slackened on the parliamentary front. Baldwin and Lloyd George exploited the debate on the Address to remind the government of their obligations under the mandate and Balfour declaration.[129] Elliot had been working for an official motion to be tabled by the Conservatives but without success : "The whips fear a repercussion from the pro-Arabs who were greatly stirred by Baldwin's letter to *The Times*."[130] He also remained in contact with the Liberals, attempting to extract from them a day for debate. But, he went on, "The Opposition Parties were disastrously hamstrung at the opening of the Session . . . the movement against Baldwin's leadership made it impossible to get his support for initiating a debate . . . Lloyd George it appears had troubles of his own."[131]

C

The meeting requested by the prime minister took place on 6 November over lunch. MacDonald looked tired and complained he was overworked and overwrought. He told Weizmann that the cabinet had met that morning and had decided to appoint a cabinet subcommittee "to consider the situation in Palestine" jointly with the Jewish leaders. In answer to M. MacDonald's question whether it was to consider the white paper, the prime minister replied: "There is no white paper". However, there was no possibility of the government retracting the document, "we cannot be expected to do that", remarked MacDonald. Weizmann did not commit himself immediately. First, he had to consult his colleagues, particularly those in America. He promised to bring a reply within twenty-four hours.[132]

The Americans, however, refused to be hustled. They insisted that all proposals be submitted to them for study in detail. They also informed London that no American representative could leave for a month. Consequently the negotiations began without them, though American observers, Dr. M. Hexter and Professor H. Laski, were present. It was not until 12 November that Weizmann officially accepted the prime minister's invitation.[133]

In view of Malcolm MacDonald's fall from Zionist grace in later years and unhappier circumstances it is of some importance to place on record the role he played in renewing relations between the Jewish Agency and the government during this period. He was, in many respects, the indispensable link between the two bodies. In constant communication with Weizmann, he relayed faithfully to his father Weizmann's opinions and consistently urged reconciliation in accordance with Zionist wishes. Apparently he even warned his father "that he will vote against him" in the forthcoming parliamentary debate.[134] Weizmann showed his appreciation':

> . . . may I on this occasion express my heartfelt gratitude to you for the great trouble you have taken in re-establishing contact between H.M.G. and the J.A. I am sure time will prove that you have rendered a great service to our cause and to the cause of Great Britain.[135]

Such importance was attached to M. MacDonald's participation in the intended negotiations that Weizmann requested from the prime minister "some way of associating your son . . . in some official capacity in the forthcoming conference. He has our complete confidence and if you will allow me to say so our most sincere affection and respect."[136] Weizmann wanted his presence in the conference as a liaison between the Zionists and the cabinet delegation. This task would allow him to report to the prime minister from his personal knowledge both the difficulties and the progress made in conference. In deference to Weizmann's request, M. MacDonald was attached to the cabinet subcommittee as Henderson's personal asssistant.[137]

To those addicted to a more cynical approach it may be argued that the Zionists were merely exploiting an intimate family relationship. That the family relationship existed is beyond dispute, and the Zionists would have been less than human had they not perceived its political potential. But to see only this factor places an altogether too machiavellian construction upon Zionist intentions. Moreover, it would be placing too high a premium on the MacDonalds' naivety to suggest that they could be deceived by so obvious a manœuvre. What emerges without question is that M. MacDonald was intrigued by Weizmann, genuinely sympathetic towards Zionism, and eager to render whatever services he could.

In all, the Anglo-Jewish conference consisted of six sessions.[138] The Jewish case was put by Weizmann on the 18th. He opened with a general résumé of the Jewish problem and then proceeded to deal in detail with the white paper. At the close of the session he handed in the Jewish Agency's criticism[139] of the white paper which, together with his own statement, could be used as a basis for the government's reply. Henderson, who was acting as chairman of the conference, promised a government reply by the following Saturday.[140] In fact, the reply (in the form of a letter from Henderson to Weizmann[141]) arrived only on 29 November. This turned out to be the first draft of what was later termed the MacDonald letter.

Early on in the proceedings it became apparent that large meetings were too clumsy a forum to conduct negotiations of this nature. Hence, on receiving the Henderson letter, Namier and Stein[142] decided to adopt new procedural methods. The subject-matter of the letter was divided into three parts. Those issues which did not involve questions of principle were to be dealt with in a separate drafting memorandum, colloquially referred to as "the flea-catching memorandum". Those aspects which touched upon the interpretation of the mandate and involved questions of a technical-legal character were to be dealt with by experts in a special legal subcommittee, while major policy questions were to be dealt with by Weizmann at the next meeting.[143] M. MacDonald was informed of the Namier-Stein proposals and Henderson's agreement obtained on 4 December.[144]

Other requests were brought forward by the Zionists. Weizmann insisted that the ultimate status of the new statement be of sufficient weight to supersede the white paper. He also argued in favour of a round table conference involving all the disputing parties as an essential preliminary to any constitutional changes; and pressed for the inclusion of TransJordan in any discussion on the future development of the National Home. To all of these points Henderson proved most accommodating, and showed open sympathy towards the Zionist contention that any new policy would fail unless the Palestine administration was radically overhauled. On this latter question the Zionists were most sensitive and attached the greatest importance. But Henderson gave them no categorical answer. Only a promise to discuss with the prime minister the enlarging of the terms of reference of his committee to deal with this question.[145]

On this aspect of the negotiations there was to be much manœuvring. The Zionists were anxious to avoid all possible contact with the colonial office. They considered that the unholy alliance between the permanent officials and the Palestine administration constituted the root cause of the trouble and misunderstanding that had occurred in the past. If now the slate was to be wiped clean and a fresh start made the whole previous system of contact between the Jewish Agency and the government had to be cast overboard. Otherwise, they reasoned, the new policy would be sabotaged and nothing gained from the present negotiations.

Two ways were considered of circumventing the colonial office. First by removing the responsibilities of Palestine from the colonial office to the foreign office.

> If that is done we shall deal with infinitely more intelligent officials . . . with men of a wider view than the rather parochial C.O. officials and more accessible to influence from America and Geneva . . . On the other hand . . . the F.O. has no possessory instincts and . . . at times Roman Catholics obtain great influence in it . . . still . . . the pros are decidedly in favour of the F.O.[146]

Weizmann too turned the idea over : "I might demand from the P.M. that Palestine be transferred from the C.O. to the F.O. or Dominions Office, so as to get rid of Passfield and his clique . . [it] needs careful handling."[147]

Any such move would naturally antagonise the colonial office, for it would be justly interpreted as a slight upon their political objectivity and departmental efficiency. That the present negotiations had in fact been removed from their control only added to the feelings of resentment nurtured by that office. This can be clearly felt from the conversation between Shiels and Dr. Hexter, where the former was positively indignant at the way the colonial office was being bypassed.[148] The project was discussed at a high level only to be rejected : ". . . quite by chance I discovered that the immediate transfer of the Middle East from the C.O. to the F.O. has been discussed—and that the idea has been dropped".[149] The words "immediate transfer" suggest a possible transfer in the future. Weizmann appeared to be privy to definite information on this point when he reported to his executive that "there had been a discussion about the transfer of Palestine to the F.O. and [it was] decided this should take place in 1932".[150] There is no evidence, other than Weizmann's statement, that such a decision had in fact been taken. Indeed Weizmann had seen Sir Robert Vansittart, permanent under secretary at the foreign office, on 4 February, and Vansittart, always a ready and understanding listener to Weizmann, had gently but explicitly turned down his proposal.[151] Perhaps the refusal was too gentle; or perhaps Weizmann wished to appease his executive on this thorny subject by delaying the decision for another year.

An unexpected difficulty intruded. No candidates were found willing to undertake the responsibility. Henderson was "tired and overworked and had other matters to attend to".[152] For the rest "there is a certain weariness, and a certain dislike on the part of ministers of continually interfering in the affairs of another department".[153] The government quashed the whole idea publicly when Shiels, in answer to a question in the House, stated : "There is no intention of transferring the supervision of the affairs of Palestine from the Colonial Office to the Foreign Office."[154]

The second method of eluding the colonial office was to be by way of a new administrative authority. From the outset of the negotiations, the Zionists envisaged the cabinet subcommittee as something to be preserved and exploited as a future instrument of Anglo-Zionist contact. The terms of reference of the present committee were quite specific and Henderson would not exceed them without prior authority from the prime minister. The idea, therefore, emerged of reappointing the present committee with more comprehensive terms of reference when the present negotiations ended. This new body would then serve as the forum for major policy decisions regarding the National Home.

When Weizmann met the prime minister they agreed that once the work in hand had finished the committee would be reappointed in accordance with Zionist wishes.[155] Weizmann then informed Passfield of the prime minister's promise. Even if one makes all the necessary allowances this must have appeared to Passfield untactful at best and unwarranted interference in the affairs of his office at worst. It was patently obvious that the colonial office would not abdicate its authority without a struggle.

Passfield reacted soon after he learned of the decision to reappoint the committee. The Zionists heard "from unimpeachable authority"[156] that the colonial office were considering administrative changes in Palestine. As the Jewish Agency had not been consulted it was all too readily assumed that the officials were presenting all concerned with a *fait accompli*. The Zionists countered by formulating a programme for the second committee, and presented it at the fifth session of the conference. It included: a development commission for Palestine; the question of TransJordan; the legislative council proposal; and the status of the Jewish Agency in relation to the Palestine administration.[157] This was an unwise and hasty step. There was no great urgency about the committee's agenda; and it would have been far more rewarding to have extracted an agreement in principle from the cabinet and bargain about details later, rather than the reverse. On 2 February Weizmann followed up this initiative and sent the prime minister a spirited reminder of his previous promise.[158] Two days later M. MacDonald telephoned Namier and informed him that the programme of the proposed second committee had impressed the cabinet as being "too formidable", and the decision would be postponed until next week.[159]

Weizmann made a last attempt to win cabinet support. He sent a plea to J. H. Thomas, the dominions secretary, stressing the importance of the second cabinet committee for the future of Palestine.[160] By then it was too late. Weizmann reported of a new offensive launched by the high commissioner and the civil service to sabotage his scheme. Passfield had issued an ultimatum that the colonial office would brook no further encroachment upon their province and hence "there was no alternative but to leave the question outstanding to the colonial office".[161]

But the Zionists believed that they had secured something almost as beneficial : a small inter-departmental committee to discuss the development scheme and associated subjects and which would report directly to the cabinet.[162] Unfortunately for the Zionists this scheme never left the ground. Negotiations dragged on throughout the year with little to show for them. The colonial office still blocked the way to agreement. By August Mrs. Dugdale was still drafting the terms of reference for the committee in co-operation with M. MacDonald and Amery.[163] In these circumstances the concept of a Jewish Agency-government committee which would evade the supervision of the colonial office and Palestine administration petered out.

At the third session the drafting memorandum prepared by Namier and Stein was handed in to the government.[164] However Weizmann's major policy statement had to be altered at the last moment owing to some disagreements with the Americans. Hence, his statement was more in the nature of a *critique* than a series of constructive proposals. For this reason it was decided not to forward the statement in written form immediately. According to Namier only a convenient *"note verbale"* was needed. Instead the Zionist executive and political committee "who had no share in the work of the negotiations and no real idea of what was required, wished to go on record for ages to come in a 'historic memorandum', etc., etc. Precious time was wasted for no purpose whatsoever."[165] It was not until the week before Christmas that the memorandum was handed in. Then the holidays intervened, the House rose, and further progress was made doubly difficult.

In spite of this delay the legal subcommittee had been hard at work. They held two meetings on the 11th and 18th of December. As a result the second draft of the Henderson letter was completed by 30 December. Because of previous commitments of the lord advocate in Edinburgh and Henderson in Geneva, it became vital to iron out the remaining differences with the utmost haste and to prepare an agreed draft for circulation to cabinet ministers. In consequence the cabinet committee considered the third draft of the letter on 8 January. The same evening Weizmann, Dr. Hexter, and Namier were invited to Downing Street by M. MacDonald and informed that certain changes were considered essential, apparently due to pressure exerted by Passfield. The paragraphs under contention were 11 and 12 of the Henderson letter. These considered the questions of land purchases, agricultural development, and settlement. A meeting was arranged for the following day. After at times "a queer rambling discussion"[166] certain provisional changes were agreed upon and draft four was completed. Further meetings took place on 28th and 29th January. The amendments then suggested were approved by the cabinet committee on 30 January. On 4 February the cabinet ratified the fifth and final draft of the letter and the Zionists were informed that the letter would be signed by the prime minister and not Henderson.[167] It was Passfield who insisted that Ramsay Mac-Donald sign the letter; or rather he insisted that Henderson not sign it.[168] He would, of course, have preferred to append his own signature to the letter. He was acutely conscious of the rumours, particularly prevalent in parliamentary circles, that he was about to resign his office owing to his inept handling of the crisis.[169] The negotiations had already been removed from his jurisdiction and he believed that if Henderson were to sign the concluding document it would appear as though the government were capitulating to the Jewish Agency's demands to transfer the affairs of Palestine from the colonial to the foreign office. This was a cogent political argument; but behind it sheltered the wounded vanity of the responsible minister who had been effectively shelved and bypassed for the past few months.

The final publication of the letter was not without its anticlimax. On 11 February, in answer to a supplementary question put by Sir Austen Chamberlain, the prime minister stated :

> I think under the circumstances that we had better let it go as a letter which will be published. If it were laid before parliament . . . it would give the paper a status which it is undesirable it should have . . . I am very unwilling to give this the same status as the dominating document.[170]

This reply caused something of an uproar in Zionist circles. The answer appeared to challenge the Zionists' concept of the eventual status of the new statement. That evening the prime minister contacted Weizmann in an attempt to set matters right. Weizmann told him :

> . . . We want it made clear that the letter to me containing the authoritative interpretation of the White Paper shall be the basis of the law in Palestine. Unfortunately Lord Passfield still imagined that nothing has happened or changed since the publication of the White Paper. He is causing trouble all the time. If a question is put to you in the House tomorrow, then you can still

put matters right. If you will consult the Lord Advocate he will advise you as to the formula to be used. We have to deal with excited and anxious people, and it is undesirable that there should be any misunderstanding . . . We are dealing with an administration in which we have no confidence, and in which I think you should not have any yourself.[171]

Weizmann was disturbed lest the officials of the colonial office and Palestine administration exploit the prime minister's aberration and continue to administer Palestine in accordance with the white paper when clearly the whole point of the negotiations was to amend the white paper in accordance with Zionist desires. Weizmann's phraseology is, to say the least, blunt. And one wonders how MacDonald reacted to being given instructions in quite so forthright a manner. Unfortunately, we have no record; but it would not be illogical to assume that once again he was very near to losing his patience with the Zionists.

At the last session of the conference Weizmann raised the matter again. Henderson, after consulting *Hansard* to discover what MacDonald had actually said, agreed that the prime minister should make a statement confirming the authoritative character of the letter. Anxious to substantiate the status of the letter, Weizmann requested that three points be considered : that it be addressed to him as president of the Jewish Agency [he had in fact resigned from this post on 20 October]; that it be laid before the Council of the League as an official document and an announcement made to that effect; and that the letter be despatched as an instruction of the cabinet to the high commissioner and in that form tabled and recorded in the records of the House. Henderson saw no difficulty in these requests and promised to relay them to the prime minister.[172] The same day MacDonald made the required statement to the House.[173]

On 13 February Kenworthy rose to ask the prime minister for the text of the letter, and it was duly recorded in *Hansard* as an official document.[174]

Weizmann wrote to the prime minister thanking him for the letter and setting on record yet again "how deeply we appreciate the consistent work and friendship which has been put into the negotiations by your son Mr. Malcolm".[175] He reminded the prime minister, "everything now turns upon the spirit in which the principles laid down in your letter are applied in practice . . . I have no doubt you will not lose sight of this aspect of the matter." With this parting shot the negotiations that culminated in the Mac-Donald letter came to an end.

In summing up the significance of the letter, two aspects should be borne in mind. In the short run Zionist expectations were only partially fulfilled. It is true that they had achieved an official re-interpretation of the white paper. But their scheme of direct consultation with the government on major policy questions, to which they attached the utmost importance, proved abortive. The Zionist *bête noire,* the world of officialdom, still remained on guard in Whitehall and Jerusalem, thwarting any Zionist initiative. Only five months after the letter was issued the Zionists were complaining bitterly of official indifference to the letter.[176]

But the MacDonald letter remained the legal basis for adminis-tering Palestine until the May white paper of 1939. The years im-mediately following the letter saw a consolidation of the National Home. Immigration figures rose to unprecedented heights. Capital flowed into Palestine. The material basis of the National Home was secured. Weizmann commented : ". . . it was under MacDonald's letter to me that the change came about in the Government's attitude and in the attitude of the Palestine administration which enabled us to make the magnificent gains of the ensuing years".[177] A less Anglophile Zionist version summarised the letter : "The Jew-ish people were given the possibility to continue their constructive work, although with most serious limitations, for another eight years; those years decided the fate of *Eretz Israel* [Palestine] until today."[178]

Without doubt the letter inhibited a hard policy which may have been contemplated by the officials. And this remained true until the latter years of the 1930s. When the National Home was threatened and the MacDonald letter pigeon-holed somewhere in the colonial office it was already too late. By then the *Yishuv* was able to stand on its own feet and withstand any attack upon its position. In this sense the letter more than fulfilled its function.

NOTES

1 See Cmd. 3530, *The Shaw report on the Disturbances of August 1929* (March 1930), p. 65.

2 On 24 Sept. 1928, the Jewish day of atonement, the incident at the Wailing Wall occurred whereby a screen used to divide Jewish male and female worshippers was forcibly removed by the police. From then on, tension rose steadily until the outbreaks of Aug. 1929. A narrative of these events may

be found in Cmd. 3229, *A Memorandum by the Secretary of State for the Colonies on the Wailing Wall* (Nov. 1928); and Cmd. 3530.

3 C. Weizmann, *Trial and Error* (London 1950), p. 410.

4 See Weizmann to Lord Melchett (formerly Alfred Mond; at the time he was chairman of the council of the Jewish Agency), tel., 25 Aug, 1929 W.A.; and to J. R. MacDonald, tel., 25 Aug. 1929, W.A.

5 Minutes of the third meeting of the Zionist executive, 28 Aug. 1929, W.A. A version has emerged that Passfield was reluctant to see Weizmann and conjured up many excuses before finally agreeing to a meeting. See, Weizmann, pp. 410-11, and C. Sykes, *Crossroads to Israel* (London, 1965), p. 141; Weizmann received the news in Switzerland on the 25th. By the morning of the 28th he had met Passfield in London. This hardly suggests reluctance or indifference on Passfield's part to meet Weizmann.

6 At the time of the riots Luke was acting high commissioner and Cust acting commissioner of the Jerusalem district. The usual occupants of these offices were on vacation.

   During the riots Luke had attempted to cut Palestine off from the outside world by closing down the newspapers and cutting off telegraph and telephone communications. These activities were partially thwarted by the *Haganah* (Jewish defence organisation) which maintained contact with Cairo and Beirut and then to the outside world. I. Slotski, *Toldoth HaHaganah* (The History of the Haganah), (Tel Aviv, 1964), ii, part 1, pp. 393-4.

7 Minutes of the Zionist executive, 28 Aug. 1929, W.A.

8 Passfield to Weizmann, 30 Aug. 1929, W.A.

9 Col. J. C. Wedgwood: Labour, previously Liberal, M.P., 1906-42; chancellor of Duchy of Lancaster, 1924; a fervent Gentile Zionist. Created Baron 1942.

10 Wedgwood to Passfield, 26 Aug. 1929, W.A.

11 Col. R. Meinertzhagen (1876-1967): Chief political officer in Palestine and Syria, 1919-20; military adviser to the Middle East department, colonial office, 1921-4.

12 Mrs. Dugdale to Weizmann, 28 Aug. 1929, W.A.

13 Mrs. E. C. Blanche Dugdale: Balfour's niece and biographer; the leading Gentile Zionist of her generation.

14 Mrs. Dugdale to Weizmann, 29 Aug. 1929, W.A. This letter was subsequently sent to P. Graves, foreign editor of *The Times*, and appeared in that newspaper on 31 Aug.

15 Weizmann gave public expression to these sentiments at a mass meeting held at the Albert Hall, see *The Times*, 2 Sept. 1929.

16 See Passfield's comments to Melchett, 2 Sept. 1929, W.A.

17 *The Times*, 4 Sept. 1929.

18 When the Shaw report was published, the colonial office had second thoughts about major policy questions. "What are they?" an official asked, "who decides whether the commission's report does or does not invade that ill-defined province. Best course possible is to avoid definition and keep our hands as free as possible." Colonial office minute, 19 March 1930, Premier 1/102.

19 See the prime minister's statement to the Assembly of the League at Geneva, *Manchester Guardian*, 4 Sept. 1929. On 5 Sept. Weizmann met the prime

minister at Geneva (*The Times*, 6 Sept. 1929) where he repeated the assurances.

20   Weizmann to Meinertzhagen, 9 Sept. 1929, W.A.

21   Weizmann and Melchett to Passfield, 10 Sept. 1929, W.A.
Weizmann to J. Shuckburgh, 26 Sept. 1929, W.A.
W.D., 24 Sept. 1929, W.A. These diaries were written by Miss M. Maas, Weizmann's secretary, and continue until the end of 1930.

22   Mrs. Dugdale to Weizmann, 10 Sept. 1929, W.A.

23   W.D., 27 Sept. 1929, W.A.

24   Weizmann to Melchett, 23 Sept. 1929, W.A.

25   Notes of an interview between Passfield, Weizmann, and Professor Brodetsky, 27 Sept. 1929, W.A.

26   J. S. Smuts (1870–1950): Boer general and British field marshal; prime minister of South Africa, 1919–29 and 1939–48; member of the war cabinet 1917–18; one of the statesmen responsible for the Balfour declaration.

27   W.D., 25 Nov. 1929, W.A.

28   Weizmann to Smuts, 28 Nov. 1929, W.A.

29   Notes of an interview between Smuts and Weizmann, 3 Dec. 1929, W.A.

30   *Ibid.*

31   L. S. Amery (1877–1955): Conservative M.P.; first lord of the admiralty, 1922–4; colonial secretary, 1924–9.

32   Notes of an interview between Smuts and Weizmann, 3 Dec. 1929, W.A.

33   W. Ormsby Gore: under secretary of State for colonies, 1922–4, 1925–9; colonial secretary, 1936–8; succeeded his father as Lord Harlech in 1938. An old friend of Weizmann.

34   Ormsby Gore to Weizmann, 12 Dec. 1929, W.A.

35   See C.Z.A., F13/56. The meeting was convened for 5.30 p.m., committee room 8, by Wedgwood, Hamilton and Conway. Invitations were sent to thirty-one M.P.s of whom the following attended: Wedgwood, Hamilton. Amery, Samuel, Ormsby Gore, J. de Rothschild, Maj. Nathan, Capt. Hudson, N. Day, Dr. H. B. Morgan, G. Mander, Dr. Spero, P. Harris, A. Smith, F. Messer, D. Hopkin, Lt.-Col. C. Malone, Sir A. Sinclair, H. Knight, N. Angell, J. W. Milne.

36   Sir H. Samuel (1870–1963): Home secretary, 1916, 1931–2; high commissioner for Palestine, 1920–5; leader of the Liberal party, 1931–5.

37   W.D., 17 Dec. 1929, W.A. Those present included Wedgwood, Conway, J, Buchan, A. Eden, Elliot, Sinclair, Hamilton, Hopkins and Dr. Spero. L. B. Namier and Mrs. Dugdale were also in attendance.

38   Walter Elliot: Conservative M.P.; financial secretary to the treasury, 1931–2; minister of agriculture, 1932–6; of health, 1938–40; secretary of state for Scotland, 1936–8.

39   W.D., 18, 19, and 20 Dec. 1929, W.A.
The Times, 20 Dec. 1929.

40   Weizmann to Smuts, 20 Dec. 1929, W.A.

41   Elliot to Weizmann, 25 Dec. 1929, W.A.

42   P.D., Commons, vol. 233, c. 1902, 23 Dec. 1929.

43   Elliot to Weizmann, 25 Dec. 1929, W.A.

44   Weizmann to F. Warburg (the American financier and Zionist supporter), 16 Jan. 1930, W.A.

45 W.D., 23 Jan. 1930, W.A.

46 W.D., 4 March 1930, W.A.

47 Weizmann to Elliot, 15 March 1930, W.A.

48 Mrs. Dugdale to Weizmann, 17 March 1930, W.A. This decision was taken formally at a meeting of the Mandates Society on 17 March. Among those present were: Mrs. P. Snowden, Buchan, Wedgwood, H. Sidebothan, and M. MacDonald.

49 P.D., Commons, vol. 237, c. 28, 24 March 1930.

50 Cmd. 3530. The report was overwhelmingly critical of Zionist methods in Palestine. Only in one conclusion was it in full accord with Zionist views: that the outbreak was an attack by Arabs upon Jews for which there was no excuse, p. 158. The report found that the outbreak was not premeditated and that the behaviour of the Mufti and Palestine Arab Executive offered no serious ground for complaint, pp. 158-9. The administration was absolved from blame, pp. 159-61. On immigration, they criticised the methods of selecting immigrants and claimed that the Zionists had not adhered to the principle of absorptive capacity. Zionist claims in this sphere led to Arab fears of political subordination and displacement from the land, pp. 98-112. The report contended that a landless, discontented class was being created and this constituted a source of political unrest. It concluded that no more land was available for settlement unless new methods of agriculture were introduced, pp. 113-24. In conclusion the commission found that the fundamental cause of the riots was in Arab frustrations consequent upon the disappointment of their political and national aspirations and fear for their economic future, p. 163. These conclusions were somewhat mitigated by the reservations of Mr. H. Snell. He criticised the activities of the Mufti and the Arab leadership, p. 172; and also the administration and government, p. 174. He did not accept the majority findings on land and immigration, pp. 175-6.

For the Zionist rebuttal of the report, see L. Stein, *Memorandum on the report of the commission on the Palestine Disturbances of August 1929* (Jewish Agency, May 1930.)

51 Notes of the meeting of 28 March 1930, W.A.; and for subsequent quotations. those present: J. R. MacDonald, Passfield, Hargreave, Lord Melchett, Lord Reading and F. Warburg.

52 That same afternoon at a private meeting between Baldwin, Lloyd George, Samuel and Passfield, it was decided to employ Smuts, accompanied by Sir J. Campbell, to report on the mandate. MacDonald then wired Smuts accordingly, P.P. the Beatrice Webb diaries, 30 March 1930.

53 The London Naval conference between Great Britain, the United States, Japan, France and Italy had been in session since 22 Jan. and was not to end until 22 April. At the same time negotiations were in progress with Indian and Egyptian nationalists. On the domestic side the government was even more pre-occupied with the effects of the world economic crisis.

54 See, for example, his statement in the Commons on 3 April 1930, vol. 237, c. 1466-7.

55 Weizmann to MacDonald, Lloyd George, and Baldwin, 2 April 1930, W.A.

56 W.D. 31 March 1930, W.A. The letter was drafted on 31 March together with Buchan and copies were sent to MacDonald, Lloyd George and

Baldwin. *The Times*, however, requested on abridged version before publication. Therefore, a further letter was drafted which appeared in *The Times* on 3 April while the original statement was published in its entirety by the *Manchester Guardian* on 11 April.

57 Cabinet conclusions for 2 April 1930 CAB 23/63. Passfield alone was inclined to dispense with a further enquiry. At the same meeting a cabinet committee was set up to watch over policy towards Palestine. It consisted of: Passfield; A. Henderson; T. Shaw, secretary of state for war; and Lord Thomson, secretary of state for air.

58 Notes of the meeting of 28 March 1930, W.A.

59 See W.D., 7 and 9 April 1930.

60 W.D., 11 April 1930. Some attempts were made by Lloyd George to change MacDonald's mind but with no success. See Weizmann to Warburg, 15 May 1930, W.A.

61 Sir J. Hope Simpson (1868–1962): Liberal M.P. 1922–4; member of the Indian colonial committee, 1924; served on the refugees settlement commission, Athens, 1926–30.

62 W.D., 11 April 1930, W.A.

63 L. B. Namier (1888–1960): political secretary to the Jewish Agency, 1929–31; professor of modern history at Manchester University 1931–53, Kt. 1952.

64 W.D. 3 May 1930, W.A.

65 Namier to F. Kisch (chairman of the Palestine Zionist Executive), 8 May 1930, W.A.

66 Weizmann to Warburg, 15 May 1930, W.A. Namier dubbed this duo as "the hero and the author of the [Shaw] report", Namier to Kisch, 8 May 1930, W.A.

67 See notes of the meeting of 28 March 1930, W.A.

68 Weizmann to Warburg, 15 May 1930, W.A.

69 Namier to Kisch, 8 May 1939, W.A.

70 See *The Times*, 14 May 1930. Apart from that on 12 May Weizmann met MacDonald who communicated to him the Arab demands. Weizmann felt that the prime minister did not take them too seriously, W.D. 12 May 1930, W.A.

71 Weizmann to Warburg, 15 May 1930, W.A.

72 See Namier to Kisch, 8 May 1930; and Weizmann to Warburg, 15 May 1930, W.A.

73 For the sequence of these events see Namier to Kisch, 8 May 1930, W.A.

74 Weizmann to Warburg, 15 May 1930, W.A.; and W.D., 15 May 1930, W.A.

75 MacDonald personally handled Anglo-American affairs. His desire to promote Anglo-American friendship was entirely genuine and through his efforts much was achieved. Hence his concern at the influence American Jewry might bring to bear upon his government.

76 W.D., 15 May 1930, W.A.

77 This principle was first formulated in Cmd. 1700, *Correspondence with the Palestine Arab Delegation and the Zionist Organisation, And a Statement of British Policy on Palestine.* (June 1922), p. 31. The Churchill white paper.

78 For example at a cabinet meeting held on 14 May the question of immigration was not even cited. See CAB.23/64. There was another opinion held by some M.P.s that the suspension resulted from the grave situation in India,

and that the government did not want to lose the support of the Indian Moslems. *Jewish Chronicle*, 30 May 1930

79 This view is confirmed by Beatrice Webb: "Lunn [the Dominion under-secretary] told me that the parliamentary labour party thought Sidney too much in the hands of his officials. But that is inevitable. By temperament and training Sidney belongs to the civil service." P.P., Beatrice Webb diaries, xliv, 5 Feb. 1930. MacDonald said of Passfield: "He was old, in some ways efficient, but he has the mind of a German professor and an indestructible belief in the experts who sit in the C.O." Notes of a meeting between MacDonald and Weizmann, 6 Nov. 1930, W.A.

80 M. MacDonald (1901–): Labour M.P., 1929–31; National Labour, 1931–5; National Government, 1936–45; parliamentary under secretary for dominions, 1931–5; dominions secretary, 1935–8; 1938–9; colonial secretary, 1935, 1938–40.

81 Weizmann to M. MacDonald, 21 May 1930, W.A. At a meeting of the Zionist executive that morning Weizmann had proposed convening Congress and submitting the resignation of the executive before it because the man-datory power had broken faith. Minutes of the meeting, 21 May 1930, W.A.

82 M. MacDonald to Weizmann, 21 May 1930, W.A. His letters invariably reflected the opinions of his father.

83 Weizmann to M. MacDonald, 23 May 1930, W.A.

84 Cmd. 3582, *A Statement of Policy with regard to Palestine* (May 1930), p. 7.

85 *Ibid.*, p. 8.

86 *The Times*, 29 May 1930.

87 See Weizmann to Namier, 4 June 1930, W.A. This conclusion was also prevalent in League of Nations circles, W.D., 31 May 1930, W.A. However, the government's statement to the permanent mandate's commission could only have been regarded as satisfactory by the Zionists. In it government obligations under the mandate towards the National Home were recon-firmed, *The Times*, 4 June, 1930.

88 J. R. MacDonald to M. Marcus, M.P., 10 June 1930, W.A.

89 Weizmann to Namier, 4 June 1930, W.A.

90 Weizmann to Warburg, 26 June 1930, W.A.

91 M. MacDonald to Namier, 14 June 1930, W.A.

92 M. MacDonald to Weizmann, 17 June 1930, W.A.

93 W.D., 19 June 1930, W.A.; also Minutes of the Jewish Agency executive meeting, 19 June 1930, W.A.

94 Passfield to Weizmann, 4 July 1930, W.A.

95 Minutes of an interview between Passfield and Weizmann, 7 July 1930, W.A.

96 Weizmann to M. MacDonald, 9 July 1930, W.A.; and Weizmann to J. R. MacDonald, 9 July 1930, W.A.

97 A full outline of the scheme may be found in an enclosure to a letter from Rutenberg to Sir John Shuckburgh, 15 May 1930, Premier 1/102.

98 Amery to Weizmann, 26 July 1930, W.A.

99 Weizmann to Warburg, 25 June 1930, W.A.

100 Sidney to Beatrice Webb, 15 July 1930, P.P.; also, Hope Simpson to Pass-field, 18 Aug. 1930, C.P.301(30), CAB.24/215. In this letter Hope Simpson strongly opposed Jewish settlement in TransJordan.

101 Sidney to Beatrice Webb, 10 and 24 Sept. 1930, P.P.; and cabinet conclusions

for 24 Sept. 1930, CAB.23/65.

102 Sidney to Beatrice Webb, 22 Sept. 1930, P.P.
103 Sidney to Beatrice Webb, 24 Sept. 1930, P.P.
104 W.D., 25 Sept., 1930, W.A.
105 Minutes of an interview between Passfield, Weizmann, and Namier, 1 Oct. 1930, W.A.
106 Sidney to Beatrice Webb, 1 Oct. 1930, P.P.
107 See cabinet minutes, CAB.23/65
108 W.D., 13 Oct. 1930, W.A.
109 Namier to M. MacDonald, 14 Oct. 1930, W.A.
110 Minutes of the meeting, 15 Oct. 1930, W.A.
111 See Cmd. 3686, *The Hope Simpson Report on Immigration, Land Settlement and Development*, (Oct. 1930); and Cmd. 3692, *A Statement of Policy* (Oct. 1930).
112 Entry for 26 Oct. 1930, Beatrice Webb diaries, xliv, P.P.
113 See W.D., 18 Oct. 1930, W.A.; and notes of a telephone conversation between Weizmann and Passfield, 18 Oct. 1930, W.A.
114 W.D., 20 Oct. 1930, W.A.
115 Beatrice to Sidney Webb, 21 Oct. 1930, P.P.
116 *The Times*, 22, 23 and 24 Oct. 1930.
117 Lt.-Commander J. M. Kenworthy, later Baron Strabolgi (1886–1953): Labour M.P.; a firm defender of Zionism in and out of the House.
118 Kenworthy to Weizmann, 21 Oct. 1930, W.A.
119 Amery to Weizmann, 27 Oct. 1930, W.A.
120 *Manchester Guardian*, 1 Nov. 1930.
121 *The Times*, 4 Nov. 1930.
122 W.D., 23 Oct. 1930, W.A. Smuts had also expressed his dissatisfaction with the white paper to the prime minister. See their correspondence, *The Times*, 25 and 27 Oct. 1930.
123 *The Times*, 25 Oct. 1930.
124 *The Times*, 28 Oct. 1930.
125 *Jewish Chronicle*, 31 Oct. 1930. According to Mrs. Weizmann, MacDonald told Marcus that Passfield and Chancellor 'must resign', and even suggested promoting a parliamentary attack upon his colonial secretary to force his resignation. Vera Weizmann, *The Impossible Takes Longer* (London, 1967), p. 113.
126 Sidney to Beatrice Webb, 28 Oct. 1930, P.P.
127 *Manchester Guardian*, 30 Oct. 1930.
128 J. R. MacDonald to Weizmann, 31 Oct. 1930, W.A.
129 P.D., Commons, vol. 244, c. 18, 46–7, 28 and 29 Oct. 1930.
130 Elliot to Weizmann, 7 Nov. 1930, W.A. Chancellor, the high commissioner, also considered the Baldwin-Amery-Chamberlain letter as the main cause of the recent activities of the Jews. See his letter to Shuckburgh, 16 Nov. 1930, Premier 1/103.
131 Baldwin's leadership was under heavy attack. The press lords, Beaverbrook and Rothmere, were conducting an Empire Free Trade crusade and threatening to run their own candidates against the official Conservatives. In Oct. 1930 they made good their threat and an Empire Free Trader defeated the Conservative candidate in a by-election at South Paddington, a warning Baldwin could ill afford to ignore. The split in the Conservative ranks,

The proposal to establish a Legislative Council . . . is completely ignored in the letter to Dr. Weizmann . . . on this vital issue . . . a substantial concession could have been wrung from the Government . . . Weizmann has shown too great a readiness to grasp the shadow for the substance, and his colleagues have worshipped at his shrine, regardless of the facts of the situation.[48]

The "organ of Anglo-Jewry" had always been an opponent of Weizmannism. None the less it was evident that Weizmann's handling of the crisis caused a great deal of unrest in some Zionist circles. This reached its climax during the Zionist Congress in August 1931, when he was not re-elected as president of the movement ostensibly as a consequence of his diplomacy during the winter of 1930–1.

Weizmann had to make a real attempt to salvage his reputation, particularly with regard to the charge of negligence over the council proposals. At the forthcoming Zionist Congress he fully expected to be bitterly attacked for his handling of the recent negotiations. It was, therefore, of some importance that he appear before Congress with at least one trump card.

In the early morning of 12 July the prime minister and his son Malcolm met Namier and Ben Gurion[49] at Chequers.[50] The conversation lasted five hours and ranged over a wide field of Anglo-Zionist issues. When they turned to constitutional problems the prime minister again expressed sympathy with the Zionist desire to precede any concrete proposals by a round table conference. He added, however, that before reaching a final verdict he needed additional information in order to evaluate its chances of success.

The Zionists then raised the question of political parity. "We suggested absolute equality in regard to national entities with respect to participation in all constitutional institutions and all benefits accruing from the development scheme!" The prime minister approved of this formula.

At the conclusion of the meeting the Zionists telephoned Weizmann in Basle to inform him of the substance of the discussion. Then, together with Malcolm MacDonald, they drafted a telegram to Weizmann setting on record the conclusions of the meeting. The prime minister made some slight alterations in the draft and then agreed that it be despatched on condition that it was not published. He had no wish to unnecessarily embarrass the colonial office. The text of the telegram is as follows :

B.G. and myself saw the P.M. . . . declared his full agreement parity principle between Jews and Arabs as national entities. Added in strict confidence that he himself would give much equality leaning towards the Jews. Expressed deep disappointment concerning way his letter handled by administration. Considers new H.C. [Wauchope] excellent man for post. Will see him personally and insist most emphatically on policy of law and original intention Mandate being carried out. Sympathetic Round Table conference but impossible commit himself without fuller information.

The unambiguous nature of the prime minister's pledge enabled Weizmann to go before Congress with a tangible proposal. He told the delegates : "Provided that the mandate is both recognised and respected, we would welcome an agreement between the two kindred races on the basis of political parity."[51] This did not satisfy Weizmann's critics. Jabotinsky, the leader of the Revisionists, refuted Weizmann's circumspect policy : "Our conception is, first a majority, then, of course, parliamentary institutions in which the majority is decisive."[52] The Revisionists persisted in chastising the Zionist leadership for their Fabian tactics and demanded more dynamic methods of dealing with a dilatory British government and a hostile Palestine administration. Jabotinsky, being free from official duties, could, of course, adopt a more radical tone. He was aiming to oust Weizmann from the presidency, and the Passfield white paper appeared to him as a golden opportunity to accomplish this. Hence the ferocity of his chauvinistic attack.

But Weizmann did not budge one iota from his original theme. He strongly opposed Jabotinsky, reasoning that such demands could only be interpreted by the enemies of Zionism as a declaration of intent to drive the Arabs out of Palestine. Moreover, he believed that mere numerical superiority provided no cast-iron security for the future :

> The safety of the National Home could be secured only through political guarantees by the Powers, and through establishing friendly relations with the non-Jewish inhabitants of Palestine, on the basis "of complete parity without regard to the numerical strength of either people".[53]

His espousal of parity found no explicit support in Congress. This is hardly surprising for political parity, if taken to its logical conclusion, hinted at an eventual bi-national state. And although Weizmann conditioned his proposal with "recognition and respect for the mandate"—which proved an insurmountable condition, something that Weizmann may well have realised—bi-nationalism never acquired popular support in Zionist circles.[54]

Wauchope arrived in Palestine in November 1931 to assume the post of high commissioner. His appointment was greeted by the Zionists with satisfaction. Their relations with Chancellor throughout the crisis of 1929–31 had steadily deteriorated. Chancellor himself had written : "The Jews do not accept 'No' when you say it to them the first time; but when they come to you a second time and you say 'No! damn you!' (I speak figuratively, for I am always courteous to them) they do accept it. That has been my experience."[55] That seemed to sum up their relationship : a polite, but firmly expressed, hostility. They hoped for better times under his successor.

Inevitably the question of a legislative council was raised in contacts between the new high commissioner and the Zionists. At first it appeared as though there were no need for immediate concern. Chaim Arlosoroff[56] concluded that there was no fear of having a council foisted on them at a moment's notice.[57] When he met Wauchope in the autumn of 1932 the situation had altered considerably. He was then informed that the cabinet had discussed the matter on at least two occasions in the spring and had decided to accept his, Wauchope's, advice to postpone the question. Wauchope had in fact got the cabinet to accept a long-term plan, involving fostering local administrative skills, which was to be implemented before redeeming the Passfield pledge.[58] He then proceeded to sound Arlosoroff on the Zionist attitude. Arlosoroff inveighed against Jewish participation in a council as proposed in the white paper, or indeed in any constitutional body where the Jews would be in a minority.[59] This was an obvious hint that parity might be considered, and that the Zionists did not intend to allow the prime minister's previous promise to retire into obscurity. Arlosoroff insisted that forestalling action be taken in London to counteract any imminent decision. This was deemed particularly urgent as Wauchope was expected in London in mid October for consultations with the government prior to his departure to Geneva where he was scheduled to report to the mandates commission.

Weizmann interviewed Wauchope in London. He was informed that the cabinet had definitely committed itself to a council and that the matter would not be delayed much longer. Wauchope had formed the conclusion that Arab co-operation would become ultimately impossible unless the government reaffirmed its intention to form a legislative council. At the same time he rejected the idea of absolute political parity while making it plain to the Arabs that the government stood by the mandate and Balfour declaration. And once again the cabinet approved his line.[60] Wauchope estimated that by the end of 1933 the issue would begin to mature.[61] There was, he hinted, a more than reasonable chance that when the Arabs saw what kind of a council was proposed—it was intended that the high commissioner retain extensive power to ensure the smooth working of the mandate—they would refuse to have anything to do with it.[62]

To Weizmann's mind this offered the most diplomatic way of evading the issue. It implied allowing the Arabs to make the running. In this he saw the greatest difficulty :

> There is always the possibility . . . that someone on our side will make a big row the moment the proposal is made . . . this will serve as an incentive to the Arabs to accept . . . on the theory that anything the Jews don't like must be good for them.[63]

The subtleties of Weizmannism often eluded the more forthright champions of Zionism.

They next talked of parity. Wauchope was impressed with the idea. He agreed there could be no question of strict proportional representation, but thought that the conception of parity might be stretched to include a 60–40 relationship. Weizmann seized the opportunity; he accepted Wauchope's offer with alacrity as a starting point for negotiations.

In view of past Zionist statements Weizmann's eagerness to grasp at Wauchope's suggestion represented a considerable concession. But it is doubtful whether the official Zionist leadership would have countenanced such a compromise. In this context it is important to remember that Weizmann no longer held office. His defeat at the seventeenth Zionist Congress rankled deeply and left him in an extremely bitter mood towards his former colleagues.[64] Possibly he was attempting to reassert his superiority in the field of Anglo-Zionist diplomacy. Certainly he did not want to associate himself too closely with the official leadership. He wrote to Namier, who had left office together with his chief :

I do not propose to meddle much in this matter; as you know, I adhere strictly to the view on which we all agreed . . . namely that I should keep well away from things for the next year or two.[65]

However, Weizmann's past reputation and great prestige did not allow him to play the role of a passive spectator. He continued applying his own technique and influence on events.

The Zionists had analysed the situation as follows. They were not interested in tying down the government "to official declarations in parliament . . . on the exact date and probable procedure of the Legislative Council".[66] Furthermore, Arlosoroff believed, and it may be assumed that he spoke for the Zionist leadership, that the cabinet had only agreed to a general commitment regarding the council. Cunliffe-Lister, then colonial secretary, was not interested in "political or constitutional problems" and "the initiative . . is all Wauchope's". The Palestine administration was worried about local reaction to recent constitutional changes in Syria and Iraq, and believed that if similar concessions were not made in Palestine there was a real danger of "new Arab violence directed against them".

The increasingly militant temper of the Arabs[67] caused the Zionists to harden their approach. Arlosoroff now swung away from any spirit of compromise. There was to be "no bartering, even a hint of parity would put our position in jeopardy". There would be "no Legislative Council in Palestine with Jewish participation . . . Wauchope becomes very nervous every time such a vision is conjured up".

There is here a curious parallel between British and Zionist policy making. In both cases the tune was called from Palestine. In London, far removed from the claustrophobic atmosphere of Palestine, compromise seemed possible. In Jerusalem, remote from the diplomatic merry-go-round of London, militancy was met with militancy. Ultimately the men on the spot set the pace.

By the end of 1933, Wauchope's deadline, Cunliffe-Lister confirmed the government's intention to set up a council.[68] At a Zionist confabulation Weizmann laid down the general line of policy.[69] It was inconceivable to adopt a *non possumus* attitude. It was necessary "to decide whether we wanted an exclusively Jewish country or a Judo-Arab one . . . for the present we were obliged to accept the latter". He did not want a council nor, he believed, would it come about—Cunliffe-Lister had hinted as much—but it was "important that we should not be the people to sabotage it . . . A 50–50 proposal would placate public opinion and not endanger our position." Moreover, he hinted, Cunliffe-Lister was open to such a suggestion.

Meanwhile, the cabinet had asked Cunliffe-Lister to draw up detailed proposals for the establishment of the council.[70] Cunliffe-Lister suffered no illusions as the powers or status of the council: "Provided the High Commissioner retains extensive powers and a veto I do not attach much importance to an official majority", but he went on, "As things stand now we cannot escape our commitments, and we must in due course put forward our proposals."[71] Wauchope, acting under instructions, now informed Ben Gurion that although the government would not behave surreptitiously he could state with certainty that a council would be established. The government was under an obligation to honour its pledge and, although details of the scheme had not been finalised, there was a clear decision in favour of the principle involved. Ben Gurion replied that the *Yishuv* would refuse to participate in any such body and considered that its establishment would only aggravate inter-communal relations.[72]

Weizmann refined Ben Gurion's statement at a meeting of the enlarged Jewish Agency executive. Initially the Zionists would hold their hand. If, however, the government continued without Jewish agreement the scheme would inevitably result in chaos. Then, when the government showed signs of compromise, the question of parity would be raised and MacDonald's telegram exploited to the full.[73]

Weizmann adopted this line when he met Cunliffe-Lister the following month. He recounted previous Zionist objections explaining away his acceptance of the proposals of 1922 on the grounds of "foolishness and inexperience, we genuinely thought . . . it was possible to come to an arrangement with them [the Arabs] . . . within an ordinary parliamentary assembly. But now we have learnt our lesson."[74] Weizmann then related the Chequers conversation of July 1931. Cunliffe-Lister was taken aback, he had "never heard anything about it till today". Weizmann went on to praise the virtues of parity. This would be representation based not upon numbers but upon the functions the different communities fulfilled in Palestine. It would safeguard against minority status for both sides and give practical expression to the dual character of mandatory obligations. The latter point always made a favourable impression on ministers, though not apparently upon Cunliffe-Lister, for he later wrote to Wauchope that "The Jewish claim to 'parity' . . . should be rejected. The claim of the J[ewish] A[gency] to be consulted before any bill is introduced into the Legislative Council should be refuted and there should be no departure from the present practice in the matter of consultation between the H[igh] C[ommissioner] and that body."[75] Weizmann left the meeting feeling that "it did something to clear the air . . . [and] that the . . . Council proposals may be regarded as shelved for the next twelve months". This now became the Zionist aim. Mrs. Dugdale also worked towards the same end. She told Wauchope that the Zionist executive was in no position to formulate new policy until after the elections for the next Zionist congress.[76] And Wauchope, on his return to Palestine in November 1934, informed Ben Gurion that there would be no serious discussion on the subject until after the forthcoming congress. Then the intention was to forge ahead.[77]

Clearly the Zionists were playing for time. There was little chance that the government would undergo a change of heart. The promise had been made : Wauchope was bent on redeeming it. Moreover, it is crystal clear that at the time the government had full confidence in Wauchope's judgment and sense of timing and would back him to the hilt whenever he thought the time was ripe.

Immediate Zionist tactics were to delay the decision for future generations to decide. During the mid 1930s, time, in a sense, was working in their favour. From 1933 to 1935 over 130,000 Jews officially entered Palestine stimulated by the anti-semitic excesses in Germany and Eastern Europe. There seemed little prospect of this stream of immigration drying up. This continuous *aliyah* (immigration) substantially altered the numerical relationship between Jew and Arab in Palestine in favour of the former. Every year saved strengthened the Zionist case. They argued, with considerable logic, that it was unjust to electorally freeze the population relationship when it was in a state of constant flux. Hence, they strove for postponement. If that failed they could insist on parity as the most equitable formula in view of the mass immigration now taking place and likely to continue.

In June 1935 Baldwin replaced J. R. MacDonald as prime minister. The new colonial secretary was Malcolm MacDonald, a staunch friend of Weizmann and a firm advocate of Zionism.[78] Weizmann, somewhat reluctantly, approached him with a view to quashing the preliminary discussions regarding the council which were due to commence in mid June. He opposed revealing to the Arabs any details of the scheme for they "will constitute for you and the H.C. . . . a *fait accompli*".[79] And he suggested that MacDonald re-examine the proposals as they are the "subject of serious controversy", adding that he had not envisaged "the form which is now being imported to them".

Weizmann's request did not go unheeded. MacDonald informed Wauchope that he needed a week or two to "study the papers".[80] The preliminary discussions were to be postponed until mid July. Then any discussions held would be informal and communal leaders would be warned not to divulge the contents of the soundings. Full government proposals were to be communicated to the respective parties probably in October. Beyond that date there could be no further postponement, not any material departures from the main features of the scheme.[81]

The Zionists had won a minor tactical victory. Their immediate aim of delay had been achieved. But their policy was still one of tactical withdrawal, and while the Palestine administration was as firmly committed as ever to implementing the pledge this was not the way to attain total victory. Even the manner in which they had obtained their success conjured up an image of backstairs intrigue. Weizmann was most anxious to avoid any accusation of preferential treatment. "I beg you most urgently to see to it that this matter should not receive the slightest publicity, should not even be talked about among our friends, and . . . above all, exploited as a triumph."[82]

The conduct of the administration left the Zionists uneasy. Wauchope informed them that the question of parity was to be excluded from the discussions.[83] Weizmann reacted :

. . . the JA could not be expected to take part in any discussions with these points excluded from the outset . . . I desire co-operation with HMG . . . but this does not imply reciprocal confidence . . . we ought surely not to be faced with a *fait accompli*.[84]

On 21 July Wauchope informed Shertok and Ben Gurion of the main features of the scheme.[85] Shertok summarised the chief principle underlying the proposal as "wide possibility discussion, no power decision". It is clear that the government was, within its own carefully defined framework, attempting to strike as fair a bargain as possible. Wauchope told Shertok that if the Arabs behaved unreasonably the council would be dissolved, and, in an extreme eventuality, that if the council were exploited merely as a vehicle for agitation against the mandate it would be abolished and the government would consider its pledge fulfilled.

These promises did not pacify the Zionists. Their endemic suspicion of the Palestine administration was too deep-rooted to be appeased by verbal declarations of good intent. Deciding upon the degree of unreasonableness or agitation was a matter of judgment, and the Zionists felt they had no cause to take on trust the objective evaluations of the administration. Moreover, the proposals, as enunciated by Wauchope, gave the Arabs at least 50 per cent of the seats; parity had indeed been discarded. These two factors made Zionist rejection inevitable. It was deadlock. The government had put forward its proposals; the Zionists had rebuffed them.

In September the Zionists reaffirmed their opposition to the scheme at their Congress.[86] Their uncompromising stance had some effect. Wauchope told Weizmann, "perhaps in the end the Arabs would refuse it, which might after all be the best way out".[87] Weizmann concluded that Wauchope "is by no means enamoured of the Council idea, and would not be sorry to see the thing fall through provided he could say that the government had kept its word".

This was an accurate estimation of Wauchope's view. He was clearly convinced that pledges, once given, were meant to be put into effect. If not, then the honour of the government crumbled and its word fell into disrepute. There was a certain blind logic in this train of thought; and one could almost envisage the death knell sounding for a great colonial power like Great Britain if words once spoken were not translated into action.

On 25 November the Arabs presented a memorandum to Wauchope which included the demand for a democratic government.[88] By the end of the year the position was considered serious enough to conscript the help of the parliamentary pro-Palestine committee. On 17 December the committee met under Wedgwood's chairmanship. As a result a delegation attended J. H. Thomas (he had exchanged offices with MacDonald on 22 November) the following afternoon. Thomas insisted that the details of the meeting be kept confidential, but the delegation came away "fairly optimistic and seemed of the opinion that the actual setting up the Council was very far from accomplished!"[89] Neither the Zionists nor their friends placed too much reliance upon Thomas's promises. But they decided against bringing further pressure to bear, "because if he was being honest . . . there was no need to impress him further. But if he were merely fobbing us off, there was nothing to be hoped from having other persons see him . . ."[90]

Thomas's assurances had no basis in reality. On 22 December Wauchope conveyed to the Zionists the details of the proposed new constitution for Palestine.[91] There followed no discussion. Weizmann read out a statement from a prepared typescript registering the Jewish Agency's refusal to co-operate, and the meeting came to an end.[92] The breach with Wauchope was now open and public. Only Mrs. Dugdale retained a glimmer of optimism : "Somehow I cannot believe that this ridiculous project will ever come to birth."[93]

The new year saw the Zionists swamped, if not overwhelmed, by a series of old debating points given a fresh lease of life. They had "authentic information"—which was entirely accurate[94]—that the government contemplated new legislation restricting land sales and immigration quotas. These, coinciding with the council proposals, appeared as a "studied attempt to crystallise the National Home", and understandably invoked memories of the Passfield white paper.[95]

At a tense and heated meeting with Wauchope—the government was accused of taking this action at a time when Jews "were simply drowning in their own blood"—Weizmann declared that they would fight the government to the last ditch.[96] In effect this meant standing firm on the question of a council while co-operating with the government "in all other matters in a friendly spirit".[97] Weizmann believed "we are likely to win through in the end, although we are in for a period of trouble, and the government is making it very difficult for us".

Weizmann's suspicions that the present three-pronged attack upon the National Home was premeditated lacks conclusive evidence, and he as good as admitted this to Wauchope at a later date.[98] But the government's lack of foresight in not communicating to the Zionists the proposed legislation in its earliest drafting stages —they certainly had a right to expect such consultation—could only exacerbate existing relations between the two sides. But it was more a matter of incompetence and negligence than designed malice.

Weizmann's friends in London interviewed Thomas in an attempt to salvage the situation. The more sedate atmosphere of Whitehall produced happier results. Thomas admitted his dislike of the council and that he would prefer the scheme to be dropped. To facilitate this he had put forward two suggestions which, he hoped, would cause the Arabs to reject outright the proposals. The first insisted on the eligibility of women to participate as council members. He somewhat mysteriously refused to divulge the contents of the second suggestion. We now know that the second suggestion concerned the extent to which council proceedings should be privileged or not. On Wauchope's initiative, the cabinet had agreed to so restrict council proceedings and members' privileges as to empty that body of any decisive power.[99] Hence he could confidently assure his audience that whatever happened "the powers of the Council would not be greater than a parish council".[100]

Contrary to the popular version of events there was no Zionist plan of campaign to raise the council issue in parliament. Rather, the evidence points in the opposite direction in that the initiative came from the Gentile Zionists, particularly those on the Labour benches. The Zionists were as much taken aback by this move as the government, but of course they exploited to much greater advantage the opportunity once given.

This is not to say that Weizmann and his colleagues disregarded the parliamentary scene. But they envisaged fighting the government over the broad spectrum of Palestine politics through the medium of parliamentary questions, not a full-scale debate. Weizmann's instructions to Namier concerning parliamentary strategy contain no specific reference to raising the council issue in debate.[101] Even when Namier was informed, on 6 February, that Labour peers had put down certain resolutions on the council, his initial inclination was to widen the field of discussion to extend "over the general field of Palestine politics".[102] When Namier briefed Lord Eustace Percy for the forthcoming debate the conversation ranged from land legislation to economic development. The council was not mentioned.[103]

Despite Weizmann's trepidations the debate in the Lords took place on 26 February on a motion put by Lord Snell.[104] With one exception all the participants opposed the council proposals. Only the Earl of Plymouth, under secretary of state for the colonies, put up a rather desultory defence of his government's policy. The debate constituted an expression of no confidence in the government.

Although the Zionists had achieved a remarkable, if unexpected, parliamentary victory in the Lords, they were still undecided whether or not to press their advantage in the Commons.

At a small meeting yesterday afternoon . . . the question of further action in Parliament with regard to the . . . Council was considered . . Principal matter . . . therefore, whether a debate in the . . . Commons . . . would be desirable . . . possibility that it might be discussed on purely party lines . . . felt that this risk might be overcome and a satisfactory debate secured . . . a more serious danger . . . was that Thomas might force the matter to a vote by putting on the whips and defeating the resolution . . . The suggestion . . . that it might be possible to arrange in advance between the Leader of the Opposition and Thomas for a debate which would be moderate in tone . . . In the event of such an arranged debate, there would be no vote . . .[105]

There is nothing to indicate that the Zionists took the latter suggestion seriously. Quite the contrary, on 20 March Mrs. Dugdale remarked on the "sudden resolve of the Labour party to have a Palestine debate next week. Rather annoying, but if it is to be, then we must organize some speakers."[106] This is a striking illustration of how the Gentile Zionists often outpaced the Zionist leadership. In Weizmann's words, "we neither pull strings, nor can we hold even our friends in leading strings".[107] Later, Weizmann made it perfectly clear that he had opposed any debate taking place and had informed his parliamentary friends of his view, but with little success.[108]

The debate in the Commons duplicated its predecessor. The government suffered an overwhelming setback.[109] Wedgwood took some of the credit. "I have had a successful week . . . actually slain the Palestine constitution. I got Churchill and Chamberlain and Amery and Sinclair all to speak, and they did, leaving the Rt. Hon. J. T. Dress-shirt [Thomas] in tears."[110] Melchett summarised the possible political repercussions if the government continued in its policy :

. . . it is probable that the Labour Party will raise the matter again on the CO debate where there is an opportunity for a vote.[111] In this case, we understand . . . a considerable number of Conservatives, 50–60, are likely to vote against the government, and of course all the Liberals and Labour . . . this means the majority will fall to something . . . like 60 . . . a very serious blow to them and will make it very difficult for them to force the policy through . . .[112]

It must be apparent that the Labour party's initiative did not stem wholly from unsullied, altruistic motives concerning the fate of the National Home. They used their legitimate right as an opposition to challenge the government when expedient. But also they probably recollected the events of 1929–31, and wished to pay back the government in their own coin.

It might well be asked how the government allowed itself to be manœuvred into such a *cul-de-sac*. Elliot shed some light on the circumstances. He related to Weizmann that the cabinet system had, in a sense, broken down and that government decisions had become almost entirely departmentalised.

> In general Jimmy [Thomas] would no sooner think of querying what Walter had to say about milk production, than Walter would dare to interfere with Jimmy's departmental schemes.[113]

If this be a correct assessment then Palestine policy was led, controlled and directed by the officials in London and Jerusalem. Thomas admitted as much to Weizmann.

> Jimmy stressed again that the matter matured before he came to office, and mentioned what he had done, though unsuccessfully, to hold the matter up indefinitely . . . Apparently Wauchope had threatened to resign . . . and in the circumstances Jimmy said he had no alternative.[114]

Even before the crisis broke Weizmann concluded that,

> Thomas . . . would like to protract this matter, but I am certain that he will not succeed with Wauchope, if the latter succeeds in overcoming his difficulties with the Arabs. Wauchope is determined to get the Council through and Thomas . . . has not got enough influence to prevent him.[115]

What was needed was firm leadership at the top. Instead the colonial secretary was in the dying stages of a long career and about to leave political life in the most ignominious circumstances.

There was, therefore, some excuse for Mrs. Dugdale's personal vendetta against Thomas. She wrote: ". . . evident that Jimmy Thomas will be a very bad colonial secretary from our point of view. Weak, ignorant, blustering and indiscreet. All these qualities have shown themselves . . . over Legislative Council controversy."[116]

And again, "J. Thomas has been acting most annoyingly on affairs of Palestine. I have made up my mind he ought to leave the CO",[117] while to Lord Cecil she noted : ". . . I shall not rest until Billy Gore resigns in J. H. Thomas' stead. It is not fit that the future of Zion should be in the hands of a drunken ex-engine driver."[118]

The *coup de grâce* came a fortnight after the debate in the Commons. Thomas, in reply to a question by Wedgwood, stated that the government had invited an Arab delegation to London to discuss the proposals : "In the interval no further steps towards the establishment of the Legislative Council are being taken."[119]

On 15 April two Jews were murdered on the Nablus–Tulkarem highway, the first incident in the Arab rebellion that continued sporadically until the outbreak of the second world war. Any discussion of a legislative council now became purely academic.[120]

NOTES

1   The Arab position was fairly straightforward. They demanded majority rule and self-determination from the outset. In substance this demand never altered throughout the mandatory period.

2   See Cmd. 1500, *The Final Draft of the Mandate* (Aug. 1921), articles 2 and 3.

3   S. Landman, secretary of the Zionist Organisation, to J. Shuckburgh, 1 June 1921, C.O.733/16/27373; also Weizmann to Churchill, 21 July 1921, C.O.733/16/38128.

4   Sir J. Shuckburgh (1877–1953): An Indian, then colonial office official; assistant under secretary at the colonial office, 1921–31; deputy under secretary, 1931–42.

5   Weizmann, p. 468; see also his speech before the twentieth Zionist Congress in Aug. 1937, *Manchester Guardian*, 9 Aug. 1937.

6   Prior to this an Advisory Council had functioned alongside the Executive Council. It consisted of 10 British officials and 10 nominees: 4 Moslem and 3 Christian Arabs, and 3 Jews. This council went into abeyance in anticipation of the proposed legislative council. No doubt the government felt legally inhibited from taking an earlier initiative on this question due to the fact that the League Council did not ratify the Palestine mandate until July 1922.

7   For an account of those events, see Cmd. 1540, *The Haycroft Report . . . with correspondence* (Oct. 1921).

8   See, for example, Weizmann to Sir Wyndham Deedes, 13 Dec. 1921, C.O.733/16/6286.

9   These were the conclusions drawn from an interview between Maj. H. Young, of the colonial office, and H. Sacher and S. Landman for the Zionists, 23 Aug. 1921, W.A.; see also Samuel to Weizmann, 1 July 1921, W.A.

10   See Cmd. 1700, *Correspondence with the Palestine Arab Delegation . . .* (June 1922), p. 3.

11 *Ibid.*, pp. 9–10, 15.
12 These events may be followed in Cmd. 1700; and Cmd. 1889, *Papers Relating to the Elections for the Legislative Council* (June 1923).
13 See F. H. Kisch, *Palestine Diary* (London, 1938), pp. 29, 32–4. Samuel's threat of resignation also influenced the *Yishuv* in their reluctant decision, Slotski, ii, part 1, p. 168.
14 See *The Times*, 8 Jan. 1929; 21 June 1929; and 6 July 1929. For a résumé of these negotiations, see Chancellor to Passfield, 17 Jan. 1930, C.P.108(30), CAB.24/211.
15 Chancellor to Passfield, *loc. cit.*
16 The *Brith Shalom* (Covenant of Peace) movement held that Arab-Jewish understanding was a *sine qua non* for the establishment of the National Home. To attain this end they were prepared to consider far-reaching concessions. To such an extent that the official leadership often accused them of betraying the essence of the mandate and Balfour declaration. The movement hoped eventually for a bi-national constitution. For the interim period it supported a legislative council based on full democratic principles, only stipulating that the basic interests of the Jews should be safeguarded by the mandatory power. The partisan activities of the *Brith Shalom* frequently caused the Zionists acute embarrassment. The principles of the movement were enunciated in a series of pamphlets entitled *Sheifoteynu* (Our Aspirations) issued between 1927–31.
17 Minutes of a report by H. Sacher to the Zionist Executive, 11 Nov. 1929, W.A.
18 Minutes of an interview between Amery and Weizmann, 3 Dec. 1929, W.A.
19 See Cmd. 3530, p. 108; and Weizmann's report to the British members of the Jewish Agency, 8 Dec. 1929, W.A.
20 Minutes of an interview between Amery and Weizmann, 3 Dec. 1929, W.A.
21 Mrs. Dugdale to Weizmann, 9 Dec. 1929, W.A.
22 Weizmann to Warburg, 16 Jan. 1930, W.A.
23 W.D., 9 Jan. 1930, W.A.
24 Minutes of an interview between Weizmann and Shuckburgh, 27 Feb. 1930, W.A.
25 *Ibid.*
26 Weizmann to Warburg, 15 May 1930, W.A.
27 See below, pp. 14–15.
28 According to Weizmann Shuckburgh agreed half-heartedly to the meeting. Shuckburgh finally consulted Passfield and the interview took place the same week, Weizmann to Warburg, 15 May 1930, W.A.
29 W.D., 29 May 1930, W.A.
30 W.D., 6 June 1930, W.A.
31 Weizmann to Namier, 4 June 1930, W.A.; W.D., 2 and 3 June 1930, W.A.
32 Notes of an interview between Passfield and Weizmann, 7 July 1930, W.A.
33 See below, pp. 8–10.
34 See minutes of an interview between Passfield, Prof. Brodetsky, and Rutenberg, 18 July 1930, W.A.; also, W.D. 6 June and 18 July 1930, W.A.
35 Weizmann's proposal, made on Namier's prompting, was made in a letter to Passfield, 19 Sept. 1930, W.A. For the government's rejection of it, see, P.D., Commons, vol. 244, c. 833.

36 Minutes of an Interview between Passfield, Weizmann, and Namier, 1 Oct. 1930, W.A.
37 Kisch, pp. 348–50. There is little evidence in this account that Shiels was impressed by the Zionist arguments; but apparently they had some effect.
38 Sidney to Beatrice Webb, 7 Oct. 1930, P.P.
39 Cmd. 3692, p. 13, 15. The council would consist of the high commissioner, 10 official and 12 unofficial members. The latter, as in 1922, being elected by secondary voters.
40 W.D., 23 Oct. 1930, W.A.
41 See minutes of the first session of the conference, 17 Nov. 1930, W.A.
42 Minutes of the meeting of 4 Dec. 1930, W.A.
43 Official minutes of the fourth session, 19 Dec. 1930, W.A.
44 Minutes of an interview between the prime minister and Weizmann and Namier, 24 Dec. 1930, W.A.
45 Official minutes of the fifth session, 30 Jan. 1931, W.A.
46 L. Stein suggests, "It may be—but this is only a guess—that, on the J.A. side, the primary purpose of the discussions . . . was to remove objectionable suggestions in the White Paper . . . and of implications which were manifestly unacceptable, and that the Legislative Council proposals were viewed with dislike, but I think that it was not unanimously felt that they ought to be rejected out of hand." A private communication of 4 July 1967.
47 See below, pp. 23–25.
48 *Jewish Chronicle*, 20 Feb. 1931.
49 D. Ben Gurion (1886–   ): secretary general of the *Histadruth*, 1921–35; chairman of the Jewish Agency executive, 1935–48; prime minister of Israel, 1948–53, 1955–63.
50 Minutes of the meeting at Chequers, 12 July 1931, W.A. And for subsequent quotations.
51 *ESCO Foundation for Palestine: A study of Jewish, Arab and British Policies* (New Haven, 1947), ii, p. 745.
52 *Ibid.*, ii, p. 746.
53 *Ibid.*, ii, p. 747.
54 The only Zionist groups consistently committed to a bi-national solution were the *Brith Shalom* and the *Hashomer Hatzair* (The Young Guard) party. The latter was an extreme left wing, kibbutz (communal settlement) based party.
55 Chancellor to Shuckburgh, 16 Nov. 1930, P.R.O., Premier 1/103.
56 The political head of the Palestine Zionist Executive. He worked in close collaboration with Weizmann until his assassination in June 1933.
57 Miss D. May (Weizmann's secretary) to Weizmann, 19 April 1932, W.A.
58 See CAB.24/229, C.P.124(32); and cabinet minutes for 20 April 1932, CAB.23/71.
59 Arlosoroff to Brodetsky, tel. 8 Oct. 1932, W.A.
60 See CAB.24/234, C.P.374(32); and cabinet minutes for 9 Nov. 1932, CAB.23/72.
61 The year's grace was to allow a Local Government Ordinance to be drafted and put into effect.
62 Weizmann to Arlosoroff, 28 Oct. 1932, W.A.
63 *Ibid.*

aggravated by Churchill's agitation about India, made it extremely difficult for Baldwin to initiate a debate where he would have to speak while at variance with influential sections of his own party. This, at any rate, was Elliot's view. See Elliot to Weizmann, 7 Nov. 1930, W.A. Lloyd George too was unable to command the undivided support of his party, allegiances being divided between the Simonites, the Samuelites, and the Lloyd Georgists.

132 Notes of the meeting on 6 Nov. 1930, W.A. a verbatim report of this meeting appears in Vera Weizmann, pp. 114-16.

133 Weizmann to J. R. MacDonald, 12 Nov. 1930, W.A.

134 V. Weizmann, p. 114.

135 Weizmann to M. MacDonald, 12 Nov. 1930, W.A.

136 Weizmann to J. R MacDonald, 12 Nov. 1930, W.A.

137 Henderson to Weizmann, 13 Nov. 1930, W.A.

138 These took place on 17 Nov., 18 Nov., 5 Dec., 19 Dec., 1930; 30 Jan. and 12 Feb. 1931. The government was represented by: Henderson, the foreign secretary; Passfield, the colonial secretary; T. W. Shaw, secretary of state for war; A. V. Alexander, first lord of the admiralty; Craigie Aitchison, lord advocate to Scotland; and M. MacDonald. The Jewish organisations by: Weizmann, H. Sacher, Prof. S. Brodetsky and Namier. Dr. M. Hexter and Laski were the American observers. Others who attended some of the meetings were: J. de Rothschild, C. Arlosoroff, O. d'Avigdor Goldsmid, L. Motzkin, Dr. M. D. Eder, Dr. N. Goldmann and S. Kaplansky. The joint secretary was Maj. N. G. Hind.

139 See L. Stein, *Memorandum on the Palestine white paper of October 1930* (London, 1930).

140 Official minutes of the second session, 19 Nov. 1930, W.A.

141 Henderson to Weizmann, 29 Nov. 1930, W.A.

142 Namier and Stein were the two principal drafters for the Jewish Agency. On their shoulders fell much of the detailed work.

143 L. B. Namier, *Historical Survey of the Discussions leading up to the Prime Minister's letter of February 13, 1931 to Dr. Weizmann* (London, 27 May 1931), W.A.

144 Notes of the meeting, 4 Dec. 1930, W.A. Those present: Weizmann, Namier, Henderson and MacDonald.

145 *Ibid.*

146 Namier to Kisch, 11 Dec. 1930, W.A.

147 Weizmann to Warburg, 11 Dec. 1930, W.A.

148 Minutes of the conversation, 9 Jan. 1931, W.A.

149 Namier to Kisch, 4 Feb. 1931, W.A.

150 Minutes of the Zionist executive meeting, 10 Feb. 1931, W.A.

151 See a memorandum by Sir R. Vansittart, 4 Feb. 1931, Premier 1/103.

152 Contained in a report by Weizmann to the Zionist executive, 9 Feb. 1931, W.A.

153 Namier to Kisch, 10 Feb. 1931, W.A.

154 P.D., Commons, vol. 248, c. 389, 11 Feb. 1931. The cabinet had discussed this matter on 11 Feb. Both Passfield and Henderson had submitted memoranda arguing against the transfer of Palestine from the colonial office (see C.P.27(31), and C.P.28(31), CAB.24/219). The cabinet accepted their recommendations, see cabinet minutes, 11 Feb. 1931, CAB.23/66.

155   Notes of an interview between MacDonald, Weizmann and Namier, 24 Dec. 1930, W.A.

156   Namier to M. MacDonald, 13 Jan. 1931, W.A.

157   See official minutes of the meeting, 30 Jan. 1931, W.A.

158   Weizmann to J. R. MacDonald, 2 Feb. 1931, W.A.

159   Namier to Kisch, 4 Feb. 1931, W.A.; also cabinet minutes, 4 Feb. 1931, CAB.23/66.

160   Weizmann to J. H. Thomas, 6 Feb. 1931, W.A.

161   Minutes of the Zionist executive meeting, 9 Feb. 1931, W.A. The cabinet decided on 11 Feb. 1931 not to extend the terms of reference for the committee, see cabinet minutes, 11 Feb. 1931, CAB.23/66.

162   Namier to Kisch, 10 Feb. 1931, W.A.

163   Mrs. Dugdale to Weizmann, 9 Aug. 1931, W.A.

164   The following account and quotations are taken, except where stated to the contrary, from Namier, *Historical Survey* . . ., loc. cit., pp. 2–9.

165   It must be pointed out that Namier's relations with the Zionist executive were, at the best of times, always strained. This might explain the tone of his remarks.

166   Namier to Mrs. Dugdale, 11 Jan. 1931, W.A.

167   Cabinet minutes for 4 Feb. 1931, CAB.23/66.

168   See his letter to Ramsay MacDonald, 9 Feb. 1931, Premier 1/103.

169   See, for example, the report in the *Daily Telegraph*, 7 Feb. 1931.

170   P.D., Commons, vol. 248, c. 390, 11 Feb. 1931.

171   Minutes of a telephone conversation between the prime minister and Weizmann from the Zionist office at 9.30 p.m. W.A.

172   Official minutes of the sixth session, 12 Feb. 1931, W.A.

173   P.D., Commons, vol. 248, c. 599, 12 Feb. 1931.

174   P.D., Commons, vol. 248, c. 751–7, 13 Feb. 1931.

175   Weizmann to J. R. MacDonald, 13 Feb. 1931, W.A.

176   See Notes of an Interview between MacDonald, Ben Gurion and Namier, 12 July 1931, W.A.

177   Weizmann, p. 415.

178   Slotski, ii, part 1, pp. 444–5.

2

A Note on the Whitechapel By-Election

At the time of the publication of the Passfield white paper a by-election was pending in the safe Labour seat of Whitechapel and St. George.[1] It was estimated that the Jewish electorate in the constituency amounted to more than forty per cent of the total vote. It seemed clear, therefore, that the election would be dominated by the Zionist issue then very much in the public eye.

The political storm that emerged from the white paper quickly put paid to a government notion to foist Stafford Cripps upon the constituency. He was a member of the offending government (as solicitor-general), and his chance of success seemed slender to an extreme in a constituency where the Jewish vote, hitherto reliable, now appeared dubious.[2]

The Transport and General Workers Union was closely involved in the election. Many of its members resided in the constituency and the deceased member of parliament had been president of the union. After Cripps had been dropped, E. Bevin, the Union's general secretary, was asked by Henderson to stand as the Labour candidate. Bevin refused. But the Union did agree to take the constituency under its wing and the eventual Labour candidate was Mr. J. Hall, an executive member of the Union.

Bevin had been in contact with Jewish organisations and was well aware of their hostility towards the white paper. He apparently told his chief Jewish contact, a leading member of the Palestine labour movement named Dov Hos, that he would "instruct my boys" to vote against the government if the white paper were not amended.[3] He then wrote a memorandum for the government indicating that he shared Jewish apprehensions and that unless the government would give some definite assurance to make amends he would withhold the union candidature. On 4 November he issued the government's reply: there was to be no stoppage of immigration and no crystallisation of the National Home. With this assurance Bevin entered into the campaign.

It was common knowledge that the government was concerned over Whitechapel.[4] The *Jewish Chronicle* had publicly appealed to Jewish voters "not to give their votes to the Labour candidate".[5] In November the government confirmed the impression that they were seriously rattled over their prospects in Whitechapel. Suddenly they released 1,500 immigration certificates. This convenient concession to Zionist demands after months of inactivity did not go un-noticed,[6] and was widely interpreted as an ostentatious gesture designed to win back wavering Zionist voters.

These tactics did not appease the Jews or help the Labour candidate. At a Conservative meeting on 20 November, Henry Mond, Lord Melchett's son, read out a message to the voters on behalf of his father:

> I appeal to the Jewish electors of Whitechapel not to cast a single vote for a representative of a party whose Government, and those serving them, have only shown in manifold directions their ill will to our movement.[7]

It was inevitable that the candidates themselves would make political capital from Jewish hostility towards the white paper. But now the Jews themselves took the issue into the party arena. B. Janner,[8] the Liberal candidate, was both a Jew and a convinced Zionist, and he anticipated the Jewish vote falling to him irrespective of prior political conviction. Owing to Bevin's intervention and the repeated pledges of support voiced by Hall—he had given an undertaking to vote against the government if necessary—the *Poelei Zion* (the Jewish Socialist Labour Party, affiliated to the Labour Party) had decided to back the Labour candidate. Janner complained to Weizmann, but, as might be expected, received scant comfort from him. Weizmann merely regretted that the Jewish vote would be divided along party lines.

Of all the candidates Hall had the roughest ride. He issued a special statement declaring Labour's adherence to the idea of a National Home. The statement, written in English and Yiddish, was circulated to every Jewish home in the district.[9] *Poelei Zion* organised a mass meeting in his favour, only for it to end in chaos. Attempts by H. Snell to quiet the hecklers were met with cries of: "No! We are anti-Labour, we are true Zionists!" The uproar lasted for over ten minutes, until finally the police were summoned to restore order and eject the hostile demonstrators.[10]

Major M. Marcus, M.P., speaking at the same meeting, exploded something of a bombshell. He stated that he had already seen a document, a copy of which was being sent to Dr. Weizmann that night, "which contains proposals which will materially influence the present position in favour of the Zionists". The reference is undoubtedly to the Henderson letter. As the letter was not delivered to Weizmann until the 29th one can only assume that Marcus was the recipient of an inspired leak intended by the government to reassure a mass Jewish audience of their good intentions.

This revelation caused Weizmann some anxiety. He contacted Philip Noel Baker and informed him that after Marcus's announcement Zionists throughout the world would assume that he was in possession of the government's reply and was deliberately holding it back. This would make his position untenable. Professor Harold Laski used his influence with Henderson to obtain a copy of the letter as soon as possible, and on 29 November it was delivered to the Zionists.[11]

Polling took place on Wednesday, 3 December. The Labour candidate was returned, although with a greatly reduced majority.[12] Labour lost the overall majority she had gained in the general election, and her majority over the liberal candidate had been reduced to a mere 1,088 votes. The electorate had severely impaired Labour's prestige, and without question the Zionist issue contributed most towards the damage.[13] Hence, there was little cause for Bevin to proclaim the result as a "great victory".[14] It was victory, but only just. The result must have reminded the minority Labour government that in constituencies where there was a large Jewish vote they could not afford to let the white paper pass without serious amendment. And this at a time when they were involved with the Jewish Agency in negotiations about the white paper.

NOTES

1 The election resulted from the death of Mr. H. Gosling, M.P., president of the Transport and General Workers Union. At the general election in May 1929 the results were: H. Gosling (Labour), 13,701; F. H. Sedgwick (Liberal), 4,521; T. L. E. B. Guiness (Conservative), 3,417.

2 See A. Bullock, *The Life and Times of Ernest Bevin* (London, 1960), i, pp. 455–7; also, *Jewish Chronicle*, 7 and 14 Nov. 1930.

3 M. Pearlman, *Ben Gurion Looks Back* (London, 1965), p. 71.

4   See, for example, *The Times*, 4 Nov. 1930.

5   *The Jewish Chronicle*, 28 Nov. 1930.

6   *The Times*, 18 Nov. 1930.

7   *The Times*, 21 Nov. 1930.

8   Barnett Janner (1892–   ): Liberal M.P., 1931–5, Labour M.P., from 1945; has since acted as president of Board of Deputies of British Jews and Zionist Federation of Great Britain and Ireland. Kt. 1961. Cr. Life Peer, 1971.

9   *The Times*, 26 Nov. 1930.

10 *The Times*, 28 Nov. 1930.

11 W.D., 28 Nov. 1930, W.A.

12 The figures were: J. Hall (Labour), 8,544; B. Janner (Liberal), 7,445; T. L. E. B. Guiness (Conservative), 3,417; and H. Pollit (Communist), 2,106.

13 It should not be thought that the campaign was fought exclusively on the Zionist issue. Two other problems were very much to the fore: unemployment; and adequate provision for non-provided schools, particularly Roman Catholic ones.

14 Bevin to S. Kaplansky (secretary of *Poelei Zion*), 8 Dec. 1930, C.Z.A., Z4/3555 I. Bevin tended to exaggerate his intervention in the whole affair, important though it was; see his interview with L. Glick, 18 July 1932, C.Z.A. S25/802.

3

The Question of Self-Government

The problems of representative government raised acute questions of policy for both the Zionists and the British.[1] The government was under a mandatory obligation to secure "the development of self-governing institutions" and to "encourage the widest measure of self-government for localities consistent with the prevailing conditions".[2] There developed a conflict in approach between the British and the Zionists on the method and pace needed to achieve self-government.

The Zionists interpreted the mandate as explicitly endorsing a definite priority in the establishment of a National Home. Any reading of the mandate clearly establishes that the formulation of the articles was primarily intended to serve Zionist interests. Once this had been achieved the movement towards self-government could go ahead. The British, while recognising the obligation of establishing the National Home, saw no necessary contradiction between the achievement of this aim and the immediate laying of the foundations of self-governing institutions.

Zionist objections to the concept of immediate self-government were well known at the colonial office. They argued that the standard of education and political experience of the population of Palestine did not make the experiment "expedient or opportune". As the mass of *fallachim* were illiterate and under the influence of a few *effendis*, any representative body based on such an electorate would be unfriendly both to British policy and the National Home.[3]

Landman's letter succeeded in stirring the waters of the colonial office. Clausen, an official, minuted his letter :

Although there is no intention to create at an early date a Legislative Council . . . it is definite policy of H.M.G. to allow local population as large a measure of management of affairs as compatible with J[ewish] N[ational] H[ome] . . . therefore proposed to introduce representative principle into Advisory Council at early date. Most unwise, in present situation in Palestine to refuse absolutely non-Jewish demand for some voice in management of their own affairs.

It was left to John Shuckburgh,[4] head of the Middle East department of the colonial office, to illustrate the dilemma facing British policy. In a covering note to Churchill he pointed out

> two distinct obligations. Firstly, a Jewish National Home policy; and secondly, the introduction of representative government . . . the Zionists argue they are incompatible and must therefore give preference to set up a Jewish state and ignore local opinion. Must find means of reconciling our obligations . . . a difficult task . . . must resist pressure from both sides.

Theoretically the argument was sound; in practice it carried no weight whatsoever. The Arabs consistently set their political sights too high to allow the British to reconcile the twin obligations. This, together with invariable Arab opposition to the concept of the National Home, confirmed the Zionists in their view that any move towards representative government, however insignificant and innocuous by normal colonial office standards, would be exploited by the Arabs for a concerted attack upon the National Home.

This negative posture towards representative government touched upon a sensitive Zionist nerve : public opinion. The Zionist movement, perhaps suffering from a surfeit of internal democracy, appeared to adopt a typically *colon* attitude to the question of self-government, thus laying itself open to accusations of authoritarian, anti-democratic tendencies. Weizmann, forever conscious of world public opinion, realised the implications of such a stance.

> The position in which we placed ourselves by our refusal to consider the legislative council was . . . an unfortunate one. The public heard the words "legislative council for Palestine"; it heard of Zionist opposition; the obvious conclusion was that the Zionists were undemocratic or anti-democratic.[5]

The Zionists were not opposed to all forms of representative government indiscriminately and without qualification. But they were not prepared to place the future of the National Home in the hands of Arab extremists. However, this was a flexible principle and around it there was room for much manœuvre. The Zionists did encourage the development of municipal government. Indeed they saw this as a necessary prerequisite for broader measures of self-government as it involved co-operation between the two races and experience in the arts of administration. Again, the Zionists championed the idea of parity in governmental institutions, a notion that emerged from the crisis of 1929–31. These questions will be examined later in the chapter.

The first attempt to introduce some form of representative government[6] occurred during the years 1921–3, and it arose directly as a result of the disturbances of May 1921.[7] The Zionists were convinced that concessions were being made to the Arabs at their expense. As evidence they cited the temporary suspension of immigration announced on 14 May by the high commissioner, Sir Herbert Samuel. This measure met with intense Zionist hostility,[8] and it was readily assumed that other concessions would be forthcoming, particularly in the field of constitutional reform. The Zionists formed the impression that Samuel was committed to giving the Arabs satisfaction in the form of a constitution, but that any concrete proposal would be devoid of real content. There would be the appearance of a constitution, not the reality of one.[9]

Samuel's initiative met with an entirely negative Arab response. They rejected the proposals on the grounds that "Zionist policy will be carried out under a constitutional guise".[10] Churchill, then colonial secretary, attempted a policy of appeasement, but to no avail. And he was eventually forced to remind the Arabs that government policy was to secure as large a measure of self-control without repudiating past pledges.[11] Despite the obvious lack of enthusiasm on the part of both parties Churchill went ahead with his constitutional plans. A proclamation of 1 September called for the establishment of a legislative council with an elected majority. An electoral system was organised and elections were actually held. However, the authorities met with a "large measure of non co-operation" from the Arabs and had to extend the voting period until 7 March 1923, and then again until 31 May. The Arab boycott was almost total. The situation was rapidly degenerating into a farce. On 29 May Samuel announced that "owing to lack of public response, the government have decided to suspend, for the time being, the establishment of a Legislative Council..."[12]

There can be little doubt that this admission of failure was received with satisfaction by the Zionists. The *Yishuv* had been far more vehement in its opposition to self-government than the leadership in London, and it was only after fierce and prolonged discussion within the community that eventual agreement was obtained to participate in the elections.[13] Hence Zionist interests were served, however indirectly, by the obduracy of the Arabs.

Samuel's statement terminated the first act of the council scheme. Not until the events of 1929 threw into confusion the relative stability of the preceding years was there to be another attempt.

As a result of the general upheaval of 1929 it was inevitable that fundamental assumptions concerning the mandate would come under close scrutiny. The problem of self-government was among the more important of such questions.

From the beginning of his administration Sir John Chancellor appeared receptive to the idea of representative government. During the summer of 1928 the two leading Arab factions, the Huseinis and the Nashashibis, patched up their long-standing feud and resolved to support the establishment of parliamentary government in Palestine. When Chancellor met Arab representatives in January 1929 he promised he would consider their request. In June he informed an Arab delegation of his intention to consult the colonial office on this matter. A month later he reported to the permanent mandates commission the government's intention to "examine the question with the desire to find the best possible solution".[14]

The August riots put an abrupt end to these feelers. But it seems apparent that Chancellor was anxious to initiate some form of representative government. Hence, when the question reappeared after the first shock of the disturbances had died down he once again grasped the banner of self-government.[15]

The Zionists believed that the council issue had been revived through unofficial channels. It came to their notice that Dr. Judah L. Magnus, chancellor of the Hebrew University and a leading member of the *British Shalom* group,[16] had been conducting negotiations with the Arabs with the intention of reaching an Arab-Jewish *rapprochement*,[17] and it was fully expected that Magnus would agree to a council based on full democratic principles.

Weizmann's personal attitude towards this problem was not as rigid as the official Zionist line. And indeed considerably more flexible than that of some Gentile Zionists. Leo Amery, for example, held that a purely democratic council would be fatal to the National Home, and that the Jews should have nothing to do with it.[18]

H. Sacher, then head of the political department of the Zionist Organisation, acting on Weizmann's instructions, echoed his chief's more indeterminate approach when giving evidence before the Shaw commission : "as a result of this natural process [immigration] there will be a Jewish majority in this country . . . what practical forms this . . . may take I do not intend to prophesy".[19] This was a reasonable diplomatic posture. No rigid lines had been drawn; the door was still open for negotiation.

Weizmann's motives were probably mixed. Conceivably he was concerned with public opinion, anxious to emphasise Jewish flexibility as opposed to Arab intransigence. Possibly his conciliatory attitude was to be exploited as a bargaining counter with the government. He therefore informed Amery of his inclination to discuss constitutional problems if the government would tell the Arabs that the mandate and Balfour declaration were not subject to revision and that this policy "is *chose jugée*".[20]

His uncertainty how to react can be further adduced from Mrs. Dugdale's advice. She indicated two alternatives : either total resistance or modification. Mrs. Dugdale opted for the latter, arguing that the Zionists would then enlist Conservative support "that has so far been lukewarm".[21] There was a general disenchantment in some Conservative circles concerning Labour's policy in India and Egypt, it being widely felt that the government was rushing its constitutional fences too fast. Mrs. Dugdale wished the Zionists to cash in on this feeling. Furthermore, she believed that Zionist tactics should concentrate on elaborating the local government system in Palestine and persuading London that the implementation of such a scheme must precede wider measures of self-government.

These arguments appeared to carry some weight, for Weizmann restated them in no uncertain manner,

> . . . at the beginning of the Labour regime . . . there was a tendency to grant as much self-government as possible to Egypt, Iraq, TransJordan and above all India . . . The devastating results of this policy have become manifest . . . It is quite clear that the setting up of fake democracies in backward countries . . . is mere eyewash and these institutions are breaking down throughout the Empire.[22]

Weizmann made clear his opposition to representative institutions. But he did not exclude co-operation with the Arabs in economic, social or cultural spheres. He believed that genuine joint effort in strictly non-political fields would provide the essential foundations for future political co-operation.[23] On another occasion he told Shuckburgh that no constitution of Palestine could be drafted that took into account only the 160,000 Jews at present in the country. Therefore, there could be no question of establishing a national government strictly in accordance with the present population figures, for Palestine was a country awaiting an incoming population of Jews.[24]

This was a recurring Zionist argument. It was based on the fact that it was the duty of the mandatory power to help facilitate the establishment of the National Home. This last phrase was given to widely different interpretations. The Zionists subscribed to the most lavish of them, while the government tended to define its intention by reference to many factors some of which did not rate too highly on the Zionist order of priorities.

Shuckburgh told Weizmann that "all these constitutional experiments are futile; they had broken down all over the Empire and they were not sincere".[25] However, Weizmann left Shuckburgh with the distinct impression that Passfield did not share his official's apprehensions. Passfield, no doubt, had his own preconceived ideas regarding constitutional change in the Empire. In the case of Palestine these opinions were strengthened by those of Chancellor's. During 1930 Chancellor's opinion hardened and the Palestine administration began to exert pressure systematically on the government to introduce another council scheme. Their efforts met with considerable success.

By the beginning of May 1930 discussions between an Arab delegation and the government were well under way. These caused the Zionists some concern. It was obvious that major issues such as immigration, land sales, and constitutional changes would not go by default. The prime minister told Weizmann that the Arabs were demanding "sweeping constitutional changes . . . amounting virtually to national Arab government".[26] The Arabs now had second thoughts about the legislative council and realised the mistake they had made in rejecting the proposals of 1922.

The one practical result of Weizmann's meeting with the prime minister emerged from the Rutenberg plan.[27] The prime minister suggested that Rutenberg meet Shuckburgh to fashion out the details of his programme.[28] Negotiations went ahead. At a meeting on 29 May the proposals were hammered into shape and cabled off to Chancellor in order to ascertain his views.[29] It had been agreed that two independent, democratically elected Jewish and Arab national councils be formed. Each would deal with its own communal problems. In addition an advisory committee consisting of two Arabs and two Jews would convene under the chairmanship of the chief secretary. At committee meetings subjects such as immigration and land problems would be acceptable for discussion, though the rights and functions of the Jewish Agency were not to be affected.

In effect these proposals represented no substantial concessions by the Zionists. The immediate emphasis was still on communal development leaving full representative institutions to an indefinite future. The advisory committee, although having the power to discuss highly controversial questions, had no power of decision. There could be little doubt that the Arabs would reject the Rutenberg plan out of hand. Moreover, there was no certainty that the Palestine administration would endorse the programme. Indeed the Zionists heard that Chancellor had informed the government of his disagreement, and requested that nothing be done until his arrival in London in early July.[30]

A few days prior to this information reaching the Zionists Weizmann had an uncomfortable session with Shiels in Geneva. Although the discussion surveyed a wide range of problems Shiels made no comment on the Rutenberg plan. He could hardly plead ignorance as he was present at the meeting of 20 May. His forgetfulness appears even more unusual when it is recalled that these proposals constituted the only agreed programme—if only in principle—between the government and the Zionists. Weizmann concluded : "I have gained the impression . . . that he either does not understand these things, or that he does not take them seriously.[31] The latter assumption was more probably the correct one.

The marked coolness in the British attitude can only be explained in terms of pressure exerted by the Palestine administration upon the metropolitan government. Weizmann made this clear when he met Passfield on 7 July : ". . . he [Chancellor] has gone all wrong . . . and will put forward constitutional reform which we shall certainly not accept". Passfield intervened : ". . . and we would not encourage them".[32] The pretentious nature of Passfield's remark could not have impressed Weizmann. He was already profoundly disillusioned with Passfield[33] and fully aware that the minister was tentatively rebuilding his diplomatic bridges with the Zionists and in particular with himself.

When the discussions concerning the Rutenberg proposals were resumed on 18 July the government produced a remarkable *volte-face*. Passfield denied that the government had ever approved of Rutenberg's suggestions and certain points, he claimed, were entirely unacceptable. It is quite certain that the original proposals underwent some modification, mainly as a result of the known opposition of the high commissioner. But the government had backed down. Everything, Passfield declared, hung on the Hope Simpson report. The Zionists left the meeting with the general impression "of an absolute negative to everything which we had to propose".[34] This was confirmed when the government turned down Weizmann's proposal to convene a round table conference where the government could act as "as honest broker" and where "the true spirit and intentions of both sides could be tested, and possibly the adherence of at least a section of the Arabs be gained to the idea of constructive work without which the legislative council has no *raison d'être* and could only do harm".[35]

On 1 October Weizmann again met Passfield for preliminary discussions concerning the publication of the government statement of policy. The minister, monopolising the conversation, informed Weizmann of the government's decision to establish an elective council.[36] All Zionist efforts for the past year had collapsed. But they made another belated, and in many ways typical, attempt to forestall the apparently inevitable.

In early October Shiels was in Palestine on an official visit. It is clear that the local Zionist leadership subjected him to considerable pressure.[37] In consequence he telegraphed Passfield urging him to reverse the previous decision concerning the council. Passfield commented on this extraordinary request :

> I have today a telegram from him [Shiels] . . . urging me to go back on the decision to have an elected Legislative Council, which Chancellor strongly pressed for, and had been approved by the cabinet. He is troublesome in this. After discussing with Wilson, [Passfield's permanent under secretary of state] I have decided to telegraph tomorrow that it is *too late* as I have imported it to Weizmann, and moreover I can't throw over Chancellor who convinced me and the office that an elected council however troublesome, is best, and anyhow necessary.[38]

The letter reveals Chancellor, or perhaps more accurately the Palestine administration, as the driving force behind the council proposal. Moreover, it suggests that the colonial office needed a great deal of persuasion as to the expediency of the proposal, and only reluctantly arrived at the conclusion that although "troublesome" it was, somehow, the best of two bad choices.

In the Passfield white paper the government announced its intention to establish "a measure of self-government", and that this step must "be taken in hand without further delay".[39] It was proposed to form a legislative council roughly in accordance with that of 1922. Possible boycotts were envisaged, but the government promised "that steps will be devised to ensure the election of all unofficial members in the event of non-co-operation". It did not specify what these steps would be. But other than reverting to appointed members, in which case the whole point of a council would have been lost, it is difficult to see what precise action could have been taken.

There was complete Zionist unanimity concerning the latest government proposals. Even the *Brith Shalom* concurred in the decision of the *Va'ad Leumi* (Jewish National Council in Palestine) not to participate in the suggested scheme.[40] But there was a general feeling that the Palestine administration would force the government's hand, while the Anglo-Jewish conference, convened to settle differences arising from the Passfield white paper, was in progress. Already it had come to the notice of the Zionists that a draft ordinance restricting land sales had been prepared by the administration. They argued that the subject was *sub judice* and that any new legislation on the topics then under discussion would adversly affect the present negotiations. The government refused to accept this and continued preparing new legislation.[41] The two sides deadlocked on this issue. And the fear of a constitutional *fait accompli* emanating from Jerusalem hung over the conference.

The legislative council question was first raised on 4 December. Henderson, although sympathetic to Weizmann's arguments, claimed that constitutional questions lay outside his terms of reference. And before engaging in a discussion on this topic he needed the consent of the prime minister and cabinet.[42] This dialogue was repeated at a meeting later in the month.[43] When Weizmann finally met the prime minister it was agreed that when the work in hand had been successfully terminated the committee would be reappointed with enlarged terms of reference covering the neglected topics.[44] Henderson underwrote this promise at a later session of the conference.[45]

It is not clear why the constitutional questions should have been excluded from the original terms of reference of the subcommittee. The suggestions as enunciated in the white paper were totally unacceptable to the Zionists. The point of the negotiations was to clarify disputed issues arising from the white paper and where possible to amend them. Hence, neglecting this vital section of the Passfield statement made little sense—at least from the Zionist standpoint.[46] It is arguable that the government did not want to overburden itself with too many controversial problems at one and the same time. Hence, their reluctance to include the subject in the present negotiations, and their apparent willingness to consider the topic within another framework.

The other framework—the subcommittee with enlarged terms of reference—proved to be a false starter.[47] And the net result of those negotiations was simply that the council proposals, as expressed in the white paper, still held. The white paper was not rescinded. The prime minister had made it clear from the outset that there could be no question of withdrawing the document. The MacDonald letter itself contains nothing concerning constitutional policy in Palestine. All that the government had done was to express sympathy with the Zionist case.

While the Zionists remained firm over land and immigration, they allowed the equally crucial question of constitutional government to be shelved for discussion in the distant future. This was clearly a grave miscalculation. Possibly, Weizmann, having already gained so much, was prepared to adopt a more flexible attitude concerning the council, particularly in view of the undoubted sympathy of some leading members of the government. He might also have reasoned that self-government was not an immediate danger and could, therefore, be safely left to the future.

This frame of mind, although comforting at the time, was no guarantee to future events. Weizmann, perhaps more than most, should have appreciated that ministers come and go while white papers remain the legal basis for government policy. The Zionists paid dearly for this lapse in foresight, for Sir Arthur Wauchope, Chancellor's successor as high commissioner, came to consider the Passfield pledge as weighing heavily on the conscience of England and one that had to be redeemed almost at any cost.

For the present Weizmann and his supporters came under heavy attack from their opponents within the Zionist camp.

64　He wrote of them as "ignorant of the mentality of the British negotiators . . . considered problems not on their own merits, but always with an eye to the press of New York or Warsaw . . . it is inconceivable that I could ever have sat round the table with gentlemen of this kind . . . I did not realise the enormity of what I was doing." Weizmann to Arlosoroff, 28 June 1932, W.A.

65　Weizmann to Namier, 10 Nov. 1932, W.A.

66　Arlosoroff to Weizmann, 20 Nov. 1932, W.A. And for subsequent quotations.

67　Only the Nashashibi faction was prepared to consider Wauchope's proposals and then, it was widely believed, in order to entrench themselves at the expense of the Huseinis.

68　P.D., Commons, vol. 283, c. 259, 23 Nov. 1933.

69　Minutes of the meeting of 18 Dec. 1933, W.A.

70　Cabinet conclusions for 11 April 1934, CAB.23/78.

71　See his memorandum of 28 March 1934, CAB.24/248, C.P.95(34).

72　Minutes of an interview between Ben Gurion and Wauchope, 15 Aug. 1934, W.A.

73　Minutes of a Jewish Agency executive meeting, 13 Sept. 1934, W.A.

74　Minutes of an interview between Cunliffe Lister and Weizmann, 4 Oct. 1934, W.A.

75　See his note of 11 Nov. 1934, CAB.24/251, C.P.256(34).

76　Mrs. Dugdale to Weizmann, 12 Nov. 1934, W.A.

77　Miss D. May to Weizmann, 9 Nov. 1934, W.A.

78　It was, however, as a result of this issue that the rift between the Zionists and MacDonald began to emerge. Weizmann, at the hight of the crisis, described him as "a weak man and a broken reed . . . I shall be sorry if we will have to get into conflict, particularly with Malcolm whom I like, and who is thoroughly honest but thoroughly weak." Weizmann to Melchett, 17 Jan. 1936, W.A.

79　Weizmann to MacDonald, 14 June 1935, W.A. Wauchope was to inform the Zionists of an outline scheme on 15 June, and the Arabs on the 19th.

80　Minutes of an interview between Wauchope and Shertok (then head of the political department of the Jewish Agency and a member of its executive), 16 June, 1935, W.A.

81　Minutes of an interview between Wauchope and Shertok, 27 June 1935, W.A.

82　Weizmann to Shertok, 17 June 1935, W.A.

83　Weizmann to Shertok, tel. 18 July 1935, W.A.

84　Weizmann to MacDonald, 5 July 1935, W.A.

85　Shertok to Weizmann, tel. 21 July 1935, W.A. The council was to consist of the following: 8 elected and 3 nominated Moslems; 1 elected and 2 nominated Christians; 3 elected and 4–5 nominated Jews; and 5 British officials and 1–2 commercial members. The high commissioner was to retain extremely wide powers. He had an unrestricted veto; powers of legislation when the council was not in session; exclusive financial initiative; and powers of dissolution.

86　*New Judaea*, Sept. 1935, p. 205.

87　Minutes of an interview between Wauchope and Weizmann, 10 Oct. 1935, W.A.

88　*Survey of International Affairs*, 1936, p. 722.

89　A. Lourie (then political secretary to the Jewish Agency in London) to

F

Shertok, 20 Dec. 1935, C.Z.A. S25/1378. The delegation was composed of: Wedgwood, Lord Hartington, B. Janner, T. Williams and James de Rothschild. About 40–50 members attended the previous meeting.

90   *Ibid.* He had been visited recently by S. Marks (twice), Brodetsky, T. Williams, Wedgwood, de Rothschild, R. Denman and the parliamentary committee.

91   See Cmd. 5119, *The Proposed New Constitution for Palestine* (March 1936), The structure and powers of the council closely approximated Wauchope's disclosures to Ben Gurion and Shertok in July. The Arabs had been informed on 21 Dec.

92   Minutes of the meeting, 22 Dec. 1935, W.A.

93   Mrs. Dugdale to Weizmann, 28 Dec. 1935, W.A.

94   See cabinet minutes for 15 Jan. 1936, CAB.23/83.

95   Weizmann to I. Sieff (now Lord Sieff), D. May, and Namier, 22 Jan. 1936, W.A.; also Weizmann to Melchett, 23 Jan. 1936, W.A.

96   Minutes of an interview between Wauchope, Weizmann, Ben Gurion, Shertok and Dr. A. Ruppin, 26 Jan. 1936, W.A.

97   Weizmann to Warburg, 19 Jan. 1936, W.A.

98   See Weizmann to Wauchope, 22 Feb. 1936, W.A.

99   See Thomas's memorandum, 10 Jan. 1936, CAB. 24/259, C.P.2(36); and cabinet conclusions for 15 Jan. 1936, CAB.23/83.

100 Sieff to Weizmann, 31 Jan. 1936, W.A. Sieff and Sacher saw Thomas on the morning of the 31st.

101 Weizmann to Namier, 5 Feb. 1936, W.A.

102 Namier to Weizmann, 7 Feb. 1936, W.A.

103 Namier to Weizmann, 12 Feb. 1936, W.A.

104 P.D., Lords, vol. 99, c. 750–93. The motion asked, "what is their [the government's] intention in regard to the proposed Legislative Council . . . whether they have considered the widespread objections . . . and whether they will consider . . . deferring the proposals until greater experience of local government . . . has been obtained".

105 Lourie to Wiezmann, 4 March 1936, C.Z.A., Z4/17122. Those who participated in the "small meeting" were Melchett, Brodetsky, Dr. Eder, Namier and Lourie.

106 D.D., 20 March 1936.

107 Weizmann to Hexter, 27 Oct. 1936, W.A.

108 See Weizmann's speech at the twentieth Zionist Congress on 4 Aug. 1937. A verbatim report is contained in the *Manchester Guardian*, 9 Aug. 1937. Although this may be considered as an *ex post facto* justification, it is substantiated by the evidence.

109 P.D., Commons, vol. 310, c. 1079–1173, 24 March 1936.

110 C. V. Wedgwood, *The Last of the Radicals* (London, 1951), p. 191. Wedgwood wrote this in a letter to his daughter Cynthia at the end of March.

111 Wedgwood initiated the debate during the second reading of the Consolidated Fund Bill. The House does not divide on such a debate.

112 Melchett to Shertok, 27 March 1936, W.A.

113 Lourie to Shertok, 13 March, W.A.

114 *Ibid.*

115 Weizmann to Warburg, 19 Jan. 1936, W.A.

116 D.D., 21 Jan. 1936.
117 D.D., 22 Jan. 1936.
118 Mrs. Dugdale to Cecil, 17 Feb. 1936, Cecil Papers, MS.51157, British Museum.
119 P.D., Commons, vol. 310, c. 2760, 8 April 1936.
120 Constitutional proposals did reappear in the May white paper episode of 1939. However, these took shape in an entirely different political context and will be discussed in a later chapter.

4

The Seventh Dominion

As a result of the Great War, the Zionist movement came of age. For the first time since its inception as a political organisation, Zionism gained a backer of international and world-wide repute. The political charter which Herzl had hawked around the chancellories of Europe found its consummation in the Balfour declaration. The British Empire, in its moment of supreme crisis, stamped its seal of approval on the concept of a Jewish National Home in Palestine.

Of all the great powers Britain had shown herself the most receptive to territorial solutions of the Jewish problem.[1] Now, having finally linked Zionist aims and British interests through the Balfour declaration, other, more pertinent, questions intruded. What would be the future form of the National Home? Who would act as its guide and mentor?

There can be little doubt that both the Zionists and their Gentile supporters saw the ultimate development of the National Home as a Jewish state. Initially both parties were inhibited from placing their cards openly on the table. The Zionists argued that it was necessary to wait and see how the Jewish masses would respond to the opportunity given them. Meanwhile, it was essential to create as rapidly as possible the political, economic, and cultural bases of the National Home in Palestine. Weizmann's thesis was that "States must be built up slowly, gradually, systematically and patiently".[2] But he did not abandon hope of a Jewish state in the future. That, after all, was the *raison d'être* of Zionism. The Zionists have often been accused of "double-dealing" on this question.[3] There is certainly some truth in this. But the real question to be posed is : who were the Zionists deceiving? Not the British who were fully aware of the potential of their declaration. Nor the Palestinian Arabs who, at the time, were not taken very seriously as a national entity. They were, it seems evident, setting the minds of the non-Zionist Jewish

communities throughout the world at rest and attempting to relieve
them of the onerous burden of dual loyalty.

Later during delicate negotiations with the government and an
Arab delegation, Weizmann wrote to his close friend Sir Wyndham
Deedes, first chief secretary to the Palestine administration.

> They asked me to put in a phrase that the Zionists don't intend
> to create a Jewish state in Palestine. I refused to do so . . . [for
> the] chief reason that we cannot forswear such a possibility
> which might or might not arise in some future generation. I told
> them that at present we are building Palestine but it may be that
> some day Jews may be in ascendency there.[4]

Weizmann's organic approach reflected his distrust of rigid, inflex-
ible programme-making. It was obviously early days, apart from
being politically inexpedient, to make ringing declarations of future
intent.

British politicians, too, were under no illusions as to the future
result of the National Home policy. Balfour had gone on record as
saying that by the declaration they had always meant an eventual
Jewish state,[5] and this interpretation was later confirmed by Lloyd
George in his memoirs and in the evidence he offered before the Peel
commission.[6] As to who would act as protector of the National Home
until such time as she was able to stand on her own feet, there was
little doubt, and no real alternative, that Britain would fulfil the
role.

Having settled, in their minds if not on paper, the future status
of Palestine and its relations with Great Britain, it was inevitable
that more adventurous spirits should seek to define that relationship in wider and more intimate terms. Weizmann, who of all the
Zionist leaders was most closely linked to Britain, was best qualified
to give vent to such feelings. He did so at the height of a diplomatic
controversy with the government when, stung by the government's
nonchalant attitude to the still unratified mandate, he claimed that
"our logic, our claims to justice, our dream of a great Palestine
within the orbit of the British Empire is at present scoffed at,
misunderstood".[7] The phrase is of some importance. It reflected a
distant dream, an ultimate goal to be obtained if and when all the
immediate Zionist aims were realised. Content with giving voice to
the ideal, Weizmann was too pragmatic, too concerned with the
burning problems of the moment, to allow the vision to blur the
reality. It was left to the Gentile Zionists to accord concrete expres-

sion to the image of a Jewish Palestine lying within the orbit of the British Empire.

In February 1928 Wedgwood published a small book entitled *The Seventh Dominion*. The cause Wedgwood expounded was the eventual inclusion of a Jewish Palestine within the British Commonwealth. Wedgwood was one of the foremost patrons of Zionism in England. A passionate, devoted advocate, the pages of *Hansard* are littered with his championship of the National Home. In many ways he personified the Gentile Zionist both in motivation and deed. His first contact with Zionism came during the Great War. On 3 December 1914 he met Weizmann at one of Lloyd George's working breakfasts. He was profoundly impressed. Weizmann writes of the meeting, "It became clear that every person in the room was favourably disposed, and an atmosphere was created which warmed and encouraged me."[8] Wedgwood's feelings were reinforced when he came into contact with units of the Zionist Mule Corps during the Gallipoli campaign.[9] From then on his interest in Zionism never flagged until finally, as his biographer tells us, "Zionism had come level with and passed India as Josiah's chief interest outside his own country".[10]

It is of some interest to examine the factors that prompted Wedgwood, and so many of his contemporaries, to champion the Zionist creed. A great deal stemmed from the Protestant, non-conformist tradition. He wrote :

> The Anglo-Saxon, more than any other race, wants to sympathise with the Jews, and would like to settle up for these last two thousand years . . . We are both moneylenders, and unpopular; we, too, are wanderers among strange peoples; we, too, are traders, and if we rather look down on those with whom we trade, that is only what the Jews do too. We, too, find in the Old Testament, or Torah, convenient justification for all that needs justification in our relations with mankind. We, too, can laugh at ourselves, so sure are we of being in reality the Chosen People. Having all these tastes in common, no doubt we understand the Jew better than can those to whom the Old Testament is not familiar from infancy. To the foreigner the word Jew is a hissing in the street; to us the word suggests Solomon and Moses, and a thousand cradle stories. So often have we used their names for our own children that they seem now to be our fathers, specially our Puritan forefathers . . . When my ancestors hewed down the aristocrats at Wigan Lane and Naseby they were armed with the names of Aaron and Abner; and they rallied to the charge, call-

ing on the God of Israel in the language of the prophets . . .
Moses led out from Egypt the first non-conformists, the first free
thinkers to break away from idolatry and priestly rule. Judah
Maccabeus led the first national rising against the rule of tyrants
—led it to victory 1,600 years before Swiss or Scotch or Dutch
followed in the footsteps of these Jewish peasants . . . Towards
such a people one has a feeling almost of awe, they are so well
known, and yet so old and so eternal.[11]

He believed also that Zionism would restore to the Jews that
corporate national confidence they appeared to lack. "Zionism",
he claimed, "is now doing for the Jews what the Labour Party seeks
to do for the British working class—creating self-confidence and
corporate self-respect."[12]

Wedgwood was a Labour Imperialist. He believed in the British
Empire and its civilising mission, a mission, he contended, that was
being continuously sabotaged by bigoted and narrow-minded officials. "If it be Imperialism to be convinced that the race that
spread from, and came to, these islands is the finest on earth and in
history, then I am an Imperialist."[13]

Because of the close affinity between the British and the Jews,
Zionism, in Wedgwood's eyes, was destined to spread the gospel in
the Arab East. "We can . . . immigrate the Jews until the higher
civilisation is numerous and wise enough to make democracy safe
for all."[14] Zionism, he assumed, would hold high the banner of the
Empire and all it stood for: justice, democracy, and freedom.[15]
Therefore, it was in British imperial interests to co-operate with
the Zionists as the latter would truly serve the greater ideals upon
which the Empire was founded.[16] Hence the Gentile Zionists, or
some of them, did not act purely from philanthropic motives; it was
argued that Zionism was a British interest.

There were other British interests to be safeguarded of no lesser
importance than bringing Western civilisation to the desert.

Those who do settle in Palestine are likely to be of real political
and commercial service to the Empire, for Palestine is the
Clapham Junction of the Commonwealth. The air routes, as well
as the ocean routes, east and west, and south and north, cross
here, where one flank rests on the Suez canal and the other on the
port of Haifa, the natural trade base of Mesopotamia. With pipe
line and railway debauching at Haifa under Carmel, the British
fleet can look after the Near East in comfort and safety.[17]

The link between the Protestant tradition and the Jewish re-
naissance; the debt owed by Gentile society for centuries of persecution; the recovery of Jewish self-respect; the civilising mission
enjoyed by Gentiles and to be emulated by Jews; and the strategic
considerations. All these are to be found in *The Seventh Dominion*
and all are to be discovered, to a lesser or greater degree, in the
make-up of the Gentile Zionist.

But *The Seventh Dominion* was not only an exposition of the
characteristics of a Gentile Zionist. It was also a crushing indictment of the Palestine administration which, Wedgwood, was convinced, had stifled the National Home in the cold grip of bureau-
cracy and uncompromising hostility. The solution he proposed was
simple. The alternatives of complete separation or transference
of the mandate to another power were rejected as being incom-
patible with British policy : "Therefore it must be Dominion home
rule."[18]

Wedgwood, somewhat naively, took it for granted that this was
the aim of the British government and that it was the duty of the
metropolitan government to inform the Palestine administration of
this aim and to ensure that they co-operated actively in fulfilling
the policy.[19] Such was the political programme envisaged by the
author of *The Seventh Dominion*.

The book was not received by the general public with unreserved
enthusiasm. *The Times* put on the best face, remarking, "the author
makes breezy suggestions full of good sense".[20] The traditionally pro-
Zionist *Manchester Guardian* observed that, "he and his party will
lose their case if they are going to be so frankly philistine and care-
less as to anything but commercial progress . . . his attitude to the
Arabs is absurd".[21] (Wedgwood usually referred to the Arabs as
"natives".) It was left to the *Observer* to sum up the average attitude
of the informed Englishman : "[with his] usual gay courage Colonel
Wedgwood invites the British public to think of Palestine as a future
Dominion . . . The book, which is written with an enthusiasm which
raises occasional doubts as to the author's judgment . . . closes with
a fine justification of Zionism."[22] Wedgwood was not deterred by
this lukewarm reception; nor was he content to let the matter rest
with the publication of a single book. He went ahead to initiate
practical measures to put his thesis into effect.

On Tuesday, 26 February 1929, the Seventh (Palestine) Dominion League was inaugurated at a public meeting held at the Central

Hall, Westminster. The meeting was presided over by Sir Martin Conway, M.P., and addressed by Wedgwood (who had been elected chairman of the fledgling organisation), Commander J. M. Kenworthy, M.P., Mr. Joseph Cowen and Sir Robert Hamilton. Messages of support were read on behalf of Mr. L. Hore Belisha, M.P., Dr. Drummond Shiels, M.P., and Sir Archibald Sinclair. On the whole the arguments put forward corresponded closely to those enunciated by Wedgwood in his book. There was perhaps more emphasis placed on purely British interests, but that was inevitable as the League was founded to persuade the British public of the righteousness of the cause.[23]

Wedgwood lost no opportunity of propagating his scheme. To a Jewish audience in Clapton, North London, he proclaimed their joint aim of Jewish settlement in Palestine and "the widening of civilisation and the spreading of culture".[24] He informed parliament that it was the intention of the government "to make Palestine develop into a self-governing country which shall take its place as one of the free self-governing Dominions of the British Empire",[25] a remark that went unchallenged, perhaps unheeded, by government spokesmen.

On 7 May the League held its first general meeting and elected an executive.[26] Wedgwood had plans to found branches throughout the Empire; it appeared to be succeeding. He certainly gained the support of the widely read organ of Anglo-Jewry, the *Jewish Chronicle*.

> [It] may well prove to be a vital point in Jewish history . . . [it will] utilise the Balfour Declaration and Palestine mandate . . . for the benefit both of Jews and the British Empire . . . Everything, therefore, should be done by Great Britain to encourage and stimulate Jewish effort, so that Palestine redeemed may develop into a Seventh Dominion of the Empire . . . the invitation . . . should be accepted in the spirit in which it is made, with alacrity and enthusiasm.[27]

The aims of the League were received with immediate effusiveness by the Revisionists. In October 1928 Wedgwood's aspirations were acclaimed at a Revisionist meeting in Berlin.[28] The following month the Seventh Dominion scheme was welcomed and endorsed in a formal resolution adopted by the All Palestine Zionist/Revisionist conference in Jerusalem, Jabotinsky being a party to the proceedings.[29]

Jabotinsky in particular seemed fascinated by the proposal. His biographer estimates that "the 'Dominion' concept gained his unreserved approval".[30] Certainly his ardour knew no bounds. In a letter to Wedgwood (which, incidentally, he requested be kept confidential) he visualised the project as "more than brilliant and clever—it is a service to both causes, the British and the Zionist". And, throwing all caution to the wind, "Had we today even a 99 per cent majority in Palestine, I, the extremist, would still fight every idea of independence and would insist on keeping within the British Empire."[31] In May 1928 Jabotinsky accepted the chairmanship of the newly constituted branch of the League in Jerusalem.[32]

During the days of the Sixteenth Zionist Congress an interview with Jabotinsky appeared in the *Jewish Chronicle* on the subject of the League. Once again the fervour was passionate, even evangelical :

> It would be a blessing for any land to become a partner in the British Commonwealth of Free Peoples . . . the invisible tie binding Britain and the Dominions is the most remarkable achievement in the world's political history . . . the core [not every detail, of course] of British statesmanship is a thing of almost divine inspiration ! . . . If . . . his [a British official] instructions read . . . "a Jewish Palestine is Britain's need, not only the Jews' need"— then the British official would conceive this order brilliantly . . . the main difficulty we shall have to surmount [is] the re-establishment of confidence in Great Britain and teaching our people to draw a sharp distinguishing line between a bureaucracy and a nation. And we shall succeed.[33]

Jabotinsky's predisposition towards England was wholly characteristic of certain elements of East European Jewry. His faith in the ultimate good will of the government combined with a conviction that the Palestine administration was sabotaging Anglo-Zionist relations represented the foremost view within the Zionist movement. Perhaps these feelings gave him a natural leaning towards close association with England. But it should not be forgotten that Jabotinsky represented a minority group within Zionism. His was a vociferous opposition. And where the official Zionist leadership feared to tread, Jabotinsky could, with impunity, afford to rush in.

Meanwhile, a degree of opposition, or at the best very lukewarm support, had emerged following the establishment of the League. Neither the government nor the opposition registered approval of the scheme. The reason was obvious. Great Britain held the mandate for Palestine in trust from the Council of the League of Nations. Her duties under the terms of the mandate were specific : to secure the establishment of the National Home and develop self-governing institutions which, it was hoped, would eventually lead to self-government. Great Britain's role was intended to be transient. Any attempt to impose a quasi-permanent character on her protectorate would give rise to serious international repercussions. To do this less than seven years after the ratification of the mandate would confirm suspicious minds abroad of Britain's machiavellian, imperialist plots. It was little wonder, and could have come as no great surprise to the founders of the League, that the government politely turned a deaf ear to the whole business.

In any case the mandate was a legal document and could not be altered unilaterally. Article 27 stated that "the consent of the Council of the League of Nations is required for any modification of the terms of the mandate". Wedgwood himself was plainly aware of these drawbacks. He answered his critics,

> . . . in visualising Palestine of the future as part of the British Commonwealth of Nations, we do not commit any act of disloyalty to the League of Nations or the terms of the mandate. If Palestine is to be a Seventh Dominion, it will be by the free will of its population, who will take a voluntary step in choosing for the country the status of a British Dominion after the expiration of the mandate.[34]

While Wedgwood set out the ultimate aim of the League clearly and concisely he also gave his supporters an interim task to fulfill : that of protecting the interests of the National Home. The League was also to act as a day-to-day Zionist pressure group. Indeed it might appear as though that was the most functional of the League's purposes.

The attitude of leading politicians of the day can best be gauged from the opinion of Leo Amery. He believed the movement had no immediate possibilities. In principle he favoured the idea, although he thought it somewhat superfluous while the British government actually exercised full sovereignty in Palestine. However,

> if conditions in Palestine should change, become consolidated, and, in accordance with the mandate, the question of whether Palestine is fit for self rule should arise, then Amery prefers natur-

ally that both parts of the population should retain their connection with the British Empire by joining . . . as a Dominion.[35]

Amery's approval was hedged with "ifs", "shoulds", and "in accordances". He clearly saw the project as one for future reference, and one on which no serious politician should adopt hard and fast opinions. The attitude adopted by the official Zionist leadership was equally ambivalent.[36]

The Seventh Dominion also underwent a searching analysis from Chaim Arlosoroff.[37] The article was a mixture of criticism and agreement. He greeted the publication of the book as "if most significant, still premature . . . [and] somewhat precipitate . . . like a dream devoid of any reality, a random phantasy". The arguments he presents are so Weizmann-like in character and imagery that it seems quite apparent that Arlosoroff drew his inspiration from his leader.

> And as to the discussion of the ultimate political aims of Zionism, we have had more than one opportunity . . . to point out that such a discussion today is very ill timed . . . [it] has a doubtful influence within the ranks of the movement . . . It serves to divert Zionist energies from the point where they are most wanted . . . It sidetracks the attention of the movement and turns it into barren channels. It is dangerous to occupy the mind of the movement, at any time, with the discount of promissory notes on a distant future . . . The Jew, and for that matter the Zionist, thinks too much of the Zionist state and too little of the average annual yield of his cow which may help him establish a profitable dairy, and, progressively, systematic immigration, and, ultimately the Jewish state. He hardly needs appetizers for the discussion of distant issues, such as the Seventh Dominion presents to him.[38]

Arlosoroff's viewpoint was weighty and considerable. But this was by no means his final word. For though he fervently opposed the project as an immediate practicable proposition, he offered no disagreement in principle and considered the scheme would bring important long-term economic and political benefits to the *Yishuv*.

Was Arlosoroff for or against? It must have been difficult for a British-orientated Zionist like Arlosoroff, or Weizmann, to shrug off Wedgwood's proposal as a fantastic pipe-dream. Hence the indulgence in long-term benefits. But the intensely pragmatic character of this same group would brook no deflection from the day-to-day tasks of constructing the National Home and would not dissipate the energy and resources of the movement in theoretical and time-wasting discussions.

The position, therefore, was that the League attracted only the wholehearted support of a number of back-bench M.P.s, the *Jewish Chronicle* and the Revisionists. Wedgwood himself admitted the lack of support evoked by the League at a rally held in October 1929.[39] There is little evidence that the scheme found great favour in the eyes of the general public. Perhaps it was too chimerical in conception; perhaps Palestine was too remote from public scrutiny for an ambitious panacea to attract the attention and support it needed.

In August 1929 the situation underwent a radical change. The Arab riots of the same month and the subsequent commissions of enquiry and white papers all tended to place Palestine in the very forefront of political controversy. Now, it might be thought, Wedgwood's movement would gather strength and advance to consolidate its position. In fact the reverse happened. The crisis of 1929 led to the break-up of the League, and its leaders decided that in the emerging pattern of Anglo-Zionist relations there remained little hope of realising the League's aims.

Even before the riots had terminated Wedgwood was concerned at the way Anglo-Zionist co-operation was disintegrating. In Warsaw, for example, the Jews, incensed by the lack of effective protection given to Jewish settlers by the Palestine administration, had organised anti-British demonstrations. Similar sentiments were expressed in other Jewish centres throughout the world. Wedgwood asked the general public not to regard these events "as the final disillusionment with that British-Jewish co-operation which the Seventh Dominion League seeks to support".[40] He pleaded for a few more weeks of grace to allow a commission of inquiry to present the facts of the case. Two months later, with the Shaw Commission already in session, Wedgwood called for the start of a new era in Palestine.[41] Wedgwood was clearly under the impression that the Shaw commission would verify the worst suspicions of the League. He was to be bitterly disappointed. The report of the commission came as a severe shock to both the Zionists and their Gentile supporters. Worse was to follow. Throughout 1930 the Zionists suffered setback after setback. Anglo-Zionist relations stumbled from crisis to crisis until finally, with the publication of the Passfield white paper, they ground to an official halt.

At the time the white paper was issued Wedgwood was incapacitated through ill health and unable to conduct a campaign of retribution in person. Whatever the effects of his illness upon his general morale, the devastating blow struck at Anglo-Zionist relations plunged him into the depths of deep disillusion. The League, through the pen of its chairman, seceded from the political arena.

About two years ago I helped to found a Seventh Dominion League . . . to develop a friendly Palestine and a sound prop to the Empire. We had a fair success in the House of Commons and outside; but the business was not quite approved by the Zionist Organisation. They thought that the Jews in Germany and America . . . distrusted England and would suspect the cloven hoof of Imperialism . . . but obviously that time is passed now and the League and friendship dead . . . It seems incredible that medieval race prejudice should have been allowed to destroy our chance in Palestine.[42]

In this manner the first attempts to include Palestine within the framework of the British Empire expired.

From the beginning of this venture it had been apparent that any suggestion appertaining to the ultimate status of Palestine would involve gaining the consent of the Council of the League. That being the case there were only two real alternatives. First, to attempt to revise the terms of the mandate in accordance with the aims of the League. This course of action would have necessitated complicated and protracted negotiations with the member states of the Council of the League, and the United States.[43] There is no evidence that Wedgwood and his friends seriously considered this option. And there is not the slightest doubt that the government would have rejected it out of hand.

The second alternative was to wait patiently until the mandate had been successfully realised. Until that date arrived the function of the Seventh Dominion League was to act as a catalyst, transforming a largely ignorant public into active supporters of the cause.[44] The pertinent question was how long this interim period would last.

In retrospect, the years 1921–9 (until the August riots) appeared to herald a new epoch. Since 1921 there had been no violent outbreaks of communal tension. Military and police units had been steadily reduced. Arab-Jewish relations, although not friendly, were not overtly hostile. The upbuilding of the National Home had progressed, not spectacularly, but with a steady momentum encouraging to its adherents. Of course a great deal remained to be done. Criticisms were inevitable; and they were not lacking from the Zionists and their Gentile supporters. But the general trend of development seemed to augur well for the future. Hence the termination of the mandate could be detected by those enthusiasts prepared to look hard enough and long enough into the future.

In this context it is impossible to isolate the optimistic atmosphere surrounding the League from the pervading air of expectancy so prevalent in international relations during this period. The Geneva protocol, the Locarno treaties, the Briand-Kellogg peace pact, the reparations agreements : it was an age of paper solutions to complicated and delicate problems.

The Seventh Dominion League foundered upon the harsher realities of the moment. Ahead lay a decade of violence in Palestine and rising tension in Anglo-Zionist affairs. But the dream of the League did not die with Wedgwood's letter. It remained an uncertain factor, gaining a fresh lease of life when the Peel report implanted the idea of a Jewish state upon the political scene. The commissioners came to the conclusion that "the disease is so deep rooted that, in our firm conviction, the only hope of a cure lies in a surgical operation".[45] The operation proposed was a tripartite partition of Palestine into a Jewish state, an Arab state, and the retention over a considerable area of the British mandate. This policy was immediately endorsed by the government.[46]

The catastrophic situation that had engulfed Palestine since the outbreak of the Arab general strike in April 1936 induced many people to reappraise their previous views concerning the ultimate future of Palestine. It was inevitable that the dominion scheme, or some other form of close attachment to the Empire, would be resuscitated.[47] Everything had been returned to the melting pot and all solutions were now worthy of consideration.

Among the witnesses who appeared before the Peel commission was Ben Gurion. In his evidence he explained to the commissioners why the term National Home had first been used. It embraced, he told them, a conception larger than the term Jewish state. A state implied domination over the Arabs which the Jews did not want. It also insinuated a separate political entity which, Ben Gurion argued, was contrary to the wishes of the Jews who preferred that Palestine should remain connected with the British Commonwealth.[48] It is reasonable to assume that Ben Gurion was not postulating a

Baffy: the leading Gentile Zionist of her generation.

The Webbs: Sidney found himself unable to cope with a Jewish
hurricane of his own invention.

Col. J. C. Wedgwood: the personification of a Gentile Zionist.

Malcolm MacDonald: a good friend who ultimately fell
from Zionist grace.

Jewish dominion within the Commonwealth, but rather British retention of the mandate. This was certainly his initial, instinctive reaction to the partition proposal when it first became knowledge.[49]

Nevertheless, his statement was seized upon by an organisation which took shape in Palestine during the autumn of 1936, the Palestine Crown Colony Association, as an indication of the widespread sympathy held for the Association's aims in the *Yishuv* at large. The promoters of the Association were a group of British and Dominion Jews; the chairman, Max Seligman, was a Tel Aviv lawyer, born in Swansea. By January 1937, the Association claimed to have acquired "several thousand signatures" in support of a petition setting out its object. This was, in brief, a proposal to alter the status of Palestine to that of a Crown Colony and eventually to that of a British dominion.[50] The importance of the Association was in preparing public opinion in Palestine for such a possibility, and in showing to the British authorities that if they did contemplate such a solution it would benefit from the full support of the *Yishuv*

In the autumn of 1937 the leaders of the Association informed the press that their "idea is gaining ground . . . [as] the most effective alternative to the scheme for tripartite solution". It was also reported from Jerusalem that

> many British officials are enthusiastic at a solution which, in their view, would definitely stamp Palestine as a unit of the Commonwealth, remove what to most of them is the ignominy of having their policy and actions criticised by the League, and would stabilise their own position.[51]

If ever an argument, made ostensibly to show the widespread support held for the Association's ideas, was destined to boomerang upon its upholders, it was surely this one. The Palestine administration wished for Crown Colony status to escape the nagging criticism of the League of Nations; the Jews wished for a measure of independence only in order to escape from the obstructionist clutches of the Palestine administration. On this basis the scheme carried within itself the seeds of its own rejection.

The actual extent and influence of the Association is hard to assess. It is difficult to concede to it a great deal of authority. More likely it represented a wish fulfilment on the part of a group of "Anglo-Saxon Jews" who genuinely held that the virtues of dominion status would be received with open arms by Palestinian

Jewry. At any rate, the government refused to offer the Association any encouragement whatsoever.[52] And, curiously, the Association did not even exist in a legal sense, for the Palestine administration had refused to register it. The Association remained very much on the periphery of affairs.[53]

There was, of course, a great deal of speculation concerning the recommendations likely to be proposed by the Peel commission. Partition was in the air. Weizmann received a hint of the commission's intention in December 1936. By January this had been translated into a concrete proposition.[54] Weizmann and his coterie took the suggestion in deadly earnest. At a conference held on 15 March 1937 they decided that the scheme, if offered, must be accepted subject to conditions of area and autonomy, but that membership of the League and Empire was an essential prerequisite.[55] The concern that the future Jewish state should be linked with an international body stemmed from the complex defence problems that would face the new state. Partition would involve intricate, perhaps indefensible, borders. The hostility of the Arabs was an unchallengeable fact. Therefore, the question was not merely one of setting up a Jewish state but of also guaranteeing its survival. Initially, it appears, the Zionists believed that membership of the Empire afforded them the greatest sanctuary. This sentiment soon evaporated into a premise that more diffuse links with Great Britain might be preferable and more in keeping with Jewish national ambition.

In effect there were two basic forms of argument. One was prepared to accept a Jewish state in treaty relations with Britain, with the option of deciding at a later date whether or not to join the Commonwealth; the other wished to see a Jewish dominion immediately upon the termination of the mandate. Weizmann apparently adhered to the former viewpoint. He told Duff Cooper, then first lord of the admiralty, that "most Jews would wish to see Palestine part of the British Empire after it had achieved statehood".[56]

Meanwhile in the House, rumours were rife concerning partition. Informed members believed that either a Jewish state or dominion status would be recommended. The consensus of opinion in the lobbies was "that the residents there [in Palestine] and in Britain would favour the granting of Dominion status".[57] An important group stood aloof from this conclusion. Those members who were considered as Zionist sympathisers were, on the whole, antagonistic to any scheme that smacked of abandonment of the mandate, including partition in all its many ramifications.[58]

During November–December 1937 the government's attitude towards partition underwent a radical change, from open and declared support to indecision and often undisguised hostility.[59] The assault on partition led to a belief amongst some Zionists that it was necessary to step up the campaign for a Jewish dominion. The guiding light in this exercise was Henry Mond, the second Lord Melchett. He raised the issue at a meeting of the Political Advisory Committee (to the Zionist Executive) on 2 November 1937.[60] Melchett thought that the feeling of hostility engendered in various circles to the idea of an independent state could be avoided if the Zionists disclosed their "real views" on the matter. This he proposed to do when he spoke at a luncheon at Foyle's on 18 November. Professor Brodetsky came out "strongly in favour" of the dominion proposal on the grounds that external defence was one of the problems causing him most alarm. Leonard Stein reported that, at Weizmann's request, he had interviewed Professor Coupland (a member of the Peel commission), and R. Barrington Ward and Philip Graves of *The Times*. Coupland had been entirely sceptical. He believed that the Jews would never be content within the Empire if that would mean control over their external affairs. Paradoxically, this was precisely the point that Melchett and Brodetsky found so attractive. *The Times* men were sympathetic and "prepared to help in due time", but considered it too early to do anything at the moment. Brodetsky also reported that Ormsby Gore had requested Weizmann not to raise the matter now, a view supported by Mrs. Dugdale who offered the opinion that the question was "a little premature".[61]

The committee on the whole favoured the idea and deemed it expedient to foster public opinion in the *Yishuv* in support of the plan. Melchett finally agreed to explore the views of Eden and Orsmby Gore as to the wisdom of publicising his views.[62] Emerging here is an interesting division of opinion between Gentile and Jew. The Jews were intent on pressing ahead; the Gentiles for counselling caution.

Mrs. Dugdale provided further evidence of this division when she reported the discussion to Weizmann,[63] taking the same opportunity of conveying to the Zionist leader the opinions of Walter Elliot whose viewpoint always attracted Mrs. Dugdale's greatest attention. Elliot reacted strongly against the idea and thought it might easily upset the whole partition scheme arguing "that the Jews had nothing to offer now and should wait until they had". He told Mrs. Dugdale that "Eden was [not] a good enough adviser on this matter", and tendered the advice that Melchett should consult Halifax, whom he considered "the most important man in the cabinet". Elliot brushed aside Mrs. Dugdale's objections concerning the isolation of the Jewish state by retorting "that everyone knows it can't be isolated . . . [that] the British intend to hold Haifa . . . so why dot the i's and cross the t's just now". Elliot's reasoning appeared to set the remaining doubts in Mrs. Dugdale's mind at rest, for she advised Weizmann to restrain Melchett, writing, "a word from you to Henry would stop the whole thing".[64]

Mrs. Dugdale wrote to Melchett informing him of Elliot's views. This intelligence had no visible effect upon Melchett's actions. He saw Ormsby Gore on 12 November and emerged from the interview in a mood of high elation.[65] The colonial secretary had told him to begin gradually working up a demand for the Jewish state to become part of the British Empire. This was concerned with a great change in British Mediterranean policy which was now basing itself on the eastern Mediterranean and friendship with Turkey. Ormsby Gore did not spell out in so many words this "great change" but Mrs. Dugdale knew this was the background to Ormsby Gore's request "from remarks made by Walter". Haifa was the key to the puzzle. According to Elliot the acquisition of Haifa as a naval base made it imperative for Britain to get rid of the mandate. And then, Elliot quipped, the British could "garrison Haifa with two million Jews".[66]

During this period the whole structure of Britain's military-strategic posture in the eastern Mediterranean was under consideration. Palestine was a prime factor in any future planning. The question was how best she could be incorporated into any overall strategic scheme. The Peel commission had proposed partition. But it was partition with a difference. All the vital strategic areas in Palestine were to remain in British hands under an emasculated form of the old mandate. These included : a corridor to the sea from Jerusalem to Jaffa, which would include the main lines of communication to the coast, the airport at Lydda, and the vast army supply camp at Sarafand; the four towns of Haifa, Acre, Safad and Tiberius—on Lake Tiberius there was an air staging post to the East; and the Akaba enclave.[67] With these areas under British control all other solutions could be ignored. Hence partition, based

in principle upon the Peel proposals, would appear far more attractive to the government than other, more demanding, solutions.
Indeed it is difficult not to escape the conclusion that the Royal
Commission, in drawing up their report, were as concerned with the
vulnerable nature of Britain's strategic position as with finding a
viable solution to Arab-Jewish relations in Palestine.

Certainly the Peel report was an unhappy compromise between
both. But given the existing circumstances there was only one real
alternative open to the government : retention of the mandate over
those areas she considered essential to her security. This could best
be achieved through the Peel proposals; or, of course, continuation
of the 1922 mandate. Any other postulate, such as the Seventh
Dominion, conjured up too many long-term, intricate, legal problems and diplomatic manœuvrings for it to be squared with Great
Britain's immediate political-military needs.

Although Mrs. Dugdale tended to fuse the opinions of Ormsby
Gore and Elliot as part of a general dominion plan there was, in
fact, a wide gulf between their actual intentions. Elliot adhered
strictly to partition and the Jewish state acting in close association
with Great Britain. He envisaged the Jewish garrison at Haifa as a
quid pro quo for British support of a Jewish state. Ormsby Gore
was also a partitionist. But, as was to be expected, his standing with
the Zionists had deteriorated since his assumption of office. His
extraordinary request to Melchett most certainly did not reflect
government opinion. Perhaps the effectiveness of the foreign office
campaign against partition encouraged Ormsby Gore to attempt a
last fling in conscripting support in favour of the Jewish state. But
more than likely he was trying to win back his ticket with the Zionists by making some flamboyant gesture generally acceptable to
them. His comments were certainly indiscreet and definitely
irresponsible.

Whatever the reason Melchett, encouraged by Ormsby Gore's
remarks, went ahead to canvass support in the dominions. He
wrote to Lord Tweedsmuir (formerly John Buchan), governor-
general of Canada and a former chairman of the parliamentary
pro-Palestine committee, asking him to use his influence in Canada
when the right time arrived.[68] Melchett gave the impression that the
scheme enjoyed widespread support in the cabinet : "As one cabinet
minister puts it", he then repeated Elliot's remarks about Haifa;
and, "as another puts it the Jewish state is destined to play the role
of Ulster in the Eastern Mediterranean." (I have been unable to

trace the source of this remark. It was most probably made by Ormsby Gore or Hore Belisha.) Melchett assured Tweedsmuir of complete support in Palestine,

> I have been into the question . . . with . . . the leaders of Zionist thought in Palestine . . . and have found no-one to oppose the idea at all. They all assure me the movement can be carried through . . . [to] lay the Crown of the Jewish state at the foot of the throne which holds the stone of Jacob.'[69]

Finally, as if to set the seal on the bargain, Melchett assured Tweedsmuir that Weizmann "is imbued with exactly the same ideals and aspirations".

To this exalted exposition of the situation, Tweedsmuir gave a most restrained reply.

> . . . your letter has given me the first ray of light. I have no comment to make, but if you and Weizmann think the scheme practicable it certainly has my assent.[70]

Melchett's activities continued uninterrupted. On 8 December he telephoned Mrs. Dugdale informing her that a prominent cabinet minister (it was Hore Belisha) had told him it would be a good thing if the Jews were to display openly a desire to preserve the British connexion; that there was little time for delay, and it was important to get things moving by the new year.[71]

The decidedly exaggerated nature of Melchett's activities deserve further elucidation. It was quite untrue to claim, as Melchett did, that Weizmann was 100 per cent behind his feverish agitation.[72] Weizmann's phraseology is always guarded, but he is clearly not committing himself to support of dominion status for Palestine. Mrs. Dugdale shed further light on Melchett's actions.

> I find it hard to believe we are ready for the kind of demonstration he [Melchett] wants . . . He is far from well and violently excited on account of some serious crisis in his own affairs . . . I want you to understand the psychology of this. I have known for some weeks what is taking place—and I get my information from a person who never gets excited or hysterical [the reference is to Elliot] . . . who has been watching very carefully, to warn me if the moment had arrived when we can do something. Henry . . . has only just heard the facts from B. [Ormsby Gore][73]—who was certainly both excited and hysterical when he told him—I have no

doubt that they played on each others nerves, until Henry was convinced that B. had issued a sort of S.O.S. for help from us and Henry accordingly wants to shout and scream his plan . . . irrespective of whether we are ready to do so effectively or not.[74]

Mrs. Dugdale's suspicions about Melchett's health and generally excited frame of mind were borne out when she received a letter from Lady Melchett informing her that the doctors had spoken to Melchett very seriously about his heart and had advised him to cease all Zionist work for about three months.[75]

Despite the reluctance of Mrs. Dugdale and her friends to support Melchett's campaign, his struggle to effect a great public demonstration in favour of the dominion idea flowered. In particular the established organs of Anglo-Jewry, the Zionist Federation and the Board of Deputies, took up the challenge.

In December 1937 the executive of the English Zionist Federation unanimously passed a favourable resolution.[76] On 16 January 1938 the Board of Deputies followed suit with a similar resolution which was adopted by an overwhelming majority.[77]

The same day the Board passed its resolution, the Reverend M. L. Perlzweig, a leading English Zionist, informed an audience in Manchester that

> a Jewish state in Palestine as part of the Commonwealth of the British Empire was always implicit in Zionist policy . . . [the] time has come to be explicit, and the whole Zionist movement takes its stand on this basis . . . We stand or fall with Britain.[78]

Following these resolutions L. Bakstansky, general secretary of the Zionist Federation, conducted a series of interviews with leading political personalities.[79] His aim : to ascertain their opinions regarding the dominion scheme now adopted by Anglo-Jewry. Of all the Gentile Zionists interviewed only Wedgwood and Lady Snowden were prepared to offer unconditional support. The rest adhered, in one form or another, to Weizmann's formula of a Jewish state in close association with the Empire.

Although partition had become a bone of contention in the cabinet it still remained official government policy. There was, as yet, no question of the government abandoning partition in favour of some other scheme. And, quite obviously, the government could not allow the renewal of pressure for a Jewish dominion to pass without comment. Captain A. V. M. Hudson, parliamentary secretary to the

minister of transport, aired government misgivings at a Zionist meeting in Stamford Hill, North London.[80] He remarked that he had
noticed with interest the suggestion of a Jewish dominion within
the Empire and,

> while it is naturally flattering that a body of people should
> wish to live under the British flag, we must realise that such a
> suggestion may be looked at from a somewhat different angle
> and with some alarm and annoyance by other countries who think
> that we have too much already.

He wanted it realised that there were factors which made it
extremely difficult, in fact impossible, for the government to come
forward and say they accepted the programme without any
questions asked or answered.

The quintessence of this pronouncement was that the government had noted the agitation, but felt powerless to take any initiative in the matter. The first step still remained partition; then it
was necessary to wait upon events. In many ways there was a
remarkable similarity between the government's attitude and
Weizmann's. Both were still committed to partition; both still
envisaged as a *sine qua non* of the Jewish state fraternal ties with
Great Britain.

The partisan activities of Wedgwood crystallised the difference
between Weizmann and his associates and the protagonists of the
dominion plan. Wedgwood had been inveigled into organising a
meeting in the House to found a parliamentary edition of the
Crown Colony Association. Mrs. Dugdale immediately went off in
full cry against Wedgwood's splitting tactics.[81] She defined the meeting as "some such nonsense" and sought Amery's help in dissuading
Wedgwood from continuing in his meeting. She wrote: "it isn't
important what Jos does—but I am against anything that weakens
a State idea, or puts alternatives into people's heads". This
unquestionably represents the gist of the opposition thesis to the
dominion proposal.

Wedgwood, despite all efforts to the contrary, called his meeting
for Thursday, March 24. The participants responded with a
marked degree of coolness. Arthur Lourie reported that "there was
considerable opposition expressed at the meeting, and I think it
unlikely that we shall hear anything more of this committee".[82] No
more was heard.

The dominion scheme flourished for as long as the government had abandoned hope in carrying out the mandate. From July 1937 until October 1938 the government believed the mandate unworkable, or at least its official policy was based on this assumption. In October 1938 the Woodhead commission reported failure.[83] The commission concluded that partition was not practicable but offered no alternative solution.[84] The government acquiesced in this admission of failure and promised to continue in its responsibilities to find a solution acceptable to all the parties concerned.[85] In other words, until something better cropped up the mandate was again part and parcel of British policy in Palestine. And, despite the constitutional promise contained in the May white paper of 1939 to erect a Palestinian state,[86] the mandate remained the basis of British policy until the United Nations partition decision of November 1947.

In these circumstances a Jewish dominion was no longer feasible or practical politics. Even Wedgwood was forced to say "good-bye . . . to our dreams of seeing Palestine a happy colony within the British Empire".[87] But the hope lingered on. Surprisingly, Weizmann returned to this theme during the war. He wrote :

Considering the strategic and economic importance of Palestine, the inclusion of the Jewish state within the British Commonwealth of Nations would be to the interests of both . . . Jews everywhere can gain in status and security only through the rise of a Jewish state, this would be especially the case if that State is part of the British Commonwealth.[88]

Was this a return to nostalgia? Or did Weizmann genuinely believe that in the post-war settlement such a solution was indeed conceivable? Possibly a combination of both. Certainly the May white paper, in operation throughout the war, made intimate co-operation impossible between the government and the Zionists. But it is likely that Weizmann believed that the second world war, like the first, would inaugurate a new and better era in Anglo-Zionist relations. This assumption proved to be fallacious. The war led to a weakening of Weizmann's contacts and influence in Palestine. In the *Yishuv,* underground and terrorist groups were determined on violent resistance to British rule. The future for Anglo-Zionist relations appeared darker, not brighter.

In spite of the growing conflict in Palestine between the British authorities and the *Yishuv* the dream of a Jewish dominion flared

up briefly during the investigations of the Anglo-American committee of inquiry on Palestine.[89] For the last time memoranda and
arguments were placed before an official body pleading the cause of
the Seventh Dominion. The last plea proved as fruitless as the first.
It saw the end of a well-intentioned, but quite impracticable,
scheme.

The Seventh Dominion idea was born in 1928. It was then an
ideal sponsored wholly by Gentiles but gaining little or no support
from Zionist bodies, with the exception of the Revisionists. In
1937-8, when the concept of a Jewish state was a political reality,
the initiative came wholly from the Jews. And, with the exception
of such "diehards" as Wedgwood and Kenworthy, the Gentiles
generally stood aside, counselling prudence. During the second
stage it was, appropriately, Anglo-Jewry which took the lead,
prompting, initiating, conducting interviews, passing resolutions,
leading public campaigns. Theirs was a genuine concern for the
safety and security of the proposed Jewish state. But it is difficult
to escape the conclusion that they were, perhaps unwittingly, giving
public expression to latent vested interests.

Weizmann, and his inner circle of Jewish and Gentile advisers,
took a more realistic view. They refused to commit themselves on
speculative propositions and kept their eyes firmly fixed on what
was being offered : a Jewish state.

NOTES

1   In the autumn of 1902 Joseph Chamberlain, then colonial secretary, raised
    the possiblities of Jewish settlement at El Arish in the north-eastern area of
    the Sinai peninsula. The viability of the project ultimately depended on
    diverting a sufficient quantity of water from the Nile for irrigation purposes.
    In the opinion of Lord Cromer, the British Agent in Egypt, a large enough
    water supply could not be guaranteed and the scheme died a natural death.
    As a result Chamberlain made his Uganda offer. Again the idea was re-
    jected, this time because of the fierce opposition of the Russian Zionists who
    would accept no territory other than Palestine. It should be pointed out that
    Herzl envisaged East Africa as the only realistic place for an immediate
    settlement of persecuted East European Jewry. He hoped that this would be
    first and temporary step—as his follower Max Nordau put it, a *Nachtasyl*—
    preparing the way for ultimate settlement in Palestine.
2   Weizmann, p. 253.
3   See, for example, C. Sykes, *Crossroads to Israel* (London, 1965), pp. 23-5,
    though he modified the accusation by writing, "they were engaged on a
    venture without precedent in recorded history . . . [and that] Weizmann
    retrieved Jewish honour to some extent".

4 Weizmann to Deedes, 12 Nov. 1921, W.A.

5 Notes of a conversation held at Balfour's home on 22 July 1921, W.A. Originally quoted in Meinzertzhagen, *Middle East Diary, 1917–1956* (London, 1959), pp. 103–5. None of the other participants in the discussion— Churchill, Sir M. Hankey and Weizmann—demurred from this comment. Meinertzhagen also quotes from a conversation with Balfour on 7 Feb. 1918, where Balfour registers his personal hope "that the Jews will make good in Palestine and eventually found a Jewish state", *ibid.*, p. 9.

6 Lloyd George, *The Truth About the Peace Treaties* (London, 1938), ii, p. 1139; and Cmd. 5479 (the Peel report), p. 24.

7 Weizmann to Deedes, 31 July 1921, W.A.

8 Weizmann, p. 192. Those present at the meeting were: Lloyd George C. P. Scott, Herbert Samuel and Wedgwood.

9 C. V. Wedgwood, p. 182.

10 *Ibid.*, p. 189.

11 J. C. Wedgwood, *The Seventh Dominion* (London, 1928), pp. 119–21.

12 *Ibid.*, p. 123.

13 *Ibid.*, p. ix.

14 *Ibid.*, p. 33.

15 For further examples of this facet of his Zionism, see his speeches, P.D. Commons, vol. 227, c. 1476, 30 April 1929; and vol. 264, c. 1820, 22 April 1932.

16 In this age when Empires are being shattered under the accusations of injustice and lack of democracy, it might seem anomalous, even cynical, to incorporate such terms in the text. No such connotations should be construed. Wedgwood, and those who thought like him, genuinely and sincerely believed in the above concepts and it is only in this sense that the contents of the paragraph should be interpreted.

17 J. C. Wedgwood, p. 3.

18 J. C. Wedgwood, p. 31.

19 *Ibid.*, p. 33.

20 *The Times*, 2 March 1928.

21 *Manchester Guardian*, 21 March 1928.

22 *Observer*, 22 July 1928.

23 A full report of the meeting may be found in the *Jewish Chronicle*, 1 March 1929.

24 *Jewish Chronicle*, 15 March 1929.

25 P.D., Commons, vol. 227, c. 1480, 30 April 1929; during the debate on the colonial office vote.

26 *Jewish Chronicle*, 10 May 1929. The members were: Wedgwood (chairman), Kenworthy, Sir M. Conway, Hore Belisha, Sir R. Hamilton, Mrs. P. Snowden, Mr. J. Cowen and Mr. M. Grossman.

27 *Jewish Chronicle*, 15 Feb. 1929.

28 *Jewish Chronicle*, 26 Oct. 1928.

29 *Jewish Chronicle*, 16 Nov. 1928.

30 J. B. Schechtman, *Fighter and Prophet, The Vladimir Jabotinsky Story. The Last Years* (London, 1961), p. 108.

31 *Ibid.*, pp. 108–9.

32 *Ibid.*, p. 109.

33 *Jewish Chronicle*, 2 Aug. 1929.

34 *Jewish Chronicle*, 15 Feb. 1929.

35 Unsigned letter to Jabotinsky, 13 March 1929, Jabotinsky Institute, Tel Aviv, Israel.

36 See, for example, the text of a resolution submitted to a meeting of the English Zionist Federation on 28 April 1929, C.Z.A., F13/5611; and a violent attack in the *New Judaea* (28 Feb. 1929) which disassociated the official Zionist leadership from the aims of the League.

37 See his article, "The Ninth Dominion?" *The New Palestine* (5 April 1929); and for subsequent quotations. Arlosoroff named the article such for he believed that India and British East Africa would achieve dominion status first.

38 For the similarity between this quotation and Weizmann's pronouncements on the 'ultimate aim' of Zionism see *Trial and Error*, pp. 302, 340, 417–19.

39 *Manchester Guardian*, 19 Oct. 1929.

40 Letter to *The Times*, 28 Aug. 1929.

41 *The Times* and *Manchester Guardian*, 19 Oct. 1929.

42 Letter to *The Times*, 30 Oct. 1930.

43 The U.S., not being a member of the League of Nations, had, after lengthy negotiations with Britain, signed a treaty on 3 Dec. 1924, making the U.S. a signatory to the Palestine mandate and providing for U.S. participation in all rights and benefits extended to member states of the League. The treaty was ratified on 5 Dec. 1925.

44 This apparently was Wedgwood's view. See his interview in the *Jewish Chronicle*, 15 Feb. 1929.

45 Cmd. 5479, *Report of the Palestine Royal Commission* (July 1937), p. 368.

46 Cmd. 5513, *Palestine: A Statement of Policy by His Majesty's Government* (July 1937).

47 See, for example, the leader in *Great Britain and the East*, 8 Oct. 1936, p. 498.

48 *Jewish Chronicle*, 15 Jan. 1937.

49 See, for example, his article in the *Daily Herald*, 9 July 1937. He wrote: "No Jew will accept partition as a just and rightful solution . . . The proposal of the Royal Commission . . . is to put a drastic limit to the possibilities of a Jewish return, and to condemn the rest of the country to stagnation and desolation.'

50 *Jewish Chronicle*, 22 Jan. 1937.

51 *Jewish Chronicle*, 29 Oct. 1937.

52 See, for example, minutes of a meeting between a representative of the Association, Mr. M. Schonfeld, and officials of the colonial office on 30 March 1938, F.O. 371/21855/38/1893.

53 The Crown Colony Association did find one prominent supporter in Wedgwood.

54 Weizmann's evidence, *in camera*, before the Royal Commission, 23 Dec. 1936, and 8 Jan. 1937.

55 D.D., 15 March 1937, W.A. Those present at the meeting were: Weizmann, Professor S. Brodetsky, Shertok, Namier, Dr. M. Perlzweig, L. Stein and A. Lourie. Stein's was the only dissenting voice from these general conclusions.

56 Notes of an interview between Duff Cooper and Weizmann, 18 June 1937, W.A.

57 *Jewish Chronicle*, 9 April and 7 May 1937.
58 For a detailed discussion of their views see the chapters on partition.
59 For a fuller account of the counter-attack against partition see pp. 151–52.
60 Minutes of the meeting of 2 Nov. 1937, W.A.
61 Mrs. Dugdale to Weizmann, 3 Nov. 1937, W.A.
62 Apparently the views of Eden and Ormsby Gore were negative. At least I have been unable to discover any contemporary reports of Melchett speaking at the Foyle's luncheon on such a topic.
63 Mrs Dugdale to Weizmann, 3rd Nov. 1937. W.A.
64 *Ibid.*
65 D.D., 12 Nov. 1937, W.A.
66 *Ibid.*
67 See Cmd. 5479, pp. 381, 384–6.
68 Melchett to Tweedsmuir, 17 Nov. 1937, W.A.
69 The reference is to the Stone of Scone. Tradition identifies it with Jacob's pillow at Bethel.
70 Tweedsmuir to Melchett, 30 Nov. 1937, W.A.
71 D.D., 8 Dec. 1937, W.A.; also Melchett to Weizmann, 7 Dec. 1937, W.A.
72 See, for example, Weizmann to F. H. Kisch, 8 Dec. 1937, W.A.; and to Sir O. d'Avigdor Goldsmid, 3 Feb. 1938, W.A.
73 In her letters to Weizmann, Mrs. Dugdale invariably used an alphabetic type code in order to bamboozle the Palestine security forces.
74 Mrs. Dugdale to Weizmann, 20 Dec. 1937, W.A.
75 D.D., 8 Dec. 1937, W.A.
76 See *Zionist Review*, January 1938.
77 *Jewish Chronicle*, 21 Jan. 1938; 250 votes were cast in favour of the motion, 7 against.
78 *Manchester Guardian*, 16 Jan. 1938.
79 See C.Z.A. files Z4/17043 and S25/7564. Those interviewed were Col. R. Meinertzhagen; J. C. Wedgwood; Lady Snowden; Professor C. Webster; Sir A. Sinclair; L. S. Amery; H. Nicolson.
80 *Jewish Chronicle*, 11 Feb. 1938.
81 Mrs. Dugdale to Weizmann, 20 March 1938, W.A.
82 Lourie to Weizmann, 27 March 1938, W.A.
83 Cmd. 5854. *The Palestine Partition Report* (Oct. 1938). The commission had arrived in Palestine in April 1938 to investigate and recommend boundaries for the proposed Arab and Jewish states.
84 *Ibid.*, pp. 243, 246.
85 Cmd. 5893. *A Statement of Policy by His Majesty's Government* (Nov. 1938), p. 3.
86 See Cmd. 6019. *Palestine: A Statement of Policy* (May 1939).
87 P.D., Commons, vol. 347, c. 2002, 22 May 1939.
88 Weizmann, "Palestine's Role in the Solution of the Jewish Problem", *Foreign Affairs*, Jan. 1942, p. 338.
89 W.A., Memoranda submitted to the Anglo-American commission on behalf of the Jewish Dominion of Palestine League, Jan. 1946.

5

Some Strategic Aspects

As the 1930s progressed, Britain's Near East policies became increasingly dominated by strategic considerations. In October 1935 the British position faced its first real challenge. The strategic and military implications of Italy's strike against Abyssinia hammered home both the vulnerability of Imperial communications and the necessity of safeguarding those communications by mutual understanding with the inhabitants of the Near East.

Nor would it do to underestimate the importance the Near East held in British planning throughout this period. India, and British possessions in the Far East, provide the key to the picture. "The British Empire", maintained Lord Hankey, "is pre-eminently a great Naval, Indian and Colonial power."[1] In time of war or international uncertainty the security of India and the need to keep the routes with India and the Far East open assumed enormous proportions. Lord Alanbrooke wrote :

> With the loss of India and Burma, the keystone of the arch of our Commonwealth Defence was lost and our Imperial Defence crashed. Without the central strategic reserve of Indian troops ready to operate either east or west we were left impotent and even the smallest of nations were at liberty to twist the lion's tail.[2]

It is against this strategic-military backcloth that Anglo-Zionist relations, in particular for the years 1936–9, must be assessed.

Palestine held a vital position in relation to the two routes to the Far East that led through the eastern Mediterranean. To the north she buttressed the canal from attack, while from the east she provided an easily accessible land link with Iraq and the Persian Gulf. It was the Great War that afforded Britain the opportunity of defining her intentions towards Palestine in specific terms. Asquith gave early notice that the Ottoman Empire would not escape the rigours of war. In a speech at the Guildhall, delivered a few days after the declaration of war against Turkey, he asserted,

> It is they and not we who have rung the death-knell of Ottoman dominion, not only in Europe, but in Asia. The Turkish Empire has committed suicide and dug its grave with its own hand.[3]

As early as March 1915 a cabinet memorandum had been circulated by Herbert Samuel proposing alternative regimes for Palestine after its liberation from the Turks. Samuel was pressing for the restoration of the Jews in Palestine, and on sentimental, political, and strategic grounds preferred a British protectorate within the framework of the Empire.[4] Samuel's views gained some support in the cabinet, mainly from Sir E. Grey, the foreign secretary, and Lloyd George, the chancellor of the exchequer. But Asquith was, and remained, implacably hostile to Samuel's thesis and even more to Lloyd George's support for it.[5]

Asquith's opposition must have been reinforced by the conclusions reached by the de Bunsen committee in the spring of 1915. This foreign office committee was set up to clarify British aims and policy in Asiatic Turkey in the face of rival claimants. Concerning Palestine it reported that it would be,

> . . . idle for His Majesty's Government to claim the retention of Palestine in their sphere. Palestine must be recognised as a country whose destiny must be the subject of special negotiations, in which both belligerents and neutrals are alike interested.[6]

Britain's wartime negotiations concerning Palestine, the object of much abuse and tendentious discussion, remained reasonably faithful to the frame of reference mapped out by the de Bunsen committee. The Sykes-Picot agreement envisaged an international administration for Palestine, "the form of which is to be decided upon after consultation with Russia . . . with the other allies, and the representatives of the Sherif of Mecca".[7] And even in the highly controversial MacMahon–Hussein correspondence the British high commissioner in Cairo went to some pains to emphasise that no final decision regarding the territorial extent of Arab independence could be made without respecting the interests of France. In particular MacMahon stipulated that the eventual status of the *vilayets* (districts) of Beirut and Aleppo would be subject to Allied approval.[8]

A. J. Balfour: the most eminent Gentile Zionist of his day.

Arthur Wauchope: 'Perhaps the best High Commissioner Palestine has had'

Walter Elliot: invaluable as a channel of communication.

L. S. Amery: an unyielding advocate of partition.

However, it was the Balfour declaration that constituted the foundation stone of eventual British mandatory rule in Palestine. It might, therefore, be argued that the declaration was merely a guise to mask actual British intentions to secure Palestine and safeguard Imperial communications. The motivations behind the Balfour declaration are many and complex.[9] Unquestionably some soldiers and politicians saw in Palestine an important strategic acquisition; an indispensable buffer zone not to be allowed to fall into the wrong hands. But other factors also played their part, and however one analyses the declaration it seems abundantly clear that this act contained measures of sentiment and altruism as well as *realpolitik*. At any rate, the Balfour declaration does not read as a definite British commitment to administer Palestine. Weizmann himself acknowledged that it was more "in the nature of a principle".[10]

It was the Zionists that argued most persistently in favour of a British protectorate. Weizmann rejected outright any form of condominium or French control. He told Lord Robert Cecil that "Jews all over the world strongly desired that Great Britain and no other power should have control of Palestine".[11]

But Weizmann's keenness to involve Britain in Zionist ambitions was not viewed with unreserved enthusiasm by all cabinet ministers. Balfour himself voiced preference for an American presence,[12] while Curzon expressed disquiet at the consequences of a Zionist orientated policy.[13] However, there was no acceptable alternative other than continued British rule in Palestine. The United States retreated from overseas commitments; France or Italy were ruled out by both the Zionists and the British.[14] The British, therefore, entered into their Palestinian inheritance with no deep-laid plan involving vital strategic considerations. The reasons were less dramatic, and followed almost inevitably from their conquest of Palestine and issuance of the Balfour declaration.

The advent of a Conservative administration in October 1922 led to a complete reconsideration of British policy towards Palestine. Some ministers were plainly dissatisfied with the policy embodied in the Balfour declaration. In consequence, on 27 June 1923, a cabinet committee was formed to re-examine British obligations and interests in Palestine.[15] The committee had before it memoranda prepared by the Middle East department of the colonial office, the three services, and the standing defence subcommittee of the committee of imperial defence. The majority of the reports concerned themselves with the strategic importance of Palestine, and the

H

cabinet committee's report incorporated their views.[16] It was agreed to continue with the policy of the Balfour declaration. With the exception of the general staff[17] all held the opinion that Palestine was essential for the defence of the canal, particularly in view of Egypt's recently acquired nominal independence in February 1922. The cabinet approved this policy on 31 July,[18] and, in a sense, officially endorsed for the first time the strategic importance Palestine now held in British Near Eastern policy.[19]

The feeling that Palestine was part and parcel of Britain's imperial framework and indispensable to her lines of communication began to be expressed with increasing regularity. Wedgwood's definition of Palestine as "the Clapham Junction of the Commonwealth",[20] graphically symbolises the importance that country now claimed in the British order of priorities. His Seventh Dominion League helped sharpen public and parliamentary opinion into an awareness of the strategic advantages to be gained from retaining a foothold in Palestine. The leaders of the League made no secret of the fact that they saw a Jewish Palestine serving imperial, as well as Zionist interests.[21] The League's political life was short lived and its influence nominal, but it helped create the convenient political formula linking a Jewish Palestine with British strategic fortunes.

Moreover throughout the 1920s imperial communications had been developed within Palestine itself. Aviation and transport links from Haifa to Baghdad made this a viable alternative route to India should the canal ever be threatened or fall into the wrong hands. This, together with the development of Haifa as a deep-water harbour, the laying of oil-pipe lines from Kirkuk, and the construction of oil berths at Haifa, gave Palestine a significance not easy to shrug off. Palestine had now become a strategic factor in her own right, and not merely as an appendage of Egypt.[22]

The continued development of these interests depended upon maintaining British influence in Palestine, and the most logical way of furthering this aim was by adhering to the mandate. Despite outbreaks of violence in 1920, 1921 and 1929, there was reason to assume that the British, at least at governmental level, believed that the Arabs would eventually become reconciled to the concept of a Jewish National Home. But even these slender hopes were demolished when Hitler assumed power in Germany in January 1933.

Anti-semitism was incorporated into the national life of a major European state. Other countries in eastern Europe followed suit.

The result was that Palestine, hitherto in the main a focus for Jewish idealism, now became a centre of hope for tens of thousands of European Jews. In the course of three years, 1933–5, almost 150,000 Jews officially entered Palestine.[23] The situation viewed through Arab eyes was abundantly clear. If the present rate of Jewish immigration continued unabated they, the majority national community, would be swamped and relegated to the status of a minority group. Furthermore, they considered that the British, by their adherence to the mandate, acted as the guardians of Jewish immigration. They had, therefore, to convince, even coerce, the British to abandon the fostering of the National Home.

A portent of the new Arab approach occurred in October 1933 when riots broke out in Jaffa, Haifa, and Jerusalem. The riots were aimed at protesting against Jewish immigration but, unlike those of 1929, they were directed mainly against the administration and only secondly against the Jews. Cunliffe-Lister, then colonial secretary, told Weizmann that the "Arabs would in future fight not against Jews but against the government". He expressed great anxiety at the effect an Anglo-Arab conflict would have on the "man in the street" who had no interest in implementing the Balfour declaration, or the mandate, or the MacDonald letter. It would be bound to result in an outcry to clear out of Palestine. As for India, ". . . the only element we can rely on is the Moslems. They are our friends because they need us and they are against Zionism."[24] To all this Weizmann could only repeat that a friendly Jewish population would safeguard British interests in Palestine.

This argument, however, held similar dangers to that of a double-edged sword and as such had to be wielded with considerable skill and caution. For if a few hundred thousand Jews concentrated in Palestine were capable of safeguarding British interests, surely some tens of millions of Moslems scattered from Palestine to India were immensely more capable of sabotaging those same interests. The logic of this argument apparently was overwhelming for it permeates British thinking on the Near East throughout this period. In a sense the Zionists were on safer ground in appealing to Britain's moral obligations towards them. But even this factor depreciated in value as the 1930s progressed, and the more the Zionists wavered between strategic arguments and moral obligations the more they found themselves caught in a cleft stick not of their own making.

The emerging conflict in Palestine placed Britain in a real dilemma. Previously she had been able to adjudicate upon Palestine problems more or less on their own merits. Now the situation had altered out of all recognition. The post-war settlement in the Near East, as in Europe, was being challenged. The Arab-Jewish conflict in Palestine had now to be resolved within the framework of rising international tension together with the emergence of a militant, pan-Arab nationalism influenced by the totalitarian regimes in Europe. While in the background lurked the danger of a Moslem world up in arms.

Italy represented the major threat to Britain's position in the Mediterranean. In November 1933 the cabinet had agreed that although Italy could not be viewed as a reliable friend she need not be considered as an enemy.[25] The Italian campaign against Abyssinia led to a modification of this theory. The Mediterranean fleet, now based on Alexandria, Port Said and Haifa, was reinforced. British commanders in the Mediterranean were warned that if war broke out with Italy they would have to bear the brunt of the attack for some time. The war clearly indicated both the weakness and strength of the British position in the Near East. One result was seen in the attempt to regularise British relations with Egypt, which found its expression in the Anglo-Egyptian treaty of August 1936.

By June 1936 the sanctions policy imposed by the League on Italy had been condemned by N. Chamberlain as "the very midsummer of madness", and the cabinet were searching for a formula which would enable them to restore better relations with Italy and, at the same time, would reassure their Mediterranean collaborators of their honourable intentions. Eden proposed that if sanctions were withdrawn Britain should declare that in the present state of uncertainty she would come to the assistance of those countries who had co-operated in the sanctions policy, should they feel threatened. He left the question of an eastern Mediterranean understanding with Turkey and Greece open, while the idea of a pact, which would include Italy and France, was rejected as impracticable for the moment.[26]

The chiefs of staff, who had been requested to comment on the strategic aspects of Eden's paper, poured cold water on his suggestions. They emphasised that British interests demanded a peaceful Mediterranean and this could only be achieved by returning to a state of friendly relations with Italy. The object of abandoning sanctions was to enable Britain to withdraw the extra forces she had concentrated in the Near East and return "to a state of normal distribution" in Europe and the Far East. A statement along the lines of Eden's memorandum might be construed by Italy as provocative and would postpone the return "to normal defence arrangements". Of course, it would serve British interests to have a friendly Greece, Turkey and Yugoslavia, but no extra tension should result in attaining this object. The chiefs assured the cabinet that article 16 of the Covenant remained on record to deter any future aggressive intent by Italy. Furthermore, as the assistance we would receive from Greece, Turkey or Yugoslavia would be minimal, the main burden of defence would fall upon Britain. Hence every measure should be adopted "to reduce the likelihood of war and the period of tension".[27] The cabinet noted these conclusions, and both Sir T. Inskip, the minister for the co-ordination of defence, and Sir S. Hoare, first lord of the admiralty, insisted "that no further commitments could be undertaken in the Mediterranean".[28]

The joint planning subcommittee of the committee of imperial defence examined the same question in greater depth, and their report[29] assumes an added interest for it indicates that Palestine was already included amongst the possible permutations for a British military response in the eastern Mediterranean. Three factors were either explicitly mentioned or hinted at : the question of a strategic reserve for the Near East; the need for a naval repair base in the eastern Mediterranean; and the maintenace of communications with the east.

The committee reached the conclusion that, after the experience of the Abyssinian crisis, Malta could no longer be relied upon to provide safe facilities for the navy, hence another base was necessary. Haifa, Alexandria and Famagusta were considered in turn although serious objections were raised to all three. Haifa, nevertheless, had some advantages. It had been used as a temporary base during the recent crisis, and had already been developed as a deepwater, commercial harbour. The real objection, however, was political : that of "establishing a base in territory over which we have no guarantee of permanent control". Again, Haifa was important in that she provided the first link in an alternative land route to the canal *via* Baghdad and Basra. And it was no coincidence that the project of building a modern road between Haifa and Baghdad first began to receive serious attention in the spring of 1935, when the Near East situation was beginning to boil.[30] In the event of the canal being threatened, or its approaches in the Red Sea blockaded, the land route to the east would assume a crucial character. Nor, according to contemporary observers, did this latter conjecture appear as mere fanciful speculation. In November 1937 Sir Miles Lampson, British Ambassador in Egypt, reported of the serious danger to supplies in transit through the Red Sea owing to the presence of Italian guns at the straits of Bab el Manded.[31]

The increased importance of Palestine was linked with the vulnerability of Malta. The limitations of the island port had been acknowledged long before the Italian threat to Abyssinia. Baldwin told Weizmann that Malta could "no longer be relied upon as a *point d'appui* for the great trade routes to India", and agreed that as events developed in Malta and Egypt, Palestine would grow in importance.[32] Cunliffe-Lister played the same theme. He appreciated that before long the problem would be how to convert the mandated country into a naval base.[33]

All this was very gratifying. But once the Italo-Abyssinian war had begun Weizmann realised that whatever the result the National Home would suffer. For if the Abyssinians proved victorious it would signal the triumph of a native people over a European power; while if the Italians won it would mark a decline in British prestige. Either way the Palestinian Arab stood to gain heart in his struggle against the British and the Zionists.[34]

By May 1936 the Italians had completed the conquest of Abyssinia, and throughout 1936 they consolidated throughout the Mediterranean area the initiative they had thus achieved. In Palestine, where the Arab rebellion had broken out in April 1936, the Italians were not slow to exploit an explosive situation. From their radio station at Bari blared forth an incessant and, for the British, a highly embarrassing and provocative barrage of propaganda designed to encourage the Arabs to liberate themselves from British imperialism.[35]

Nor did the Italians confine themselves to propaganda. There is no doubt that they intervened actively in the Palestine rebellion. They quite certainly supplied the Arab insurgents with funds, guns and ammunition. There is at least one recorded incident of £40,000 being handed over by the Italian consulate in Jerusalem to an intermediary of the Mufti as early as April 1936.[36] Furthermore, according to Zionist intelligence, the Italian consulate in Damascus was overstaffed with chauffeurs and mechanics who occupied themselves in their ample spare time in fund-raising, gun-running, and gang-raising activities on behalf of the Palestine rebels.[37] The British were well aware of these activities, though, during the summer of 1936, they regarded them merely as "mischievous . . .

[and] on too small a scale and too difficult to substantiate by chapter and verse, for it to be of any real use for us to attempt to take it up with the Italian government".[38]

The Italians were also in contact with the Zionists and attempted to win them over from a British connexion. Mussolini had told Weizmann : ". . . the more he watched the situation the more he felt convinced that there would be no improvement unless the Jews had a state of their own . . ."[39] In June 1936 Theodoli, the Italian representative at Geneva, inveighed "in the most violent terms about England and the most friendly terms about us . . . [he] repeated again and again . . . 'A National Home is no solution of the Jewish problem in Palestine. What the Jews need is a Jewish state which England will never give them.' " Dr. N. Goldmann, the recipient of this information, reached the understandable conclusion that Theodoli was volunteering the services of Italy to obtain a Jewish state.[40]

Again, in July of the same year, Captain Dadana, head of Italian propaganda in Cairo, assured a representative of the Jewish Agency that the parliamentary regime in England was too weak to give the Jews a state. On the other hand, Italy was not afraid of the Arabs and knew how to deal with them—as in Tripoli—and would aim at creating a Jewish state in Palestine. However, this could not be achieved immediately. Italy intended ultimately to dominate the Mediterranean and would soon be in a position to take Egypt and expand even further. Britain would be unable to stop her. Meanwhile, Italy was anxious that the Jews settle the Gajjam area in Abyssinia. This would serve Italy economically and politically and foster sympathetic opinion for the Jews in Italy. As a *quid pro quo* Italy would undertake to establish a real Jewish state in Palestine.[41] These comments somewhat embarrassed Weizmann; and he went to some pains to emphasise that his alleged flirtations with Italy always emanated from "the other side". And, he added, the British government was always informed of the contents of the conversations.[42]

Italian concern about a Jewish state *per se* must be taken extremely lightly. They were obviously keen to mobilise Jewish economic ability, agricultural technique and financial resources in the settlement of Abyssinia. Without doubt they exploited the tension in Palestine to their own advantage and attempted to play off both sides against the middle. Indeed their diplomacy would have been short sighted had they not pursued such a policy.

These conversations took place before the Peel commission's investigations and report. The commission recommended partition, thus placing a Jewish state on the political map. Previously the Italian overtures had been made *in vacuo*. Now a Jewish state was a viable possibility, hence it is not surprising that the gist of the above conversations reappeared in September 1937 soon after the report was issued. On 10 September the Italian representative at Geneva, Mr. Bova Scoppa, met Dr. Goldmann. Four days later the discussions were resumed with the participation of Weizmann. These conversations were more restrained and less bombastic than those of the previous year. The Italian denied that his country was backing the Arabs, or even endorsed the Arab attitude towards Zionism. Italy wanted two things : to be a guarantor of the future Jewish state; and that the Jews remain neutral in the power struggle ensuing in the Mediterranean. If so, "Italy will view with much sympathy its [the Jewish state] creation and . . . development".[43] It is evident that the Italians were suspicious lest the Jewish state be exploited by the British as a platform for a containment policy against them in the eastern Mediterranean. This was not an over-estimation of British government intentions.

The so-called Gentleman's Agreement of the 2 January 1937 momentarily reduced Anglo-Italian tension. Only a month after the Agreement had been concluded the committee of imperial defence had before it a memorandum prepared by the joint overseas and defence subcommittee enquiring whether the cabinet ruling of November 1933 was still operative.[44] During the discussion Chamberlain remarked that it would be "unfortunate to signalise the conclusion of the Anglo-Italian Agreement by installing 15-inch guns in the Mediterranean". A comment that seems to personify the government's attitude towards Italy during this period.

On 24 February the cabinet approved the following recommendations of the C.I.D. : that the Mediterranean is a vital link in imperial communications; that Italy cannot be counted upon as a reliable friend, "but in present circumstances need not be regarded as a probable enemy"; and, that "no very large expenditure should be incurred on increasing defences of these [Red Sea and Mediterranean] ports, but some steps taken to improve their efficiency".[45] This strange combination of unease at Italy's intentions coupled with anxiety not to provoke her unduly found further expression in a report of the chiefs of staff.[46] It emphasised the vital importance of keeping open imperial communications and acquiring extensive naval dock facilities in the eastern Mediterranean. But it saw the solution in the restoration of friendly relations with Italy, not in provoking her.

Yet, despite official protestations of good intent, relations between the two countries deteriorated rapidly. In April 1937 it was decided to concentrate all main base facilities at Alexandria, while Haifa would serve as a base for light naval forces.[47] There is some evidence to indicate that the admiralty already had its sights fixed firmly on Haifa. Mrs. Dugdale noted in her diary that "Admiral Chatfield had pitched in a terrific memo, about Haifa—he must always have it for the British navy",[48] while a week later Ormsby Gore disclosed to Weizmann "that the Admirals had been after him with regard to Haifa".[49]

Throughout the summer of 1937, while the recommendations of the Peel report were being digested by the responsible government departments, there was little change in the overall situation. But during November–December 1937 events took a sharp turn for the worse. On 6 November Italy joined the anti-comintern pact. The chiefs of staff then reiterated that a peaceful Mediterranean was an essential prerequisite for the safeguarding of British interests, and this implied a return to amicable relations with Italy by diplomatic means thereby reducing the number of Britain's potential enemies.[50] A month later, on 11 December, Italy withdrew from the League of Nations. The response to this act was immediate. The chiefs put on record their opinion that the military situation then confronting the British Empire was "fraught with greater risk than at any time in living memory, apart from the war years".[51]

The impression this warning left on British policy was reflected, among other things, in the preliminary moves to abandon partition, and the extension of diplomatic feelers to Italy which resulted finally in the Anglo-Italian Agreement of April 1938.

The Zionists were naturally concerned over the impending talks with Italy. They suspected that Palestine would be used as a bargaining counter in the negotiations. Weizmann asked Chamberlain for assurances. The prime minister was most emphatic : "This question will not even come up; I shall not allow it to be raised . . ."[52] Nevertheless reports continued to appear in the press suggesting that the maintenance of the *status quo* in the Mediterranean was an essential condition for the conclusions of an agreement, and this contradicted the government's declared position on partition.[53] At the same time it was learned that G. W. Rendel[54] was accompanying the British delegation to Rome as an expert on Arab affairs. This fact alone caused great consternation, for Rendel was considered, rightly so, as the inspirer of the foreign office attack on partition, and in general as the arch-opponent of the Zionists at that office.

In the event Palestine was not specifically mentioned in the published text of the agreement.[55] The omission was rectified by Chamberlain in parliament. He informed the House that Palestine had been the occasion of discussions between Lord Perth, the British ambassador in Rome, and Count Ciano, the Italian foreign minister. As a result oral pledges were given that Italy would abstain from creating difficulties or embarrassing the government in Palestine, while in turn the government would protect legitimate Italian interests there. When pressed further Chamberlain added : ". . . the matter was not considered to be quite of the same order as the other matters which are made the subject of written exchanges, but we ourselves are perfectly satisfied with the oral declaration which we have received . . ." This, however, was only part of the truth. Herbert Morrison, in opening the debate for the opposition, suggested that Palestine was included in the discussions but that agreement was found to be impossible, hence the vague nature of the oral assurances.[56] This supposition received indirect confirmation from Rendel himself. He later recollected that "It soon became clear that, owing to the complexities of the Zionist question, it would be useless to try and include Palestine in our discussions."[57]

The agreement had only a marginal effect on Italian activity in Palestine. Both the British and the Zionists continued to grumble that Italy was keeping the pot on the boil.[58] The foreign office admitted some renewed Italian activity from June 1938, but added gratefully : "Had Italy been as active in the same manner as she was prior to the Anglo-Italian agreement the Palestine situation would have been rendered much graver."[59] It was an admission of failure, even if gracefully phrased.

When the idea of partition began to lose ground, the first reports of cabinet differences reached the Zionists in November 1937,[60] it became more vital than ever for the Zionists to persuade the government that from a strategic-imperial point of view the Jews were a safer bet than the Arabs. In early May 1938 the *Haganah*, the then illegal Jewish defence organisation, prepared a memorandum setting out the role the *Yishuv* could play in Britain's imperial defence plans.[61]

The memorandum came at an opportune moment. Specifically,

Britain's military problem in the Near East was in organising a swift and effective response to any local threat without weakening her commitments elsewhere. Previously she had laid great emphasis on the Indian army. This had not proved a satisfactory arrangement. The army in India, from an administrative, financial and technical standpoint, was unable to function efficiently in areas where communications with India were difficult. Hore-Belisha, secretary of state for war, when introducing the army estimates on 10 March 1938 stated plainly that the existing relationship between the army at home and in India was no longer geared to meet present-day requirements. To rectify this, an inter-departmental enquiry between the war office and the India office had been set up with the aim of reorganising the Indian army to enable it to match imperial requirements elsewhere.[62]

In this context progressive military planners were thinking in terms of an autonomous strategic reserve for the Near East with a local industrial-military base. There can be little question that such a reserve would have fulfilled a crucial function for Britain's sorely pressed army, for there was virtually no correlation between her military obligations and her capacity to act. In 1938, for example, the year of Munich, "the United Kingdom had no more than two divisions actually available for service on the continent".[63] During the Anglo-French staff talks of April 1938, this particular pigeon came home to roost. Halifax told the French :

> . . . that in present circumstances, with the best will in the world, the greatest measure of help that they could immediately hope to contribute . . . after considering their other military commitments at home and abroad . . . would be two divisions . . . these divisions would not necessarily be completely equipped with material regarded as essential for modern war, and they might also be short in certain effectives.

Chamberlain went even further.

> He wished . . . to make it clear at this stage that HMG had no desire to commit themselves to sending two British divisions to France on the outbreak of war. The most he could definitely say was that this possibility was not excluded if the Government of the day decided accordingly.[64]

Some months later, at the time of the Czech crisis, Hore-Belisha noted : "All we could do at the outset would be to provide a force of two divisions . . . inadequately equipped for any offensive operations".[65]

During these years Palestine was a constant factor in occupying British troops. At the height of the disturbances the army had in Palestine the equivalent of two divisions.[66] In fact it seems that 40 per cent of Britain's total field force, the equivalent of what was being tentatively offered to France in the event of a European war, was tied down in Palestine. These figures perhaps lay bare the notion often put out by the Zionists that in dealing with the Palestine disturbances only two choices lay before Great Britain : either the appeasement of Arab extremism; or, continuing with the construction of the National Home. But there was a third choice of primary importance : that of protecting the home base. This priority headed the list in all the calculations of the chiefs of staff and decisions of the cabinet.[67] And this of necessity involved a very careful juggling of Great Britain's meagre military resources.

The *Haganah* now proposed that the *Yishuv* play the key role in a Near East strategic reserve. They had the necessary technical and scientific know-how, were unreservedly pro-British, and were proving themselves in the strictly military sphere. The document was shown to a number of military experts. Liddell Hart, who found himself in agreement with the fundamentals of the memorandum, undertook to show it to "two or three army chiefs"; and the document was widely canvassed in military and political circles.[68] There was, in fact, a marked feeling of sympathy in favour of utilising Jewish military capabilities among some army chiefs at the time. General Haining, commander-in-chief in Palestine, 1938-9, told Liddell Hart that we ought "to press on with the policy of creating a Jewish state, and arming it, as a bastion of the British Empire in the Middle East".[69] And General Ironside, commander-in-chief designate in the Middle East, noted in a letter to Orde Wingate[70] on 8 June 1939 : "If the crisis in September [1938] had developed I had made up my mind to arm the Jews and withdraw most of the troops."[71]

Inevitably there was a clash between military and political opinion. And as one commentator notes, the summer of 1938 produced a curious paradox. While Britain was preparing a political retreat from the mandate and the Peel recommendations, military co-operation with the *Haganah* in Palestine reached its zenith.[72]

The activities of Captain Orde Wingate helped establish a basis for future Anglo-Jewish military co-operation. The policy of the *Haganah* to Arab acts of violence was summed up in their slogan *Havlaga* (self-restraint). There was no organised policy of retaliation. However, in the face of growing Arab violence, self-restraint proved an increasingly difficult policy to sustain. The *Haganah* began straining at the leash and were distinctly moving towards a more activist approach. It was clear that a redefinition of self-restraint would have to be formulated.[73]

Wingate canalised *Haganah* enthusiasm into directions beneficial to the British and ultimately of immense profit to the *Haganah* itself. He persuaded two successive army commanders in Palestine, Wavell[74] and Haining, of the practicability of his Special Night Squads scheme. The S.N.S. consisted of *Haganah* members with a stiffening of British officers and N.C.O.s. His policy was one of active defence. To seek out the raiders in the countryside, to lay in ambush for the gangs, and, whenever possible, to destroy the rebels in their village bases.[75] The policy proved to be an outstanding success.[76]

Wingate himself was a passionate Zionist. He admitted that he had adopted Zionism "as a religion".[77] Mrs. Dugdale wrote of him : "Lucky for us that Wingate's fanatical Zionism gets the better of his sense of duty as an Intelligence Officer. He is clearly one of the instruments in God's hand."[78] He had grandiose ideas about future Anglo-Zionist co-operation,[79] and his undying ambition was to command the future Jewish army.[80] By the winter of 1938–9 his political opinions, well known to the British authorities, constituted a considerable source of embarrassment to them, and in consequence he was transferred out of Palestine in May 1939.

His political instinct was not as sure as his military touch. The bellicose advice he tendered to the Zionists on how to tackle the Chamberlain government seemed to exemplify the soldier dabbling in politics.[81] Weizmann concluded : "Much as I admired and loved Wingate, I did not think that his diplomatic abilities in any way matched his military performance or his personal integrity."[82] The real value of Wingate's work lay in giving free rein to Jewish martial ability within the framework of overall British planning, even if it was only for a limited period and with limited aims.

A further attempt to link a Jewish Palestine with Britain's fortunes ensued from Weizmann's contacts in Turkey. Weizmann was of the opinion that Turkey held the key to the security of the eastern Mediterranean. He believed that Jewish influence could help in bringing Turkey into the British orbit. He had direct access to Atatürk through a certain Dr. Ginsberg, Atatürk's dentist and *homme de confiance*.[83] The Zionists and Atatürk's emissaries were in contact during the autumn of 1938, and Weizmann was able to gauge what the Turks wanted, how the Jews could help, and what role Turkey could play in the overall strategic picture.

The Turks were angling for financial aid and had approached the Zionists for assistance in raising a loan.[84] Weizmann believed that the cost for supporting a Turkish-centred Balkan grouping[85] would amount to approximately £50 million. He told M. Mac-Donald that the Jews could help provide a portion of that sum. When informed of this information and Weizmann's impending visit to Turkey the colonial secretary saw the "first glimmer of hope in the last few weeks".[86] Some days later Weizmann met Halifax. The conversation turned on the Turkish question. Halifax explained that while over the Czech settlement there might be some discussion, there existed no difference of opinion over the importance of the Bosphorus. Here Jewish and British interests coincided.[87] Weizmann, therefore, went to Ankara with the distinct expectation of receiving British support. In fact the British attitude was one of indifference, of wait and see. They neither objected nor approved,[88] though no doubt if something of substance would have emerged from the visit they would not have withheld their support.

The visit, however, was inconclusive.[89] Weizmann tended to blame the Turks : ". . . [they] were under the naive impression that I was in control of vast fortunes, and was merely putting them off".[90] But from contemporary reports it is clear that he returned from Ankara satisfied, believing that he had brought back something tangible to bargain with.[91]

The decisive factor appears to have been the government's attitude. The Zionists could only help in raising a loan, the main burden of which would fall upon government resources. This implied some sort of co-operation. But at the time the government was not forging closer links with the Zionists. Quite the contrary, they were in the process of disengaging from past commitments. Hence, although there existed a coincidence of interests at the Bosphorus, the securing of those interests would be attained by individual, not joint, effort. Elliot had hinted as much when he said that a Jewish loan would not give the Zionists any particular pull with the government, it would only mean "some good Jewish money would be sunk into Turkey".[92]

It was also not clear to what extent Britain wished to commit herself to Turkey. Only a year earlier the government had rejected a proposal from the Turks to conclude a Mediterranean pact. It was then argued that Italy had always been contemplated as being party to any agreement, and that in present circumstances it was difficult to imagine a pact except in the most simple and non-committal form. Such a pact, containing mere generalities, would contribute little towards solving Mediterranean problems.[93] Since then the Anglo-Italian agreement had been concluded and rati-fied.[94] In the immediate months after the Munich settlement there was no compelling necessity for the government to alter its policy. In fact the government persisted in its previous line of not taking any provocative measures in the Mediterranean.[95] It was only after the German occupation of Prague in March 1939 and the Italian invasion of Albania in April of the same year, that Anglo-Turkish negotiations began in greater earnest, culminating in the Anglo-Turkish mutual assistance agreement of 12 May 1939.

Neither was the situation as simple as Weizmann imagined. While in Turkey Sir Percy Loraine, the British ambassador, told him that the Turks were asking only for half a million gold pounds *per annum*. The smallness of the sum astonished Weizmann.[96] But it transpired later that the Turks were asking for considerably more : credit for war material to the sum of £35 million; a bullion loan of £15 million "at as early a date as possible"; and extra credit for £10 million "to cover expenses . . . indicated in point one and to deblock all frozen balances".[97] These sums raised complex prob-lems for the British who were preoccupied with foreign-exchange problems of their own.[98] The negotiations dragged on, inconclu-sively, throughout the summer of 1939.

The Turks also approached the Zionists over arms and munitions.

The Turks say that they had repeatedly urged the French to arrange for part of the Skoda works to be moved to the Balkans. They had wanted some branch to be set up in or near Turkey . . . They were most definite—and this was said both by a leading member of their Foreign Office and a high army officer—that if the British government would permit the establishment of ammunition and arms factories in Palestine the Turks would undertake to cover all their requirements from it and . . . induce their Balkan allies to do the same . . .[99]

Weizmann naturally assumed that the Jews, with their great reservoir of scientific and technical talent, would take the lead in the establishment of such industries.

The Turkish proposals coincided with similar suggestions enunciated in the *Haganah* memorandum. Even then Liddell Hart had warned that, "About greater things, such as artillery, etc., there is no possibility . . . of bringing Palestine into the picture."[100] Nothing further was heard of these ideas. The political implications of allowing the Jews to set up and run an arms industry in Palestine were too far reaching to warrant its implementation.

There was another aspect to Weizmann's Turkish activities. By the end of the 1930s, it was becoming obvious that Great Britain intended to rely upon the Arab countries in order to secure her strategic-imperial interests. Weizmann pointed in another direction. He expounded the theory of "the outer circle". He argued that the security of the Near East depended almost entirely upon the posture adopted by the "outer circle" countries : Turkey, Iran and Afghanistan. To this group he added the eastern Mediterranean seaboard countries. Once Britain had won over these countries to her side the Arab East would be neutralised, and the possible defection of the Arab world to the Axis powers minimised.[101]

The nucleus of such a combination seemed already to be in existence. This was in the so-called Saadabad pact of July 1937, which pledged the signatories, Turkey, Iraq, Iran and Afghanistan, to mutual consultations in international disputes affecting their common interests. But this was essentially an agreement between Moslem countries. Iraq would certainly not associate herself with a Jewish Palestine, and as M. MacDonald reminded Weizmann there was a strong pro-German sentiment in Afghanistan stimulated by "the Palestine question which outraged Moslem religious susceptibilities".[102] However, for the British, the logical line of action to be deduced from "the outer circle" scheme was not to ignore, but to implement it. And they could best achieve this by excluding the Zionists from their calculations. Thus the outer circle, instead of restraining the inner circle, as the Zionists argued, would now strengthen it.

In retrospect these manœuvres by the Zionists, however, ingenious and well planned, appear as so much beating in the air. Partition was officially buried in October 1938. The government, in a final attempt to reach a compromise, convened a tripartite conference to meet in London early in the new year. If it should fail the government would impose its own solution.

Before the conference met at St. James's Palace in February 1939, the chiefs of staff

> emphasised the need to convince Egypt and the Arab states that it was to their interest to observe their treaty obligations and, where there was no treaty, to maintain friendship with Great Britain. On this depended the security of our forces and of our lines of communication. The retention of our hold on the Middle East was essential to our whole scheme of Imperial Defence.[103]

These sentiments were relayed faithfully by M. MacDonald to the Zionists during the course of the conference.[104]

As anticipated the conference ended in deadlock, and the government imposed its own solution in the form of the 1939 May white paper. The government statement clearly indicated that in weighing the potential nuisance value of Jew or Arab the government had tipped the scales heavily in favour of the latter. Halifax made this patently plain during the conference discussions.

> They could not assess the nuisance value of the Arabs, but he was disposed to set his estimate higher than Weizmann's. The feeling in India . . . would be very difficult to control. None of them could put it less than a great dead weight . . . at a time when they were unable to carry any extra weight.[105]

And as if to rationalise his theory :

> In the world today there was a contest between the profoundest philosophies of human life . . . [and] if this diagnosis be correct, they would see how necessary it was for them to reconcile administrative necessity and fundamental and eternal spiritual claims and rights.

On a less inspired but equally effective plane it was frequently argued that in the event of an armed conflict with Germany the Jews would have no option but to support Britain; there was no such guarantee with the Arabs.

The white paper did not satisfy the Arab extremists. But the British prognosis proved reasonably accurate. During the war, apart from incidents of an essentially secondary importance, the Arab East maintained a sullen neutrality in favour of the Allies.

I

It is with the issues raised in this chapter kept in mind that one can turn to a more detailed examination of Anglo-Zionist diplomacy in the years immediately prior to the outbreak of war.

NOTES

1 Lord Hankey, *The Supreme Command: 1914-18* (London, 1961), p. 46. Quoted by E. Monroe, *Britain's Moment in the Middle East, 1914-1956* (London, 1965), p. 11.

2 A. Bryant, *Triumph in the West* (London, 1965), p. 415; E. Monroe, p. 12.

3 *The Times*, 10 Nov. 1914.

4 J. Bowles, *Viscount Samuel* (London, 1957), pp. 172-7.

5 See H. H. Asquith, *Memories and Reflections* (London, 1928), ii, pp. 59-60, 65-6.

6 Cmd. 5974, *Report of a Committee Set Up to Consider Certain Correspondence between Sir Henry MacMahon and the Sherif of Mecca in 1915 and 1916* (March 1939), p. 51.

7 See, An Agreement between England, France and Russia, CAB.37/147, No. 19.

8 See, Cmd. 5957, *The Text of the Correspondence between Sir Henry MacMahon and the Sherif Hussein of Mecca, July 1915-March 1916* (March 1939), and in particular enclosures,

No. 4, MacMahon to Hussein, 24 Oct. 1915.
No. 6, MacMahon to Hussein, 14 Dec. 1915.
No. 8, MacMahon to Hussein, 25 Jan. 1916.

The *vilayet* of Beiruth extended down to the north of Jaffa and hence included part of Palestine. However, it is true that Palestine was never explicitly mentioned in the correspondence which was distinguished by a woolly turn of phrase inviting misunderstanding and dispute. Needless to say MacMahon himself denied that Palestine was included in "his pledge". Before the mandate was ratified he explained the reasons for phrasing his letter as he did, ". . . in my letter to Hussein of 24/10/15 it was my intention to exlude Palestine from independent Arabia . . . I hoped the wording was clear for all practical purposes . . . my reasons for specific mention of Damascus, Homs, Hama, and Allepo were, (a) the Arabs attached vital importance to these places, (b) I could, at the time, think of no place further south for purposes of definition . . . it was fully my intention to exclude Palestine as it was to exclude the more northern coastal tracts of Syria . . . I did not use the Jordan as a frontier because I thought at some later stage of the negotiations a more suitable frontier line east of Jordan and west of the Hedjaz railway might be considered desirable . . . also, at the moment, very detailed definition did not seem called for . . . I must also make mention that I never received from Hussein any message or letter to make me suppose he did not understand that Palestine was excluded from Independent Arabia." MacMahon to Shuckburgh, 12 March 1922, C.O.733/38/13471.

9 The most authoritative work on this involved topic is L. Stein, *The Balfour Declaration* (London, 1961); and, for an earlier study of the origins and

motives of the declaration, C. Sykes, *Two Studies in Virtue* (London, 1953). See also M. Vereté, "The Balfour Declaration and its Makers", *Middle Eastern Studies* (Jan. 1970); and D. Barzilai, "On the Genesis of the Balfour Declaration", *Zion*, XXXIII, No. 3-4 (Jerusalem 1968).

10 M. Vereté, p. 65.

11 Stein, pp. 391-2; also Weizmann, p. 242.

12 Stein, pp. 605-6. Stein devotes a complete chapter to "The Idea of an American mandate for Palestine", pp. 605-20. He makes it quite clear, however, that although Balfour, and others, toyed with the idea, Lloyd George was adamant in insisting on retaining the spoils of war. For further information regarding Balfour's views on America see, Mrs. Dugdale, *Arthur James Balfour* (London, 1939), ii, p. 171.

13 *Ibid.*, pp. 474-5, 544-6.

14 See, Resolutions on Palestine of the Imperial War Cabinet, CAB.24/72; also Stein, p. 612.

15 See cabinet minutes for 27 June 1923, CAB.23/46. The committee consisted of: The Duke of Devonshire, chairman; Curzon; the Earl of Derby; Sir S. Hoare; Viscount Peel; L. S. Amery; Sir Philip Lloyd-Greame; Viscount Novar; E. F. L. Wood; and Sir. W. Joynson-Hicks.

16 See C.P.351(23), CAB.24/161.

17 I have been unable to trace the memorandum submitted by the general staff setting out their reasons for minimising the strategic importance of Palestine. It may well be that they were influenced by the relative ease with which the British repulsed a Turkish attack upon the canal in February 1915, and believed that British interests could best be secured by retention of the canal zone and the Sinai peninsula. At any rate, their main conclusion was included in the cabinet paper just quoted.

18 Cabinet minutes for 31 July 1923, CAB.23/46.

19 An accurate account of these discussions first appeared in R. Meinertzhagen, pp. 133-5; and, J. Marlowe, pp. 93-4.

20 Wedgwood *The Seventh Dominion*, p. 3.

21 See, for example, their speeches at the inaugural meeting of the League, *Jewish Chronicle*, 1 March 1929.

22 For a summary of the growth of imperial interests and the importance attached to them, see, Wedgwood, p. 3; and J. Marlowe, *Rebellion in Palestine* (London, 1946), p. 133.

23 *The Palestine Blue Book for 1936*, p. 127. The above figures do not include illegal immigrants. One commentator concluded that for the year 1935 approximately 10,000 illegal immigrants entered the country, see T. R. Feiwel, *No Ease in Zion* (London, 1938), p. 171.

24 Notes of an interview between Cunliffe-Lister, Weizmann and Ben Gurion, 30 Nov. 1933, W.A.

25 See cabinet minutes for 14 July 1937, CAB.23/89; also, I. S. O. Playfair, *History of the Second World War, United Kingdom Military Series: The Mediterranean and Middle East* (London, 1954), i, p. 2.

26 A memorandum by Eden on the problems facing H.M.G. in the Mediterranean as a result of the Italo-League dispute, 11 June 1936, C.P.165(36), CAB.24/262.

27 A report by the chiefs of staff, 18 June 1936, C.P.174(36) CAB.24/263; the

chiefs followed this up with a similar memorandum of 29 July 1936, C.P. 211(36) CAB.24/263.

28 See cabinet minutes for 23 June 1936, CAB.23/84.

29 A report by the joint planning subcommittee, 21 July 1936, C.P.211(36) CAB.24/263. And for subsequent quotations.

30 See C.P.37(38), CAB.24/275.

31 Lampson to Eden, 12 Nov. 1937, C.P.283(37) CAB.24/273, appendix 11.

32 Notes of an interview between Baldwin and Weizmann, 30 June 1934.

33 Notes of an interview between Cunliffe-Lister and Weizmann, 14 Oct. 1935, W.A.

34 Weizmann's evidence before the Royal Commission. A verbatim account of the ninth session held in *camera*, 26 Nov. 1936, W.A.

35 See, for example, the questions asked in the House about the Bari broadcasts: P.D., Commons, vol. 325, c. 1618–19, 28 June 1937; vol. 329, c. 368 and 837, 17 and 22 Nov. 1937. These examples were taken almost at random and could be repeated many times over. The Bari broadcasts to the Arabs began in May 1934, long before the Arab rebellion broke out. They were used by the Italians to soften Arab opinion in preparation for their Abyssinian campaign and it was only after Britain took the lead at Geneva against Italy that the radio campaign was stepped up. See, S. Armenian, "Wartime Propaganda in the Middle East", *Middle East Journal* (Oct. 1948), pp. 417–19.

36 Contained in Weizmann's report to the Zionist executive, 1 March 1937, W.A.

37 Minutes of a Jewish Agency executive meeting, 19 Feb. 1938, W.A.; also, Notes of an interview between Ormsby Gore and Weizmann, 25 Feb. 1938. For further information regarding Italian activities in Palestine, particularly in the propaganda and educational fields, see, H. Sidebotham, *Great Britain and Palestine* (London, 1937), pp. 187–9.

38 See Rendel's minute to a foreign office memorandum on Italian activities, 21 Aug. 1936, F.O.371/19983/3334/5292.

39 Notes on Italian aims and ambitions in the Eastern Mediterranean, 15 July 1936, W.A. This conversation took place on 17 Nov. 1934.

40 *Ibid.*

41 *Ibid.*

42 Weizmann to Hexter, 27 Oct. 1937, W.A.

43 A report of two conversations with the Italian representative in Geneva, 29 Sept. 1937, W.A.

44 Extracts from the minutes of a C.I.D. meeting on 11 Feb. 1937, C.P.65(37) CAB.24/268.

45 Conclusions of the cabinet, 24 Feb. 1937, CAB.23/87.

46 A review of Imperial defence by the chiefs of staff subcommittee, 26 Feb. 1937, C.P.73(37) CAB.24/268.

47 Playfair, p. 9.

48 D.D., 13 July 1937.

49 Minutes of an interview between Ormsby Gore and Weizmann, 19 July 1937, W.A.; see also *Evening Standard*, 17 Aug. 1937, where a report of this conversation appeared.

50 Playfair, p. 11. For a general idea of the views of the general staff and war

office on furthering better relations with Italy, see R. J. Minney, *The Private Papers of Hore-Belisha* (London, 1960), pp. 101–3.

51 Playfair, p. 11.

52 Notes of an interview between the prime minister and Weizmann, 10 March 1938, W.A.

53 See for example, *Sunday Times*, 27 March 1938.

54 Sir G. W. Rendel (1889–   ): head of the eastern department of the foreign office, 1930–38; British minister to Bulgaria, 1938–41.

55 Cmd. 5726. *The Anglo-Italian Agreement of 16 April 1938*. It should not be forgotten that the main aim of the agreement, on the British side at least. was to reduce Italian involvement in the Spanish civil war. For it was this protracted struggle that constituted the main obstacle to amicable Anglo-Italian relations in the Mediterranean.

56 P.D., Commons, vol. 335, c. 538–9, 2 May 1938.

57 G. W. Rendel, *The Sword and the Olive* (London, 1957), p. 135.

58 Weizmann to M. MacDonald, 12 July 1938, W.A.; also, Notes of an interview between Weizmann and M. MacDonald, 13 Sept. 1938, W.A.

59 A foreign office memorandum on Anglo-Italian relations, 2 Oct. 1938, *B.D.*, third series, iii, p. 313.

60 See above, pp. 151–52.

61 The following passage, except where stated otherwise, is based upon: E, Galili to M. Shertok, 18 May 1938; and A memorandum on the place of *Eretz Yisrael* (Palestine) in the Imperial framework of the Middle East, June–July 1938, C.Z.A., S25/957.

62 See Minney, p. 93; and, B. Liddell Hart, *The Defence of Britain* (London, 1939), p. 263.

63 W. K. Hancock and M. M. Gowing, *The History of the Second World War. United Kingdom Civil Series, The British War Economy* (London, 1949), p. 67.

64 A record of the Anglo-French conversations held on 28 April 1938, *B.D.*, Third series, i, pp. 201, 208–9.

65 Minney, p. 138.

66 Playfair, p. 14; also Maj.-Gen. Sir C. W. Gwynn, *Imperial Policing* (London, 1939), p. 374.

67 See, for example, A Review of Imperial Defence by the Chiefs of Staff, 26 Feb. 1937, C.P.73(37) CAB.24/268; a meeting of the C.I.D., 5 July 1937, C.P.183(37), CAB.24/270; minutes for cabinet, 14 July 1937, CAB. 23/89; and, A report by the Chiefs of Staff, 19 Oct. 1937, C.P.183(37), CAB.14/271.

68 It was seen by Sir H. Creedy, permanent under secretary at the ministry of war, and the director of the operations department, both of whom voiced agreement with the principles contained in the memo., E. Galili to Ben Gurion, 22 July 1938, C.Z.A., S25/957. It was also seen by Lord Gort, Galili to Ben Gurion and Shertok, 13 June 1938, C.Z.A., S25/957, Mrs. Dugdale showed it to Amery who in turn passed it on to Sir M. Hankey, and requested that the proposals be shown to Sir T. Inskip.

69 B. Liddell Hart, *Memoirs*, ii (London, 1965), p. 141.

70 Maj.-Gen. Orde Wingate (1903–44). He was on service in Palestine from 1936 to 1939, holding the rank of captain.

71 C. Sykes, *Orde Wingate* (London, 1959), p. 209.

72 Y. Bauer, "From Co-operation to Resistance: The Haganah 1938-46", *Middle Eastern Studies* (April, 1966), p. 187.
73 See Y. Bauer, *Diplomatiya Umachteret BeMedinyut HaTsionit* (*Diplomacy and the Jewish Underground in Zionist Policy*) (Jerusalem, 1966), pp. 17-18.
74 Wavell himself was no Zionist. His biographer writes: "Wavell could hardly be less sympathetic towards Wingate's unabashed Zionism, but he was quick to appreciate the military soundness of the S[pecial] N[ight] S[quads] . . . which Wingate elaborated with ferocious eloquence. He gave it his consent . . . [and] they operated ruthlessly and with considerable success . . ." John Connell, *Wavell, Scholar and Statesman* (London, 1964), p. 196.
75 See, 'The Organisation and Training of the Special Night Squads', the Liddell Hart Papers.
76 See, A report by Haining on military operations for the period May-July 1938, the Liddell Hart papers; and, Connell, p. 196 For a detailed account of the actions and fate of the S.N.S. see, C. Sykes, *Wingate*, Chapters VII, VIII and IX.
77 The Shertok diaries, 3 June 1937, C.Z.A., Z4/17034.
78 D.D., 23 Jan. 1938.
79 See his memorandum, "Zionist Policy and the Partition Plan, July 1937", W.A.; also Sykes, *Wingate*, p. 182.
80 Sykes, *Wingate*, p. 139; he first offered his military services to Weizmann in a letter of 31 May 1937, W.A.
81 D. Joseph to Weizmann, 10 Oct. 1938, W.A. The text of this letter is quoted in Sykes, *Wingate*, pp. 182-4.
82 Weizmann, p. 490.
83 D.D., 28 June 1938. Weizmann's confidence provoked Mrs. Dugdale into noting: "I felt they are right who say the Jews are all powerful—and yet *how* impotent."
84 D.D., 13 Oct. 1938.
85 A Balkan pact had been concluded on 9 Feb. 1934 between Turkey, Yugoslavia, Greece and Rumania. Bulgaria had stood apart. This proved to be a very fragile affair, and now, according to Weizmann, the Turks were attempting to revitalise the pact with the inclusion of Bulgaria in its defence arrangements.
86 Notes of an interview between M. MacDonald and Weizmann, 13 Oct. 1938, W.A.
87 Notes of an interview between Halifax, M. MacDonald and Weizmann, 17 Oct. 1938, W.A.
88 See F.O.371/21880/10/5239.
89 Weizmann arrived in Ankara on 27 Nov. and was back in London by 11 Dec.
90 Weizmann, p. 461.
91 D.D., 12 Dec. 1938; also, Notes of an interview between Halifax and Weizmann, 24 Jan. 1939; W.A.; and, Liddell Hart, *Memoirs*, ii, p. 212. See also the record of his conversation with the Turkish prime minister, 29 Nov. 1938, W.A.
92 D.D., 1 Nov. 1938.
93 See Notes of a meeting of ministers, 2 Sept. 1937, C.P.208(37), CAB.24/271.
94 It was concluded on 16 April and ratified on 16 Nov. 1938.

95 See cabinet minutes for 22 Nov. 1938, CAB.23/96.

96 Weizmann, p. 461.

97 Sir H. Knatchbull-Hugesson (British ambassador in Turkey), to Halifax, tel. no. 12, 14 July 1939, *B.D.*, Third series, vi, pp. 353–5.

98 Halifax to Knatchbull-Hugesson, tel. no. 444, 2 Aug. 1939, *B.D.*, *ibid.*, pp. 567–8.

99 Weizmann to Amery, 25 April 1939, W.A. Similar letters were sent to T. Williams on 25 April, and to Sir A. Sinclair on the 27th.

100 E. Galili to M. Shertok, 18 May 1938, *op. cit.*

101 Official minutes of the fifth session of the St. James's conference, 14 Feb. 1939, C.Z.A., S25/76321. For hints of a similar character, see, Weizmann's interview with M. MacDonald, 13 Oct. 1938, W.A.; with Halifax, 17 Oct. 1938, W.A.

102 Official minutes of the fifth session of the St. James's conference, *op. cit.*

103 Playfair, p. 16.

104 Official minutes of the fifth session of the St. James's conference, *op. cit.*

105 *Ibid.*

6

The Debate on Partition

I. The Proposal

On 19 April 1936 Arab riots broke out in Jaffa.[1] A curfew was imposed on the area and emergency regulations brought into force. The following day an Arab national committee was organised and a general strike declared throughout Palestine. On 25 April a supreme Arab committee was established, subsequently known as the Arab Higher Committee.[2] In this manner the Palestine disturbances, which were to continue intermittently until the outbreak of the second world war, began.

The question of a Royal Commission arose on 1 May when Shertok brought "disquieting news regarding government policy".[3] The next day Wauchope admitted to Weizmann that Shertok's suspicions were grounded in fact, and that London was contemplating sending a Royal Commission to Palestine. In fact, it was Wauchope who was pressing London for a Royal Commission "as the most helpful way of preventing spread of disorders".[4] Weizmann's immediate reaction was negative. He told Wauchope the Jews will fight any suggestion of a Royal Commission. Mrs. Dugdale commented, "I know he contemplates a possible boycott of it."[5] Weizmann's concern was to postpone any final decision until he arrived in London on 17 May. Meanwhile, every effort was to be made to hold up a cabinet decision.

Mrs. Dugdale saw Amery at the House on 11 May and requested that he impress Baldwin, before the cabinet met at 6 p.m. the same day, that firmness is required, not concessions. She then advised Hankey in the same manner.[6] Whether Mrs. Dugdale's intervention had any effect is not clear; but the cabinet did decide to postpone a decision on the Commission until its next meeting.[7] Weizmann cabled Lord Swinton and Thomas pleading for a postponement.[8] He informed Simon Marks, "You must consider advisability telling

Grobman [the nickname employed by the Zionists to describe Thomas] we think appointment commission concession to violence. Repetition experience '29. Therefore we shall not co-operate . . ."[9]

But the decision had already been taken. Elliot informed Mrs. Dugdale that the cabinet had decided in favour of a commission on 13 May. He added, he alone had fought against the decision and "all the friends so lavish in assurances had given way, including Billy O.G.".[10] Elliot continued,

> that once the Cabinet had agreed to a Royal Commission it was probably war between Jews and them, and that he and I must revise techniques of what he tells me. It would be impossible for him to give me information which I should be bound to use against his colleagues.

Mrs. Dugdale concludes, "I fear this is true. I must simply trust him, tell him everything, but never consult him."[11] Despite Elliot's misgivings he continued to be a most prolific source of information on government affairs and consistently fed cabinet confidences to the Zionists through Mrs. Dugdale.

On 18 May Thomas announced the appointment of "a Royal Commission which, without bringing into question the terms of the mandate will investigate causes of unrest and alleged grievances either of Arabs or of Jews . . . The first condition that His Majesty's Government have laid down before there can be any commission is that law and order must be restored."[12] Weizmann remained dissatisfied. He told Baldwin the commission was "a foolish and useless thing".[13] But the government had decided and remained adamant in its decision.

The Zionists, keeping all options open, bowed to the inevitable, and, in their own words :

> . . . make a virtue of necessity. Since any further attempt to prevent the commission was foredoomed to failure, we should get what advantages we could . . . [by] adopting a positive attitude towards it, saying that provided the terms of reference did not cut at the roots of the Jewish National Home we had an open mind on the subject.[14]

Zionist hostility to the Royal Commission stemmed from past experience concerning previous inquiries, in particular the commissions of 1929-30. It was apparent to Weizmann that the disturbances of April 1936 presaged a far more ominous future than did those earlier riots. "Chaim thinks we are at the beginning of much trouble, which should be made to end in a final re-settlement of many outstanding things."[15] That being the case there was no need to repeat the mistakes of 1929 which led to a break-down of Anglo-Zionist relations. "What," Weizmann asked Baldwin, "was the commission going to investigate?"[16] Thereby implying that there was no necessity for any investigation, only a need to subdue the riots and implement the mandate wholeheartedly.

But having reconciled themselves to the principle of a commission, the Zionists, like the government, had to wait upon events until order had been restored. During the interim period the government was concerned with suppressing the disturbances which by now had spread to the countryside where armed bands were conducting widespread guerrilla operations.

Meanwhile, Zionist relations with the government were often strained. The first bone of contention was over the question of immigration. The Zionists were fearful lest immigration be suspended pending the enquiries of the Royal Commission. The immigration schedules for 1936 were well below par for those of previous years.[17] And the evidence now reveals that the government, pressed initially by Wauchope, was seriously considering a temporary suspension.[18] The cabinet, however, concluded that such a step would be tantamount to a surrender to violence, and that no such recommendation could be made until law and order had been restored, a view to which Wauchope eventually subscribed.[19] Even then there was no adverse decision. On 28 October, after the strike had collapsed, it was decided, on Ormsby Gore's recommendation, not to suspend immigration during the investigation of the Royal Commission.[20] Of perhaps greater significance in the long run were the inescapable indications that the government was receptive to the idea of altering the basis of immigration policy and determining the rate of immigration according to political, not economic, factors.[21] Although Ormsby Gore denied this charge, he did envisage the Royal Commission recommending far-reaching changes in immigration policy, and knew "nothing in the mandate which would preclude the government from accepting such recommendations if made".[22]

The second point of disagreement concerned the intervention of the outside Arab rulers as mediators between the government and the Arab Higher Committee. This activity, acquiesced in by the

government, continued throughout the summer of 1936. In October
the Arab strike was brought to an end, ostensibly as a result of their
intervention.[23] The Zionists objected in principle to any form of
interference by the outside Arab states, and considered they had no
locus standi in Palestinian affairs. As Namier put it, "if the Arab
kings had the right to intervene to stop the strike, next time they
could intervene to start one".[24]

Although these disputes were not directly related to the debate
on partition, the suspicion engendered by them helped colour
Anglo-Zionist relations for the coming period and emphasised a
growing gulf between British and Zionist interests.

By September 1936 there were approximately 20,000 British
troops concentrated in Palestine. Wauchope warned the Arab
Higher Committee that if order was not restored drastic military
action was planned.[25] The end of the strike was in sight, but satisfactory political solutions had yet to be formulated.

One suggestion came from Sir Stafford Cripps. He argued that
"British imperialism can no doubt crush the national aspirations of
the Arabs . . . but when this has been done the problems will still
remain unsolved . . . it is clear that . . . there must be a compromise
on both sides". He proposed a three-part programme the crux of
which was that two independent, autonomous states, Jewish and
Arab, should be established within a Palestinian federation. The
crucial questions of land and immigration policy were to be determined by the independent states, not the federal authority.[26]
The Cripps plan was immediately assailed by Wedgwood.

> Divide Palestine into two and let the Arabs rule one half and
> the Jews the other. There is about this something of the wisdom
> of Solomon . . . I doubt if even Sir Stafford Cripps and Sir
> Arnold [Wilson] together could trace the jigsaw line of the fence
> . . . Fermanagh and Tyrone are simplicity itself beside Palestine.[27]

Wedgwood's attitude is interesting for it illustrates the instinctive
dislike felt by a majority of Gentile Zionists to any talk of partition.
Here, in embryo form, were the seeds of future controversy.

On 12 October the Arab strike was brought to an end. The Royal
Commission left London on 5 November and arrived in Jerusalem
six days later to begin its inquiries.[28] The first hint of partition came
during Weizmann's evidence at an *in camera* session of the commission on 23 December 1936.[29] During an exchange between Sir

Laurie Hammond and Weizmann the question of cantonisation arose. Weizmann was sceptical, regarding the suggestion as no panacea for Palestine's problems. "First . . . it is against the mandate itself . . . Secondly, it would cause very considerable difficulties . . . we cannot place all the reliance upon the administration." Sir Laurie insisted : "It depends on what the cantonisation was," Weizmann replied, "I would only like to say no avenue should be left unexplored. This is such an important question and the task of the commission is so difficult, if a proposal is put forward I can promise you we will give it our most careful attention."

Later, during the same session, Professor Coupland refined Sir Laurie's suggestion,

> With regard . . . that something a little more drastic than can-
> tonisation might conceivably be considered, something has been
> suggested to us on the lines he was perhaps contemplating, that
> instead of having a bunch of cantons, you could have two big
> areas, developing the possibilities of self government . . .

Weizmann would not commit himself, nor was he expected to. He felt that what was required "is development, more room and more possibilities". On being pressed more closely by Lord Peel he continued,

> I really do not understand the proposal yet; it is merely a sug-
> gestion which I think Professor Coupland himself is not absolu-
> tely clear about, as to how the division is to be made, and, there-
> fore, I repeat what I said before, that if there were a definite
> suggestion before me, I would try my level best to consider it.

The subject was returned to on 8 January 1937, this time in a completely clear and unambiguous manner. Coupland :

> . . . Looking ahead and supposing for the sake of argument,
> that your hopeful prospect of harmony proves unrealisable in the
> course of the next five or ten years, what practicable alternative
> might there be? With that question in your mind, would you
> comment on this scheme which really deserves to be called more
> than cantonisation; it is really partition of a federal basis . . . if
> after a period of federal partition the only solution, or a solution
> seemed to be effective partition, meaning that in due course and
> under a treaty system, these two blocks of Palestine became in-
> dependent states of the type of Egypt and Iraq in treaty relations

with Great Britain, that is really the ultimate point on which I want to get your view.[30]

Weizmann raised the formal point that such a proposal was against the mandate. Coupland retorted, "it implies the termination of the Mandate". Weizmann hedged :

> perhaps in five or ten years' time, [it] would be an easier thing than [in] the present situation. I think it is based on the erroneous conception that we have large tracts of land to-day in one block . . . let me think of it. I would not like to close the door on any proposal . . . brought forward with the authority of this commission.

Coupland insisted :

> It is not Cust's proposal,[31] nor Cripps' . . . but the idea that, if there were no other way to peace, might it not be a final and peaceful settlement—to terminate the mandate by agreement, and split Palestine into two halves, the plain being an independent Jewish state, as independent as Belgium . . . and the rest of Palestine, plus Transjordania, being an independent Arab state, as independent as Arabia. That is the ultimate idea.

Sir Laurie Hammond : "With a British Entente."
Weizmann :

> Yes, I appreciate that. Permit me not to give a definite answer now. Let me think of it . . . Of course it is cutting the child in two . . . I appreciate the spirit in which the suggestion has been put to me, and perhaps, I may be given an opportunity of coming back to it.

How did Weizmann react to the idea of partition? Immediately after the hearing he told his private secretary that "the long toil of his life was at last crowned with success. The Jewish state was at hand."[32] Later the same month Weizmann met Coupland at the Jewish Agricultural settlement of Nahalal. After their discussion Weizmann told the waiting settlers : "Today we laid the basis for the Jewish state."[33]

His faith in partition did not diminish upon his return to England. Moreover, he successfully canvassed new adherents. "The Jews would be fools not to accept it, even if it were the size of a table-cloth. This Chaim strongly feels. He says Leon Blum is also strongly in favour."[34]

Weizmann accepted partition in principle. He told Ormsby Gore : "The really important question was one of details."[35] Those details were already under discussion by the commission and included questions such as the period of transition for the termination of the mandate and the future boundaries of the Jewish state. This information had been procured from Heathcote Amery, Peel's secretary, by Elliot, and relayed to Mrs. Dugdale. Moreover, Weizmann confided to her that if a satisfactory plan could be worked out he was prepared to consider the stoppage of immigration for a year, but insisted upon internal defence being in Jewish hands, and the inclusion of the Rutenberg works and the Emek [Vale of Esdraelon] in the Jewish sector.[36]

Whatever Weizmann's private inclinations he maintained a prudent front in his relations with the government. He informed Ormsby Gore that "the proposal [is] rather lacking in definition . . . before I could offer . . . any decided opinion . . . [it would be necessary] for me to know a good deal more about its details".[37]

Weizmann had disclosed to Amery the confidential nature of Coupland's proposal and requested him to sound out government feeling. Amery met Ormsby Gore on 16 February and found him "very sympathetic to the general idea of the scheme". He confided to Amery that the commission were seriously considering the proposal, but he was not sure "whether they would have the courage to come down flat-footed in favour of so bold a scheme".[38]

Weizmann was encouraged by this news. "The more I think of the situation the stronger grows my belief that there is no other way out of the deadlock which has been created."[39] For the remainder of the month Weizmann pressed the case for partition. He discussed raising the issue in the press with the noted journalist, Herbert Sidebotham.[40] In Paris Blum said he was prepared to argue "our case" with Eden and Halifax with whom he was on "very friendly terms". In Geneva Professor Rappard, vice-chairman of the permanent mandates commission, promised to fight strenuously any attempt "to re-interpret the mandate in a sense unfavourable to ourselves. On partition . . . he was favourable, provided this was properly done."[41] In London some M.P.s, headed by Victor Cazalet,[42] intended forwarding a memorandum (drafted by Namier) to the commission advocating a Jewish state.[43]

It is clear that Weizmann was resolutely committed to partition; and his views were generally accepted by the Zionists in London. In Palestine there were difficulties. Mrs. Dugdale wrote : "What makes me most nervous is the growing rift between Chaim and B[en] G[urion] . . . who is making most foolish and intransigent speeches in Palestine . . . We all try to soothe Chaim who is very angry."[44] All his efforts were directed to mobilising wide-spread support for the scheme. On 2 March he received definite confirmation that the commission would recommend a Jewish state as one solution.[45] Amery, an enthusiastic supporter of partition, asked Mrs. Dugdale whether we "could . . . call it Judea". She recorded, somewhat disheartedly, "All this seems to me premature."[46]

But partition had gained an important convert. Wauchope told Weizmann "he had now come round to support partition".[47] They even discussed details. Wauchope offered no real dissent from Zionist claims which included "a territory which would permit the Jews an immigration of 50,000–60,000 a year . . . the whole coastal plain from Ras el Nakurah to the southern boundary . . . the Galilee and contiguity with Lebanon . . . the Hulah and the Emek . . . in the south the Jews would want the Negev and Akaba." These requests might appear ambitious, but Weizmann and Shertok were perfectly aware that in order to get the scheme accepted in principle by the Zionist movement they needed the widest possible degree of latitude in their territorial bargaining.

Amongst Weizmann's entourage there was a general feeling that, in spite of the many difficulties, the scheme should be accepted. There remained the question of tactics. Weizmann's attitude was unambiguous : ". . . we should make it clear that we did not look favourably upon the scheme. We were keeping an open mind, but the details were of the greatest importance, and we would be prepared to consider the scheme if these details were not obviously unsatisfactory."[48] Another factor was emphasised. It was considered important that the scheme should not be regarded as Zionist inspired, but one to which the Zionists had reluctantly acquiesced only from want of a better alternative.

Such tactics demanded a very delicate touch. In the coming negotiations the Zionists were not always equal to the task they had set themselves. Often, by emphasising the difficulties and asserting their minimum territorial demands, the principle of partition was lost in a mire of detail. As a result some Gentile supporters gained the impression that the difficulties were too great to overcome and advocated a policy of perseverance in the mandate, much to the chagrin of Weizmann and his followers.

On 26 April Coupland disclosed to Weizmann the main features of the scheme.[49] He informed him that the report would be unanimous[50] and would be presented to the government early in June. Coupland's disclosures appeared "fairly satisfactory"; all the north was included and there would be complete independence. Weizmann was willing to go as far as possible with this scheme, but he confided to Mrs. Dugdale that he would not break the Jewish Agency on this question. Mrs. Dugdale was not quite so certain. "I think he may have to be [a] Michael Collins."[51]

Coupland's optimism was short-lived. By mid-May rumours were prevalent that the northern frontier would no longer be contiguous with Syria.[52] This was confirmed on the receipt of a telegram from Jerusalem stating that the commission means to withhold the whole of upper Galilee : "If this is so," Mrs. Dugdale recorded, "it is fatal and Jews cannot acquiesce."[53] Coupland later wrote to Weizmann "that there were last-minute changes in the Report".[54]

Both Namier and Mrs. Dugdale were of the opinion that Weizmann, then in Paris, should conscript the services of Léon Blum, prime minister of France, to persuade the British that the Jews must have Galilee *in toto*.[55] Weizmann was outraged at the prospect of losing Galilee and refused to consider any state without control of the headwaters of the Jordan and the *Hulah* concession. If these were not conceded he intended to adopt a policy of passive resistance and thus wreck the scheme altogether.[56]

On 29 May Weizmann saw Blum. Blum told him he would not have any Arabs on the Syrian-Lebanese border, and "would say so". Mrs. Dugdale concluded : "We may have saved the situation."[57] This was an over-sanguine evaluation of Blum's influence. There is little evidence to suggest that the British heeded French strictures concerning Palestine. Indeed the inability, or unwillingness, of the French to curb the Mufti's activities in the Lebanon and Syria throughout the Palestine disturbances was a source of continual friction between the two countries.

Meanwhile, it had become necessary to test parliamentary opinion. Weizmann, through the good offices of Sir Archibald Sinclair, organised a private dinner party for 8 June with Churchill as the principal guest.[58] Others invited who attended were, Amery, Attlee, Wedgwood, Cazalet, and James de Rothschild. Lloyd George sent apologies regretting his inability to attend, but expressing his willingness to abide by anything the assembly decided upon.[59]

After the formalities had come to an end, Weizmann opened the

K

discussion by recounting what had occurred before the Royal Commission. He added that here there were two ex-colonial secretaries
(Churchill and Amery) who, in their time, had been unable to
influence the administration. Churchill interjected : "Yes we are all
guilty men. You know [to Weizmann] you are our master—and
yours, and yours [pointing to other members of the party]—and
what you say goes. If you ask us to fight we shall fight like tigers."
Weizmann, duly encouraged, put his case for partition. He had not
committed himself, but if the mandate was unworkable he could
see no other way. The essential criteria were : an immigration of
50,000–60,000 *per annum*; the need for adequate as well as defensible frontiers; and sufficient scope for development for another
twenty years. He appreciated that the mandate had not been given
a fair trial. But that case had been fought out before the Royal
Commission. Now they were faced with a definite plan. It was
possible to destroy it. But then what would happen? Was there any
viable alternative to partition?

Churchill began to monopolise the conversation. He voiced
emphatic disapproval of the scheme. He warned that the government was untrustworthy. They were "a lot of lily-livered rabbits".
They would "chip off a piece here and there" and Weizmann's
dream of an immigration of 50,000 would be smashed from the outset. This proposal was incubating a bloody war. The only thing the
Jews could do was "persevere, persevere, persevere". He had told
the Royal Commission to continue to allow immigration in accordance with economic absorptive capacity, and "by all means let us
have a Jewish majority in Palestine". However, if Weizmann told
him to shut up, he would : "He would stay at home and be broken-
hearted about it." He realised they had let the Jews down in the
past and it was shameful they should wake up only when the Jews
came to them in dire distress.

Attlee was shocked at the idea of partition. It was, he felt, a concession to violence, a confession of failure, and a triumph for
fascism. But if the Zionists agreed to the proposal he would not
fight it. Wedgwood and Sinclair voiced similar views. Cazalet
remained silent.

Only Amery came down fully in favour of partition. And,
although the other speakers had agreed to bow before Weizmann's
policy, Amery's contribution must have appeared to the Zionist
leader the most positive of the evening. He argued that to go on as
hitherto was impossible. It was easier to build a Jewish state than

to change the administration, and the Jews would make an enormous success out of their state.

Churchill had a last fling. The whole project was "a mirage". The question assumed acuteness only when the British were down and everyone thought they could trample on them. "But the time would come and the Jews must hang on." If the government felt they had to humour the Jews then perhaps they might make some concessions; otherwise they would certainly let them down again.[60] On this note the evening ended.

The objections to partition voiced at the dinner party were quite representative of Gentile opinion. In essence it implied continuation of the mandate. Partition, apart from the very considerable technical difficulties involved, was viewed as condoning the failure of the government to implement pledges given in good faith. Moreover, the authority of the Empire had been challenged, and that challenge met, not by restoring its prestige, but by a surrender of responsibility. This was a poor example to set and would, inevitably, lead to disastrous results in other parts of the Empire. Wedgwood's line that "six months of resolute government"[61] would make all other plans superfluous undoubtedly expressed what many thought, as did Churchill's polemics, whatever the state of intoxication he attained.

But Churchill's advice of perseverance in the mandate was becoming increasingly irrelevant in the face of a combination of rising anti-semitism in Europe, violent Arab opposition in Palestine, and a weakening of Britain's international position. As Mrs. Dugdale realised later in the year, "My uncle's document is now a historic piece of paper. It has given us 400,000 Jews and a few friends and that is all—But we must make that enough."[62] The growing realisation of this fact led to a divergence of opinion between the Zionist leadership and their Gentile supporters. For while the Gentiles were expressing their opposition to partition, hitherto oppositionist Zionists were adopting the case for partition.

Ben Gurion now declared that he favoured partition under certain minimum conditions which included full sovereignty, all of northern Galilee, and some token rights in Jerusalem.[63] His adherence was important to Weizmann, for he led the major faction within the Palestinian labour movement and their support was essential when the issue came before the next Zionist Congress.

The Zionists' minimum requirements were communicated to Ormsby Gore on 15 June.[64] They came under four headings. First, an area sufficient for substantial immigration and industrial and agricultural development. This would include the whole of Galilee, the Emek, the Beisan area, the coastal plain from Ras el Nakurah to a point just north of Gaza, and a defensible eastern frontier. It also stipulated that the state should include the Rutenberg Palestine Electric works. Secondly, Haifa and Jerusalem. The Zionists were prepared to guarantee British military needs in Haifa, but insisted that the town and harbour remain in Jewish hands. On Jerusalem there could be no question of renouncing its new Jewish quarter. A British corridor was proposed linking Jerusalem with the Jewish state. This would incorporate the air bases of Lydda and Ramleh and the army supply camp at Sarafand. Thirdly, the Negev. The Zionists considered this an area of tremendous strategic importance with considerable industrial and commercial potential. They argued that if given to the Arabs the area would remain undeveloped. Therefore, they suggested it remain under British control but open to Jewish development and settlement. If, they added, the British refused responsibility "we would have to claim it". And fourthly, sovereignty. The new state would enjoy full sovereignty in treaty relations with Britain. The real point at issue here was immigration. The Zionists were not prepared under any circumstances to leave immigration to the whims of the present Palestine administration, "even for the shortest period". Weizmann summed up : "Unless these conditions are met . . . it is, in my view, unlikely that the scheme would prove workable, and I doubt whether any responsible Jewish leader could ask his people to consider it."

On 22 June Mrs. Dugdale saw the Royal Commission's report. Her contact was again Elliot. They met at the Savoy Grill—about midnight—where Mrs. Dugdale was given an opportunity to study the report.[65] Her first reaction was that there was "nothing in all this that cannot be adjusted by negotiation—provided this immigration idea does not spoil all[66]—. . . We are only at the beginning of our troubles."[67]

When the Zionists next met Ormsby Gore they recapitulated in no uncertain fashion the points made previously in Weizmann's letter.[68] Ormsby Gore replied that their considerations concerning Jerusalem were contrary to the report which envisaged the city as remaining under mandatory control. At the end of the meeting Weizmann requested an advance copy of the report. Ormsby Gore raised initial difficulties, but then agreed to submit the request to the cabinet for approval.

Ben Gurion had emphasised the strong feeling of hostility towards partition that existed in the Zionist movement. This was not just diplomatic shadow-boxing. Large and influential sections of the movement were expressing their opposition to partition. Basing themselves on Jewish historical and religious rights and the indivisibility of Palestine, they considered that one partition had already been made—in 1922—and would consider no further mutilation of the ancient homeland.[69] This view was personified by the *Jewish Chronicle* :

> Partition is completely and irrevocably out of the question . . . [it is] not in the sphere of practical politics. No Zionist, who *is* a Zionist, will look at or touch it. It is an evil and intolerable thing which revolts alike our dearest sentiments and our common sense . . . Jews will have none of it . . . and the sooner it is buried and out of site for ever the better for all concerned.[70]

Weizmann reacted :

> . . . I can see from the news . . . that the floodgates of demagogic eloquence are wide open and the zealots are gnashing their teeth and clenching their fists . . . The Zealots since time immemorial have brought misfortune on the heads of our people, but I am sure they will not succeed this time. Either the project of division is sound and "viable" then it will be accepted, or it is unsound then we shall reject it. To make political capital out of the thing before we know how it looks is folly, but you cannot save some people from their own stupidity. I can hear my old friend Ussishkin[71] raging and tearing about "Uganda" . . . But it won't wash . . . It is the reality of life as against the obscurantism of a few who may sway certain delegates at the Congress but who will be disavowed by the . . . facts.[72]

Serious opposition also came from the United States, where the agitation was led by Rabbi Stephen Wise. Weizmann pleaded for unity.

> It is very essential that we should all stand united, keep cool heads, and not burn our boats on either side . . . our general conclusion was : here is a new line of thought—an audacious proposal; it contains within it the germs of a great future, but also grave dangers; everything will depend on details . . . [it is] wrong to let things go by default by simply saying no . . . we should have

fallen between two stools and taken upon ourselves the responsibility for almost certain failure within the next 25 years . . . I
feel that to return to the old machine, which is a constant source
of friction with petty officials who are trying their best to sabotage our work . . . would be like going back to bondage. It is our
destiny to get Palestine and this will be fulfilled . . . our job is to
make the best of such an opportunity in our own house, with our
forces, as a small sovereign state, leaving the problem of expansion and extension to future generations. There is no absolute in
this world, everything is in a state of flux. This is my own honest
conviction, but . . . to the world we stand uncommitted . . . it may
be either a Solomon's judgment or a caesarian operation; it
depends on how it is carried out.[73]

Clearly there was intense feeling against partition which severely
limited Weizmann's diplomacy whatever his "honest conviction".
At Weizmann's back stood the *neinsagers*, inhibiting his negotiations and allowing little room for manœuvre. These were not the
most auspicious conditions to guarantee success.

On 1 July a new crisis broke. Weizmann had requested an
advance copy of the report. This was refused, though Ormsby Gore
had received cabinet permission to communicate advance copies
"to such persons as he might consider in the public interest".[74]
Weizmann elevated the issue to one of confidence and good faith
on the part of the government. A bitter telephone conversation
ensued between him and Ormsby Gore.

Weizmann :

So you want to strangle us in the dark? . . . I am not "everyone"; I happen to be President of the Jewish Agency. You cannot take decisions affecting the fate of millions without consulting their representatives. We are not going to be bumped off in
the dark; we shall fight you from San Francisco to Jerusalem;
what you are doing now is an unfriendly act.

Ormsby Gore :

If I may say so respectfully, I think you are making rather
heavy weather over things . . . If you are going to treat this as an
unfriendly act, you will make things very difficult for me, who
have been doing my best for you, and would like to go on doing so.

Weizmann :

Our experience in past years with similar reports and statements has not been very encouraging. But this time you are giving
us even less time for consideration than Passfield in 1930.

Ormsby Gore :

Passfield was not dealing with a Royal Commission.

Weizmann :

No, with something much less important. It is precisely because this report is of such vital importance that we are so anxious
to have an opportunity of seeing it in time—and that as much
for the government's sake as our own.[75]

Why Ormsby Gore, an old and trusted Gentile Zionist, refused
Weizmann is difficult to grasp. Paradoxically, this might have constituted the reason. Some months after his appointment as colonial
secretary he confided to Weizmann the personal difficulties he confronted in office. "He was told there would be no peace so long as
he was at the colonial office; . . . he is reminded of his Zionist past
. . . cartoons depicting him as being in the pocket of Weizmann . . .
and that he has to be very careful."[76]
Mrs. Dugdale smoothed matters over. She contacted Elliot and
requested he speak to Neville Chamberlain about the affair. This
he did. And Ormsby Gore wrote to Weizmann a note chiding him
"for going off the deep end" but couched in very friendly terms.[77]
But the report was still withheld and Weizmann's anger remained
unappeased.[78]
The report was published on 7 July, accompanied by a government statement.[79] The substance of the report came as no surprise
to the Zionists. But in the statement it was proposed to restrict total
immigration to 8,000 for an eight-month period commencing
August 1937.[80] This threw the Zionists into utter confusion. Mrs.
Dugdale, who witnessed the scene, recorded : ". . . [I] found all in
an uproar—B[en] G[urion] especially . . . B.G. was all for this
[break with the government] . . . he spoke really like one demen-
ted . . . fulminating . . . [and] referred to the 'bloody British'."
Namier told him how far his outburst showed lack of self-control.
"He [B.G.] was terribly upset . . . rushed into the room where I was
and apologised in the most affecting way."[81]

The question of immigration was of absolute importance to the Zionists and they consistently interpreted the six-monthly schedule as a yardstick of government good faith. The proposal to place an arbitrary ceiling on immigration meant abandonment of the principle of absorptive capacity and its substitution for one of political considerations. The Zionists could not accept this. Whereas absorptive capacity is given to reasoned discussion on ascertainable facts, political considerations deal in speculative assumptions on what might happen if . . .

Mrs. Dugdale attempted to influence Ormsby Gore :

> This has completely changed the atmosphere, and co-operation with HMG is now in grave danger. Feelings pent up for eighteen months have burst their dams, and it is impossible to say where the flood will carry them . . . may be nearing a stage where leadership is impossible.[82]

Neither this plea nor Weizmann's personal intervention[83] had any effect. The clause on immigration remained as a dangerous precedent.

Weizmann's immediate impression of the report was fairly favourable.

> . . . on the whole it is not bad. The boundaries although they follow the general lines of what I have shown you are more skimpy than I thought. Somebody asked me what he should write about the boundaries. I advised him to place at the head of the articles "Standing room only !" On the other hand it is a beginning of a new chapter in Jewish History. The Kingdom of David was smaller; under Solomon it became an Empire. Who knows? *C'est le premier pas qui compte!*[84]

Some days after he had digested the report he concluded that it served as "a basis for negotiation with HMG".[85]

The Zionists' position was clear. Given adequate conditions they would accept the scheme. Once again, Ormsby Gore proved remarkably receptive to Zionist demands. To all of Weizmann's points which included sovereignty, the inclusion of Jewish Jerusalem, population transfers, territorial additions to the Jewish state, the inclusion of the Rutenberg works, and the shortest possible transition period, he raised no real difficulty.[86] A day later Ormsby Gore reminded him that, it is quite impossible for me to enter into specific undertakings of any *kind* at this stage. The confidential conversation of the other day must, of course, be treated as informal, and any conclusions you drew from it should be regarded as purely provisional and tentative. Specific undertakings . . . I am not in a position to give without consulting the cabinet.[87]

On 20 July the Lords debated the report.[88] There was no thoroughly convincing exposition of government policy. Peel's contribution was pedestrian, Dufferin's untactful : his speech consisting mainly of defending the new political level of immigration. The Archbishop of Canterbury made a valuable contribution arguing in favour of partition and pleading for the inclusion of Jerusalem in the Jewish state. The speech that dominated the debate was that of Samuel, and it was wholly negative. "The commission seems to have gone to the Versailles treaty and picked out all the most awkward provisions it contained. They have put a Saar, a Polish corridor, and half a dozen Danzigs and Memels into a country the size of Wales." Numerically the speakers for and against the government were evenly matched, but the most authoritative contributions spoke against partition.

The impressive nature of Samuel's speech pervaded the debate in the Commons.[89] Here the reception to partition was even less enthusiastic than in the Lords. The overwhelming majority of Gentile Zionists spoke in terms highly critical of partition. Morgan Jones, Sinclair, Wedgwood, Tom Williams, Churchill and Lloyd George all expressed doubts.[90] Only Amery took a line close to that of Weizmann. He argued for "preliminary approval of the broad general principle", and that the final partition scheme (no one regarded the Peel proposals as definitive) should take into account future Jewish needs in conjunction with the European situation. In fact, an enlargement of the Jewish area.

The House refused to approve the government's policy. Instead it resolved :

> That the proposals contained in Cmd. 5513 relating to Palestine should be brought before the League of Nations with a view to enabling H.M.G., after adequate inquiry, to present to Parliament a definite scheme taking into full account all the recommendations of the Command Paper.

In effect this was a decision in favour of delay. The Zionists needed expeditious action; their friends gave them another inquiry.

Why had the government agreed so passively in the opposition amendment? They had an indestructible majority in parliament and were involved in a policy debate of considerable import. It appears that the government, like the Zionists, had no desire to make Palestine a source of party bickering. Above all, they did not want to divide the House on such an issue. In this sense the government could be held to ransom by minority, but strident, voices. This was appreciated by the government. During the debate Chamberlain told Ormsby Gore : "I will not have a party vote on Palestine—you must get out of it as best you can."[91]

Both the government and the Zionists were dissatisfied with the outcome of the debate. Ormsby Gore reported that "the cabinet was furious. They had slowly been brought up to the idea of partition, and now there was a very serious chance of the whole thing falling through. The Samuel view was gaining a lot of ground in the cabinet."[92] Elliot also believed that Zionist hopes had received a blow.[93] Mrs. Dugdale recorded that "it makes acceptance of the principle of partition very much less likely",[94] and that "he [Namier] agrees the debate was a great misfortune, and I hear the others are coming round to that point of view—and feel they have done their work too well in pointing out the defects of the partition scheme".[95] Zionist logic in emphasising the negative aspects of the scheme distorted their acceptance of the general principle involved. The consequences of this made government vacillation inevitable. But the Peel proposals presented a real quandary for the Zionists : they could neither accept them nor ignore them. What was required was a carefully balanced evaluation. And this, it appears, was rarely forthcoming.

Meanwhile, Weizmann had to go before the twentieth Zionist Congress and plead his case for partition. He faced a difficult task for there was mounting internal opposition to the scheme. On 4 August he delivered his key speech. He defined the present position of the Jews in terms of a Talmudic saying : "If the jug falls upon the stone, woe to the jug. If the stone falls upon the jug, woe to the jug."[96]

Then followed a passionate, emotional attack upon the government :

> I say this, I who for twenty years have made it my life work to explain the Jewish people to the British, and the British people to the Jews. And, I say it to you, who have so often girded at me, and attacked me, just because I have taken that task upon myself.

But the limit had been reached. We cannot even discuss such proposals [the Peel proposals], there is no psychological criterion for immigration. Gates are opened or closed on definite principles.

I say to the mandatory power : you shall not play fast and loose with the Jewish people. Say to us frankly that the National Home is closed, and we shall know where we stand. But this trifling with a nation bleeding from a thousand wounds must not be done by the British whose Empire is built on moral principles —that mighty Empire must not commit this sin against the people of the Book. Tell us the truth. This at least we have deserved.

He told the delegates that the scheme, as proposed by Peel, "is unacceptable [prolonged applause]. I speak of the idea, the principle, the perspectives which the proposal opens out . . ." For the acceptance of any scheme, he laid down two basic criteria. "Does it offer a basis for a genuine growth of Jewish life? . . . of our young Palestinian culture . . . [for] rearing true men and women, for creating a Jewish agriculture, industry, literature, etc?—in short all that the idea of Zionism comprises." And "Does the proposal contribute to the solution of the Jewish problem, a problem pregnant with danger to ourselves and the world?" He continued : "If the proposal opens a way, then I, who for some forty years have done all that in me lies, who have given my all to the movement, then I shall say Yes, and I trust that you will do likewise."

By all accounts it was a memorable occasion. Mrs. Dugdale, admittedly subjective, wrote : "The birthday of the Jewish state . . . He spoke for two hours. It was not a speech, it was an inspired utterance. He will never rise to these heights again—we shall never hear the like of it again . . . I sat next to him on the drive back . . . he never asked for the compliments he usually wants after a speech. I asked him whether he knew this morning that he would be able to do this—he answered he knew some parts would be good . . . So ends a great day."[97]

Congress resolved that the Peel proposals offered no basis for discussion, but empowered the executive "to enter into negotiations with a view to ascertaining the precise terms of His Majesty's Government for the proposed establishment of a Jewish State".[98] It was a notable success for Weizmann. He had captured the "prontras"[99] at Congress; he had now to bring them something substantial.

An incident occurred during Congress which greatly impaired

Anglo-Zionist relations. Mr. Meir Grossman, leader of the extreme right-wing Jewish state party, delivered a scorching attack on Weizmann during the course of which he produced a verbatim account of the Ormsby Gore–Weizmann conversation of 19 July.[100] The purpose of this revelation was to discredit Weizmann by indicating that, prior to appearing before Congress, he had committed himself to the government's partition proposals subject to minor alterations. Relations were further exacerbated when the *Evening Standard* published a highly sensationalised, if reasonably accurate, account of the meeting. The headline spoke for itself : " 'The Admirals are after me about Haifa'—what Ormsby Gore is alleged to have told Weizmann."[101]

In view of Ormsby Gore's unambiguous instructions regarding the nature and conclusions of the meeting[102] it was only to be expected that he would take umbrage at these public disclosures. He told Elliot he was "very annoyed" and suspected that the theft of the document had been "accidental on purpose".[103] Weizmann cabled his apologies and despatched Namier to London in order to "explain matters".[104] This had no visible effect. Ormsby Gore replied that he had been done "great harm and mischief".[105] Weizmann was naturally perturbed at this turn of events and did his utmost to make amends. He sought advice from Namier, Stein and Mrs. Dugdale, on how best to repair the damage. Mrs. Dugdale replied :

> do not sound too long or too apologetic . . . You are not accountable to Billy for the arrangements you choose to make in your own office, in respect of your own archives, and it is an impertinence on Billy's part to teach you "your duty" in this matter. The only thing for which you need express regret is the *stealing* of the notes.[106]

And in this vein Weizmann answered Ormsby Gore's criticisms.[107]

How to evaluate this essentially trivial affair? For the contents of the conversation were not sensational; only the manner of their publication. The meeting, obviously, had been a diplomatic feeler, designed to gauge the actual opinions of both sides concerning the realities of partition. Moreover, the talk seemed to indicate a meeting of minds. Leakages, however deplorable, were an accepted part of the game and other precedents were well known, the most startling of all being Mrs. Dugdale's access to the Peel report fully two weeks before publication and while it was still being discussed in cabinet.[108]

Two main factors were involved. First, it underlined the vulnerability of Ormsby Gore's personal position and indicated that the government, although publicly committed, were by no means one hundred per cent behind partition. In a previous interview Weizmann found Ormsby Gore

> a very chastened man . . . [he] said he was being blackguarded by everyone . . . [the] situation was intolerable. He had decided to resign . . . after this parliamentary session, return to private life . . . he could not carry the burden of office . . . he had two firm supporters in the cabinet: Lord Swinton and Malcolm MacDonald.[109]

And later Mrs. Dugdale wrote of him as "a badly frightened man".[110] What emerged was cabinet indecision and a shaky colonial secretary. Ormsby Gore was personally committed to partition. But did he have the necessary authority to impose his views on a hesitant cabinet? This question must have aroused great anxiety among the Zionists.

Secondly, the palpable nervousness displayed by Ormsby Gore in reacting to the Grossman affair resulted in a temporary breach in relations with Weizmann. Weizmann made every attempt to bridge the gulf. But there was a deeper significance than in merely re-opening relations with a colonial secretary. The diplomatic successes that Weizmann achieved stemmed, in large measure, from the personal relationships he forged with Gentile politicians. In particular he was greatly reliant upon Gentile Zionists of long standing. Ormsby Gore figured prominently in the latter category. "Why," Weizmann once asked, "was it later a completely invariable rule that politicians who were enthusiastically for the Jewish Homeland during elections forgot about it completely if they returned to office?"[111] It was a bitter, perhaps unfair, reproach. But there was an element of truth in it. The estrangement with Ormsby Gore was symptomatic of a parting of the ways between Zionist needs and government policy. In the stresses that inevitably arose, not even the good offices of Gentile Zionists were of much help.

On 14 September Eden informed the League Council in Geneva that the mandate "has become definitely unworkable", but that Britain was not committed to any particular partition scheme. The intention of the government was to appoint a special commission to visit Palestine and draw up specific proposals for partition.[112] The latter part of this announcement came as "an utter surprise" to the Zionists.[113] They were not happy about the appointment of another commission. There was always the danger that the commission would act as a tool of the colonial office, cutting away even the minimum proposals of the Peel proposals until nothing of substance remained. This, in Zionist eyes, would automatically rule out its credibility as a negotiating body. Despite this obvious drawback, Weizmann still held that the government's commitment to partition was the all-important factor.

His attitude becomes clearer in a letter to Rabbi Stephen Wise. He wrote that until a definite partition plan materialises the mandate stands and "must continue to be carried out in letter and spirit". And further, that the partition scheme "must be . . . designed to serve the same objects of the mandate and Balfour declaration . . . It must not be a sham."[114]

On the same day that Weizmann wrote this letter Mr. L. Andrews, acting district commissioner for Galilee, was shot and killed as he was leaving the Anglican Church in Nazareth.[115] It signalled the prelude to a period of great violence and unrest in Palestine. Mrs. Dugdale's observation that this "makes partition a certainty"[116] was clearly mistimed. In effect is meant more delay. Ormsby Gore, reporting to the House on the decision to send a further commission to Palestine, enumerated the various measures taken to combat the resurgence of terrorism, and concluded that the "immediate and primary duty of the Palestine government is to combat terrorism and to restore the effective authority of the British administration throughout Palestine".[117]

Weizmann realised that speed was essential. He told Sir John Simon, chancellor of the exchequer, that it was necessary to push the policy through "as quickly as possible". Simon agreed, indicating that within a year they might reach the first stage in the construction of a provisional government. He disclosed that the cabinet was unanimous in its intent to establish a Jewish state—"if [the Arabs] wanted their State they could have it; otherwise they would get nothing". He added an ominous proviso : "if there were no European explosion".[118]

With the cabinet still officially in favour Weizmann was apprehensive lest his parliamentary supporters duplicate the spoiling tactics they had employed to such good effect during the parliamentary debates. Time had not mellowed their opinion. Churchill commented : "The more I think of the Partition Scheme, the more sure I am it is a folly."[119]

The Zionists' general line of approach was as follows : "Chaim considers that we should now concentrate on the parliamentary people here, and persuade them that the only hopeful thing is to attempt to improve the scheme and not destroy it."[120] Weizmann wrote to Sinclair,

> I am perfectly convinced . . . that the mandate cannot be revived, and that partition will go through. I am equally convinced that the best service our friends can render us is to see to it that the partition scheme is a sound one, and not to try and hinder it. You know we have spoken repeatedly about the possibilities of improving the Partition scheme, . . . and I can see that the government is not unresponsive to our ideas . . . I therefore appeal most earnestly to you to help in this direction . . .[121]

The remark Elliot had made to Mrs. Dugdale concerning Britain's need to abandon the mandate in order to retain Haifa as a naval base garrisoned by two million Jews[122] tended to lull the Zionists into a false sense of security. Even Weizmann was affected :

> I do expect the Commission to come soon, and I believe contrary to the general scepticism prevailing in our ranks, that H.M.G. is more than ever determined to carry partition to a successful conclusion . . . the slogan was in cabinet circles that a bastion must be erected there which would lean on at least two million Jews.[123]

It might well be that Weizmann's absence from London during the winter months—from 25 October until the second week in February he was either in transit or in Palestine—coloured his evaluation of political developments in London. For his information he was wholly reliant upon protracted correspondence with his colleagues. Often these conflicted in their interpretation of events. Eventually he was compelled to write,

> Of late there has been such a correspondence that I do not know from which end to begin . . . I cannot believe that it [the political situation] is so catastrophical as . . . in the letters of Henry [Melchett] and Baffy [Dugdale]. When one is faced with so many contradictory statements, it would be very unwise to draw conclusions and I am waiting rather impatiently for Baffy to come here and tell me all by word of mouth.[124]

The contradictory statements revolved around rumours that the government was contemplating a *volte-face* in its partition policy.

NOTES

1   For the background and general course of these events, see: Col. No. 129. *Report by H.M.G. to the League of Nations on the Administration of Palestine, 1936*, pp. 5–20, 22–37; Cmd. 5479 (The Peel Report), chaps. 3, 4.

2   The Arab High Committee, headed by the Mufti of Jerusalem, Hajj Amin al-Husaini, re-iterated as a condition for ending the strike the demands made on 25 Nov. 1935: prohibition of Jewish immigration; the cessation of land transfers from Arabs to Jews; and the establishment of a National government responsible to a representative council.

3   D.D., 1 May 1936, W.A.

4   See, A Secret despatch from Wauchope to Thomas, 29 April 1936, C.P. 132(36), CAB.24/262.

5   D.D., 2 May 1936.

6   D.D., 11 May 1936.

7   See cabinet minutes for 11 May 1936, CAB.23/84.

8   Weizmann to Lord Swinton and Thomas, tel. 15 May 1936, W.A.

9   Weizmann to Marks, tel. 16 May 1936, W.A.

10 D.D., 14 May 1936. Elliot's information, as usual, was correct. See, cabinet minutes for 13 May 1936, CAB.23/84. His interpretation was perhaps not so accurate as Thomas was inclined to wait for Weizmann's return to England before reaching any decision.

11 D.D., 14 May 1936.

12 P.D., Commons, vol. 312, c. 837, 18 May 1936. Thomas had earlier the same day communicated to Weizmann his intended statement.

13 Minutes of an interview between Baldwin and Weizmann, 19 May 1936, W.A.

14 Minutes of the London Political Advisory Committee, 8 June 1936, W.A.

15 D.D., 23 April 1936.

16 Minutes of an interview between Baldwin and Weizmann, 19 May 1936, W.A.

17 See Cmd. 5479, pp. 206–7.

18 See Wauchope to Thomas, tel. 14 May 1936. CAB.24/262, C.P.138(36); and memoranda by Ormsby Gore, 4 July 1936 and 26 Aug. 1936, CAB. 24/263, C.P.190(36) and C.P.225(36).

19 Cabinet conclusions for 15 July and 2 Sept. 1936, CAB.23/85.

20 Cabinet minutes for 28 Oct. 1936, CAB.23/86.

21 See D.D., 9, 20 July 1936; also minutes of (Zionist) Political Advisory Committee, 1 July 1936, W.A.; and Weizmann to Ormsby Gore, 1 July 1936, W.A.

22 Ormsby Gore to Weizmann, 10 July 1936, W.A.

23 For a detailed discussion of this episode see, N. A. Rose, "The Arab Rulers and Palestine, 1936. The British Reaction," *Journal of Modern History* (June 1972).

24 Minutes of an interview between Ormsby Gore, Weizmann and Namier, 30 Sept. 1936, W.A.

25 See *The Times*, 12 and 18 Sept. 1936.

26 *Manchester Guardian*, 8 Sept. 1936. The other two points were: temporary limitation of immigration of both Jews and Arabs to the 1925–9 average;

and temporary cessation of land purchased by Jews. These issues were to be agreed upon before ultimate discussions opened and to cease to operate if negotiations broke down.

27 *Manchester Guardian*, 11 September 1936.

28 The commissioners were: Lord Peel, chairman; Sir H. Rumbold, vice-chairman; Sir L. Hammond; Sir W. Carter; Sir H. Morris; and Professor R. Coupland. Mr. J. M. Martin, secretary. Their terms of reference were to "ascertain the underlying causes of the disturbances which broke out in Palestine in April 1936, to inquire into the manner in which the mandate for Palestine is being implemented in relation to the obligations of the mandatory towards the Arabs and Jews . . . whether they have legitimate grievances . . . if such grievances are well founded . . . and to make recommendations for their removal and for the prevention of their recurrence." In Palestine the commission heard 60 witnesses at 30 public sessions, and 53 witnesses at 40 private sessions. In London they heard two witnesses at one public session and eight witnesses at seven private sessions.

29 Verbatim report of the 31st meeting, 23 Dec. 1936, W.A. And for subsequent quotations.

30 Verbatim report of the 51st meeting, *in camera*, 8 Jan. 1937, W.A. And for subsequent quotations.

31 The reference is to a proposal made by Archer Cust, "Cantonisation: A Plan for Palestine', *Journal of the Royal Asian Society* (1936).

32 Quoted by Sykes, *Crossroads*, p. 201. Sykes's source of information was Y. Sacher, Weizmann's private secretary.

33 This well-known story was first told in M. Weisgal and J. Carmichael, *Chaim Weizmann. A Biography by Several Hands* (New York, 1963), pp. 240–1; and subsequently in Sykes, *Crossroads*, pp. 202–3. The first account is based on a recollection as retold to Mr. A. Eban by Prof. Coupland in 1946. Both authors place the meeting in the beginning of Feb. 1937. This was clearly impossible as Weizmann returned to England on 31 Jan.

34 D.D., 1 February 1937.

35 Minutes of interview, Ormsby Gore, Weizmann and Shuckburgh, 2 Feb. 1937, W.A.

36 D.D., 2 Feb. 1937.

37 Weizmann to Ormsby Gore, 12 Feb. 1937, W.A.

38 Amery to Weizmann, 17 Feb. 1937, W.A.

39 Weizmann to Amery, 18 Feb. 1937, W.A.

40 Weizmann to Sidebotham, 18 Feb. 1937, W.A.

41 Weizmann's report to his London Executive on his visits to Paris and Geneva, 1 March 1937, W.A.

42 Lt.-Col. Victor Cazalet (1896–1943); Conservative M.P., 1924–43, and a close associate of Weizmann.

43 London Executive to Ben Gurion, tel. 21 Feb. 1937; also D.D., 2 March 1937.

44 D.D., 2 March 1937. For Ben Gurion's initial reaction to partition, see above, pp. 82–3.

45 D.D., 2 March 1937.

46 D.D., 9 March 1937.

47 Minutes of interview between Wauchope, Weizmann and Shertok, 14

L

March 1937, W.A.; also, Minutes of a meeting held at the Zionist Federation, 15 March 1937. Those present: Weizmann, Shertok, Namier, Brodetsky, Stein, Mrs. Dugdale and Perlzweig.

48 Minutes of the meeting held at the Zionist Federation, 1 March 1937, W.A.

49 D.D., 27 April 1937.

50 It has generally been accepted that the Peel report was unanimous. However, quite another version concerning the unanimity of the commissioners emerges from a letter by Rumbold to his son: ". . . what happened was that towards the end of our labours I found myself confronted with a scheme or plan of partition containing such glaring defects and features that I had to decide whether to split the commission and write a minority report or swallow my objections. I was disgusted at the way this particular scheme had been worked out behind my back. This was due to Coupland—an intriguing little professor—Peel never a strong chairman seemed to have abdicated any authority he possessed—probably because cancer had got its grip upon him—and I got no support from him. So I decided to sacrifice my convictions for the sake of unanimity." Letter dated 10 Feb. 1938, the Rumbold Papers. (At the time of writing in the possession of Mr. Martin Gilbert, Merton College, Oxford.)

51 D.D., 27 April 1937.

52 D.D., 21 May 1937.

53 D.D., 25 May 1937.

54 D.D., 29 May 1937.

55 D.D., 21 and 25 May 1937.

56 D.D., 28 May 1937.

57 D.D., 29 May 1937.

58 Sinclair to Weizmann, 27 April and 25 May, 1937; Weizmann to Sinclair, 30 April 1937, C.Z.A., Z4/17320.

59 Notes of a dinner conversation, 8 June 1937, W.A. And for subsequent quotations.

60 Churchill's ardour was explained thus by Mrs. Dugdale: "Winston seemed to have inveighed against partition . . . in his most brilliant style, but very drunk, fulminated against HMG and in favour of Zionism for three hours. Chaim oddly impressed with this performance, and anxious to exploit it in some undefined way. I pointed out that these people were in no sense a team . . . they knew little or nothing about the subject, and that partition must not be made the catspaw of English politics . . . they agreed reluctantly . . . Victor [Cazalet] . . . *more* than confirmed my impressions about Winston's state and wild talk . . ." D.D., 9 June 1937.

61 D.D., 9 April 1937.

62 Mrs. Dugdale to Weizmann, 22 Dec. 1937, W.A.

63 D.D., 9 and 29 June 1937.

64 Weizmann to Ormsby Gore, 15 June 1937, W.A.; and for subsequent quotations. A copy of this letter was also sent to Churchill.

65 D.D., 22 June 1937.

66 The report recommended a political high level for immigration of 12,000 a year for the next five years. See, Cmd. 5479, p. 367.

67 22 June 1937, D.D.

68 Minutes of an interview between Ormsby Gore, Sir C. Parkinson (permanent

under secretary at the colonial office, 1937–40), Weizmann and Ben Gurion, 28 June 1937, W.A.

69 A minority opposition to partition came from the proponents of bi-nationalism, though for entirely different reasons. Thus at the Congress in August 1937, an unnatural opposition emerged between the extreme left-wing *Hashomer Hatzair* (The Young Guard Party), and the *Mizrachi* (religious group) and other right-wing Zionist bodies.

70 *Jewish Chronicle*, 30 April 1937.

71 M. Ussishkin was the veteran Russian Zionist leader who led the opposition to partition at Congress.

72 Weizmann to B. Katznelson (a Palestine labour leader), 27 June 1937, W.A.

73 Weizmann to Wise, 29 June 1937, W.A.

74 See cabinet minutes, 30 June 1937, CAB.23/88; and D.D., 30 June 1937.

75 Notes of a telephone conversation between Weizmann and Ormsby Gore on the morning of 1 July 1937, W.A.

76 Minutes of an interview between Ormsby Gore and Weizmann, 30 Sept. 1936, W.A. Namier was also present.

77 D.D., 1 July 1937.

78 See Weizmann to Ormsby Gore, 4 July 1937, W.A. Quoted in *Trial and Error*, pp. 478–83.

79 Cmd. 5513.

80 *Ibid.*, p. 3.

81 D.D., 7 July 1937.

82 Mrs. Dugdale to Ormsby Gore, 7 July 1937, W.A.

83 Minutes of an interview between Ormsby Gore and Weizmann, 7 July 1937, W.A.

84 Weizmann to Mrs. A. Paterson (Lorna Wingate's mother), 7 July 1937. W.A.

85 Weizmann to Mrs. A. Paterson, 13 July 1937, W.A.

86 Minutes of an interview between Weizmann, Ormsby Gore and Lord Dufferin, 19 July 1937, W.A.

87 Ormsby Gore to Weizmann, 20 July 1937, W.A.

88 P.D., Lords, vol. 106, c. 599–674.

89 P.D., Commons, vol. 326, c. 2235–2367, 21 July 1937.

90 For further expressions of Gentile Zionist hostility to partition see: Wedgwood's interview in the *Jewish Chronicle*, 16 July 1937; his letter in *The Times*, 21 July 1937; and his pronouncement that "Partition may now be dead", in *Daily Telegraph*, 29 July 1937. An article by Scrutator (H. Sidebotham), *Sunday Times*, 11 July 1937. An article by Churchill, "Partition Perils in Palestine", *Evening Standard*, 23 July 1937; and "Why I am Against Partition", *Jewish Chronicle*, 3 Sept. 1937. Also Strabolgi in the *Jewish Chronicle*, 30 July 1937. Their parliamentary correspondent in the same issue reported that "many M.P.'s are of the opinion that the proposal for partition presents almost insurmountable difficulties, and quite a number believe that such a scheme is not now likely to be brought into effect."

91 D.D., 22 July 1937.

92 Minutes of a conversation between Ormsby Gore and Melchett, 22 July 1937, C.Z.A., S25/7563.

93 D.D., 22 July 1937.

94   D.D., 21 July 1937.
95   D.D., 22 July 1937.
96   A verbatim report of his speech appeared in *Manchester Guardian*, 9 Aug.
      1937. And for subsequent quotations.
97   D.D., 4 Aug. 1937.
98   *Manchester Guardian*, 11 Aug. 1937.
99   "Prontras" was Weizmann's definition of those Congress delegates who
      could not make their minds up which way to vote. He compared them with
      "a woman who needed good weather for lifting the potatoes and cold to dry
      the land: 'we must pray for a warm frost,' she said." D.D., 10 Aug. 1937.
100   *Jewish Chronicle*, 13 Aug. 1937; see above, p. 138.
101   *Evening Standard*, 17 Aug. 1937.
102   See p. 139.
103   D.D., 9 Sept. 1937.
104   Weizmann to Ormsby Gore, tel. 18 Aug. 1937, W.A.
105   Contained in a letter from Weizmann to Ormsby Gore, 4 Sept. 1937, W.A.
106   Mrs. Dugdale to Weizmann, 2 Sept. 1937, W.A. The Zionists suspected that
      the minutes of the meeting had been stolen from their office by a Revisionist.
107   Weizmann to Ormsby Gore, 4 Sept. 1937, W.A.
108   See above, p. 134.
109   Notes of interview between Ormsby Gore and Weizmann, 7 July 1937, W.A.
110   Mrs. Dugdale to Weizmann, 2 Sept. 1937, W.A.
111   Weizmann, p. 323.
112   *The Times*, 15 Sept. 1937.
113   D.D., 14 Sept. 1937.
114   Weizmann to Wise, 25 Sept. 1937, W.A.
115   *The Times*, 27 Sept. 1937.
116   D.D., 1 Oct. 1937.
117   P.D., Commons, vol. 327, c. 24, 21 Oct. 1937.
118   Minutes of an interview between Sir John Simon and Weizmann, 15 Oct.
      1937, W.A.
119   Churchill to Samuel, 3 Oct. 1937, The Samuel Papers, 100/19, Israel State
      Archives, Jerusalem.
120   Lourie to Shertok, 19 Oct. 1937, C.Z.A., S25/7563.
121   Weizmann to Sinclair, 19 Oct. 1937, W.A.
122   D.D., 12 Nov. 1937; see also p. 86.
123   Weizmann to Dr. L. Lipsky (a prominent American Zionist), 5 Dec. 1937,
      W.A.
124   Weizmann to Lourie, 29 Dec. 1937, W.A.

7

The Debate on Partition

II. The Withdrawal

Weizmann did not ignore the reports reaching him concerning a change in British policy. But he was dependent upon second-hand information and his lack of direct contact with the government did tend to blunt his critical faculties. It was only on 9 December that Mrs. Dugdale got leave from Elliot to inform him of the latest developments in the cabinet.[1] Elliot had warned her well in advance of an impending Foreign Office attack on partition.[2]

> W[alter Elliot] . . . told me that last week Anthony Eden launched an attack on the policy of the Peel report in the form of a F.O. memo from himself . . . taken straight out of any Arab nationalist paper—advocates no partition, Jewish minority for ever . . . The basis is not . . . hostility of Germany or Italy—W. had so far heard nothing of that—but the Arab kings. Chapter and verse in the annexes giving recent evidence of their violent opposition—especially Ibn Saud. Anthony is prepared to wipe away all H.M.G.'s policy in past years as if it had never been . . .[3]

Ormsby Gore told Elliot that the real author of the memorandum was Rendel. Elliot added that "Anthony is a very tired man—obsessed with the weakness of England".[4] Elliot's interpretation of Eden's paper was somewhat exaggerated. Eden was pointing out that in face of "growing opposition from the majority of the Palestinian Arabs and the whole Arab world partition can only be imposed by force . . . [and] that the possibility of an alternative solution should not be excluded from the terms of reference of the new commission". To underline his suggestion he included reports from the foreign office, Egypt, Iraq, Yemen and Saudi Arabia all emphasising the adverse effects a partition would bring.[5]

Cabinet discussion of the memorandum had been postponed, but

Ormsby Gore hinted that if it were accepted he would resign,[6] and wrote a well-argued memorandum suggesting that partition should go ahead and that delay and uncertainty would only worsen the situation.[7] Such a threat, if carried out, would have severely embarrassed the government and might well have inhibited acceptance of Eden's memorandum. The balance of forces inside the cabinet was not favourable towards partition : "On our side would be Billy (a broken weed), Walter, Ernest Brown, probably Kingsley Wood . . . cannot count on the service ministers—they want peace in the Middle East, so long at Britain keeps her hold on Palestine."[8] The split in cabinet opinion reached the ears of Melchett : "I rather gather some members of the cabinet are beginning to get frightened at the possibility of a serious breach in the friendly relations between the Mohammedan world and the British Empire if partition is pushed through."[9]

The Chiefs of Staff had, by the end of the year, issued an unambiguous warning concerning the potential military dangers facing the Empire and were pressing for diplomatic solutions to relieve the growing military threat.[10] In the context of Palestine this implied terminating the Arab rebellion, if possible by agreement with the Arab nationalist leaders, thereby reducing Britain's overextended military commitments. Hence a coalition between the services and the foreign office emerged against partition. This was a formidable alliance.

Conscious of the anti-partition momentum, Elliot began to think in terms other than of a Jewish state. He moved towards a form of cantonisation involving the continuation of the mandate but complete Jewish control over immigration, internal security, land sales, and escape from the Palestine administration. This scheme was dubbed the Dugdale-Elliot "Hindenburg line".[11]

On 8 December the cabinet resumed its discussion on Palestine. It was decided not to reverse the declared policy. A technical commission would be appointed and sent to Palestine, although its terms of reference would not preclude the possibility of abandoning partition. But the spirit of the discussion lacked fire or enthusiasm. Chamberlain "knows nothing about Palestine, and is all in favour of delay . . . perhaps twelve months".[12]

Elliot graphically described the new approach :

. . . [It is] like the Gallipoli expedition—the orders were to try and force the Dardenelles. Winston took that to mean : "Go on

—heads down and force the Dardenelles"— . . . the others interpreted it to mean : "Have a crack . . . but if you can't do it never mind—it wasn't a very good idea anyway, and we will try something else" . . . that is the spirit in which the commission will go out . . .[13]

Weizmann, by now, was well aware of the hostility towards partition shown by the foreign office and the services. He asked Ormsby Gore : "What are the real intentions of the government?" He complained of a lack of political resolution. In Palestine the belief was widely held that partition was merely "a stratagem of the government designed to pave the way for another solution".[14] He warned against the "liquidation of the National Home and the virtual handing over of the country to the clique of so-called Arab leaders who organised the disturbances of last year . . . Jews are not going to exchange their German or Polish ghetto for an Arab one !"[15]

But in spite of the sincerity of Weizmann's pleas, they were couched in an unconvincing political lexicon. "To throw us to the dogs may seem good 'realpolitik' to some—it would certainly not add to the spiritual armament of the Empire."[16] In a period where power politics counted the language of spiritual obligation appeared increasingly anachronistic.

Weizmann's personal belief in partition did not falter. In a letter to the American Zionists he related in cold, precise terms the political situation : the conspiracies against partition; the inactivity, even tergiversation of the government; the threats against the National Home :

> It is a veritable Witches' Sabbath . . . But I feel it my duty to tell you that all that has happened during the past few months and what is happening now in the political as well as in the security sphere has strengthened my conviction that partition offers the only practicable solution of our problem in its present phase, the only solution which, as far as I can see, will not under existing conditions involve the liquidation of the National Home.[17]

He emphasised :

> I have considered and reconsidered the problem in the light of all that was said against it, I have discussed it with detached observers here and abroad and I feel more than ever that it is the only solution we have.

Weizmann's position was clear. He no longer believed it was feasible to resuscitate the old mandate. The Peel commission had, *inter alia*, recommended a series of palliatives which struck deeply at the previous interpretation of land settlement and immigration.[18] Hence, although the commission had promoted partition it had killed the 1922 mandate. Weizmann realised the consequences of this decision. If the government decided in favour of continuing the mandate it would do so only on the basis of a thorough revision of its previous interpretation, inevitably to the detriment of the National Home. There remained only one viable alternative: partition.

On 23 December the government announced its decision to send a "special body" to Palestine to advise on future boundaries.[19] The Zionists viewed this statement with a great deal of scepticism. This evolved firstly, from the prolonged interim period deemed unavoidable between the commission's investigations and its report; and secondly, from the instructions to the commission to include the minimum number of Arabs in the Jewish state. As Amery remarked, "[this] might be taken as a hint to whittle down the area of the Jewish state".[20] In Palestine the new body was christened the "Re-Peel Commission".[21]

Ormsby Gore tried to reassure the Zionists that government intentions were sincere and that it still viewed partition as "the best and most hopeful solution". He denied the "mischievous reports" that the government was contemplating a reversal of its declared policy, but emphasised "that many months must elapse before a scheme of partition could be put into effect".[22]

These protestations did not convince Weizmann. In January 1938 Mrs. Dugdale and Cazalet were on a visit to Palestine. Both urged Weizmann to return to England to urge upon the government the seriousness of the situation. He wrote to Ormsby Gore analysing "the elements which have contributed to . . . such a sudden change in the attitude of H.M.G.". He had no doubt this was due to pressure from outside Arab rulers. After submitting Arab nationalism to a highly critical analysis he concluded, "they [the British] overestimate the quality and force of Arab nationalism and underestimate the actual and potential forces of the Jews in Palestine and of their supporters outside". Weizmann drew attention to the perils involved in persisting in a policy of vacillation and doubt :

I know the Jewish people fairly well and I am confident that 95% of Jewry would accept partition on the basis of an improved proposal of the Royal Commission, but they will not take a mutilated project which may be concocted in the offices of the Palestine Government! Should an attempt be made to force such a proposal upon us, then the group of Zionists, which has been leading the movement for twenty years in the spirit of co-operation with Britain which you yourself helped to instil, must go out into the wilderness.[23]

There was little room for sublety or finesse in his diplomacy. He even rejected the Dugdale-Elliot "Hindenburg line", and outlined his campaign as "to buy more land, occupy it and hold it".[24] To the *Va'ad Le'umi* in Jerusalem he spoke in terms of "a big creative force . . . sufficiently strong to offer resistance" if the Jews were treated as scapegoats.[25] Cazalet, who normally accurately reflected Weizmann's view, told his parliamentary colleagues that if there is an attempt "to wind up the Jewish state . . . the Jews will declare themselves an independent state . . . [and] produce 100,000 young men to look after their own frontiers".[26]

The implications of such statements are not clear. It would have been entirely foreign to Weizmann's political *Weltanschauung* to embark on an independent coup of this nature. But the situation was critical. Much was at stake. And, no doubt, Weizmann turned over this possibility among many others.

His forceful language was not based on conjecture. Information had come to light which indicated that even Ormsby Gore—a staunch partitionist—was debating concessions to the Arabs at the expense of the Zionists. On 4 February Nuri Sa'id reported on his conversations with Ormsby Gore to the Mufti at El Zok in the Lebanon. Zionist intelligence penetrated the meeting, and a report was relayed to the Jewish Agency.[27] Nuri was reported as saying that Ormsby Gore was now of the opinion that the Peel proposals allotted too great a territory to the Jews, and that the Arabs might well ask for part of Galilee and the area south of Jaffa. When confronted, Ormsby Gore vehemently denied this accusation and advised Weizmann to press for Galilee "and they would yet get it".[28] It is quite certain that Nuri, for reasons of personal prestige, deliberately inflated the colonial secretary's willingness to come to terms with the Arabs. But the damage had been done; the seeds of mistrust were sown.

Weizmann arrived in London during the night of 16–17 February. He had come for a very specific purpose : to impress upon the government the gravity inherent in Palestine affairs and to urge upon ministers perseverance with partition. But he arrived at a most inopportune moment. In February 1938 the Austrian question began to boil, culminating in the *Anschluss* on 12 March. Three days after Weizmann's arrival, Eden, the foreign secretary, resigned from the government after disagreements with Chamberlain about Anglo-Italian and Anglo-U.S. relations. Ministers were now continually enmeshed in international and internal crises of prime importance. It became a question of priorities, of conflicting national interests. And in the given situation it was inevitable that the problems of Palestine should take, at best, second place. This was impossible for the Zionists to accept, overwhelmed as they were by the enormity of the tragedy then overtaking European Jewry. Weizmann, towards the end of his visit, began to appreciate that "the British cabinet [is] worried by a great many deeply disturbing matters and hadn't begun to understand the Palestine position".[29] Unfortunately for the Zionists the years 1938-9 were punctuated by a series of six-monthly international crises, each, it seemed, more acute than the other. They had been dealt, by factors beyond their control, an impossible hand to play with all the trump cards stacked against them.

On 19 February Weizmann gave a full account of the latest developments to members of the Jewish Agency executive.[30] Why, he asked, had the foreign office waited nine or ten months[31] before launching an attack "not only on partition, but on the whole policy of Zionism"? He linked the reversal in government policy indirectly with the Hitler-Halifax talks of November 1937 : "not necessarily that Palestine had been discussed on that occasion, but it was clear that the trip had been a dead failure, and the government was jettisoning every unnecessary burden; and for the moment we seemed to be a liability to be disposed of".[32] Weizmann also revealed the formulation of a new partition scheme prepared by the Palestine administration which corresponded very closely with that suggested by Nuri to the Mufti.[33]

Weizmann believed that his diplomacy was handicapped by another factor.

My other trouble is that I find myself dealing with Pharaohs who "know not Joseph" . . . their standards and outlook . . . differ widely from those which animated Balfour . . . Everything seems to be overlaid with a kind of surrealism . . . the doctrine of temporary expediency, opportunism . . .[34]

The widening gap, at the personal level, between Weizmann and the leading ministers of Baldwin's and Chamberlain's governments severely limited his political style. Without doubt this was a contributory factor in the Zionists' failure to make a real impact on the government during this period.

Weizmann met the colonial secretary on 25 February. Ormsby Gore immediately set off upon an apologia of recent events :

> . . . He had a very bad winter, both personally and from a political point of view . . . Politically, the Foreign Office had launched a terrific onslaught on the whole policy of Zionism. Eden himself was rather innocent . . . he had his hands full with Italy, Germany and Japan, and . . . so far as Palestine . . . had simply followed the view of his officials. The Colonial Office was in constant struggle with the Foreign Office which was the senior department. His own name was mud . . . his Zionist past always being thrown in his face. Telegrams had been pouring in to the Foreign Office . . . from Baghdad, . . . Turkey, . . . the U.S., . . . [and] Egypt, the cumulative effect of which had been all against the policy of the Colonial Office.[35]

Weizmann manœuvred the discussion into an examination of the sources of the foreign office attack. He believed that the Cairo embassy acted as the clearing house for anti-partition agitation. At the centre of this cabal stood the Oriental Secretary, Smart,[36] whose close family links with Palestine Arab nationalists made him immediately suspect.[37] The ambassador, Sir Miles Lampson, was considered to be under the influence of Smart, and on his advice had recommended a five-year standstill in Palestine. Such biased sources, Weizmann contended, provided no reliable data upon which to test the strength of Arab feeling on the Palestine question.

The anti-Zionist character of the Cairo embassy was confirmed by Mrs. Dugdale : "So Miles Lampson has an adviser in the heart of Mufti's camp . . . Smart. Came away certain that Chaim was right when he said the 'smell' comes from this *milieu*. Miles makes no secret that he wants a standstill in Palestine for five years . . . No doubt about Smart being our enemy."[38] There is little doubt that the Cairo embassy was pressing, and pressing most strongly, the Arab case. Government papers for the period reveal a continuous stream of memoranda and letters from Lampson arguing in this sense.[39] Whether Smart was Lampson's *éminence grise* is another matter. There were well-founded rumours that Lampson preferred hunting and sailing on the Nile instead of attending to his ambassadorial duties.[40] On the other hand the Zionists did tend to adhere to a conspiracy theory of politics. No doubt there was more than an element of truth in all this. But the "cabal" theory alone cannot stand as an explanation for the change in British policy. There was unquestionably a genuine fear of the consequences of surrendering to Zionist demands in the face of pan-Arab, possibly pan-Moslem, hostility. This fear permeated through to sections of the highest echelons of the British military and political establishment. In a sense it is irrelevant to pose the question (as the Zionists always did) whether or not this fear was grounded in reality, for it was never put to the test. It existed; and the machinations that the Zionists assumed were sponsored by the Cairo embassy played with good effect upon the apprehensions at Whitehall.

They returned to the question of future boundaries. Weizmann stressed that the sense of the parliamentary debates and informed opinion had been that the Royal Commission had offered the Jews too little and not, as the government imagined, too much. "We still had friends in Parliament who would not allow us to be betrayed in this way, and in Palestine there were 450,000 Jews who would fight to the last ditch. Let the government . . . face the task of shooting down Jews."

It was by no measure a satisfactory interview. Weizmann was on the defensive throughout. And his threats, however pungently expressed, betrayed fundamental flaws in the Zionist position. Hitherto the government had explained its Zionist commitment in terms of moral and political obligations. Now it was being asked to weigh a Zionist threat against an Arab threat. In the context of Britain's extensive Arab and Moslem interests, and her deteriorating military-strategic position in the Near East, there could be little doubt on which side the scales would fall.

Weizmann continued his diplomatic exertions. Mrs. Dugdale wrote : "Our affairs are on the move. Chaim is conducting a series of conversations, all of them triumphant in a way, for he is above even his best form—and making a tremendous personal impression on people who have never seen him before."[41]

This was a highly coloured impression of Weizmann's activities. His appointments diary for this period reveals no new significant contacts. He did manage to breach the foreign office where he met the new permanent under secretary, Sir Alexander Cadogan, who admitted "his utter ignorance" of Zionist affairs but agreed to arrange an interview with Halifax.[42] Extra pressure was needed before the interview materialised.[43]

The meeting finally took place on 9 March. Nothing of significance emerged. But Halifax impressed Weizmann : "he felt, for the first time, . . . there might be something of the quality of understanding that A.J.B. used to display."[44] And this despite a renewed foreign office attack upon the Zionist position.[45] Weizmann also met the prime minister; again with no meaningful results.[46] He told Chamberlain that the government must not "chop and change" its policy, and that any proposal less than the Peel recommendations would "lead to disaster". Chamberlain fell back on generalities. "Why are you so uneasy? Why do you worry so much? We are committed to partition . . . on the general lines of the Peel report." The one firm commitment Chamberlain made concerned the forthcoming Anglo-Italian negotiations.[47]

Weizmann returned to Palestine to prepare his evidence for the Woodhead commission.[48] He was then sixty-four years of age, not in the best of health and given to moods of despondency. The strenuous physical effort of incessant travelling together with the mounting crisis in Zionist affairs left their mark on his spirit.

> I am distressed the Jews don't understand the apocalyptic nature of the times . . . Part of us will be destroyed and on their bones New Judea may arise ! It is all terrible—but it is so—I feel it all the time and think of nothing else . . . A new leader should arise in Israel now who should sound the call; we are already old and used up I'm afraid . . .[49]

It was in this mood that he faced the Woodhead commission and the coming negotiations.

Before doing so he renewed contact with Haining. "He is a staunch friend and understands the position very well. When it comes to a question of frontiers he will no doubt give his opinion and it is most likely to be favourable."[50] When they met later in the month Haining told Weizmann there was "no need to worry about Galilee", and that the Arabs had as much chance of securing the area south of Tel Aviv "as to bring the moon down". He believed the commission should "sketch out an outline and leave it to H.M.G.

and the military to fix the boundaries".[51] Weizmann also found the new high commissioner, Sir Harold MacMichael, equally sympathetic. "I found him very reasonable, *very* modest and friendly . . . [he would] advise the Jews to press for the 'beginning' of the States quickly but would not urge 'finishing it' . . . his mind, therefore, runs on the creation of a nucleus with a big mandatory area in reserve."[52]

In May 1938 Malcolm MacDonald succeeded Ormsby Gore as colonial secretary. The news was received with some relief by the Zionists.[53] In Palestine the British clamped down on the rebels[54] and Weizmann returned to England in a somewhat easier frame of mind. He told MacDonald that "the government was now doing the right thing. There was at last co-ordination . . . between the High Commissioner, the Administration and the military, such as had not existed three months ago."[55]

Weizmann turned to the work of the Woodhead commission and government policy. It was apparent that the commission was uneasy on two main questions : the inclusion of Galilee in the Jewish state; and the question of a large Arab minority within that state. On both these issues the Zionist position was absolutely clear. Galilee was considered indispensable. And, Weizmann argued, it would be in the Jewish interest to treat their Arab minority well for as a nation they were *sui generis* in having hostages throughout the world, including most of the Arab countries. He continued : "the spirit of the administration . . . was defeatist . . . cheaply cynical . . . [and] generally antagonistic". In consequence the work of the commission had been thrown out of focus. MacDonald agreed and improved upon this denunciation : "our trouble all along had been that we were dealing with a tenth-rate administration".[56]

The chief criterion for the success of any scheme was the possibility of bringing into Palestine a million and a half Jews within a short period of time. This figure, Weizmann explained, represented the younger generation of the five to six million Jews in central and eastern Europe for whom emigration was a matter of life or death. Only within this context would the Zionists examine the Woodhead proposals.

It has generally been accepted that the Woodhead commission was not of the same calibre or distinction as the Royal Commission. This is undoubtedly correct; but it is an unfair comparison. Not only was the Royal Commission exceptional in the quality of its members, but its main recommendation was accepted in principle by the Zionists. This alone would have been sufficient to enhance its reputation in Zionist eyes. The Woodhead commission had a much more mundane task to perform. Nevertheless, Weizmann was on the whole "impressed with them as a body competent to do their work".[57]

And, significantly, the Zionists held out greater ambitions for the Woodhead commission. They did not want the commission merely to act as a technical body : "[It] should not simply bring in a verdict and leave it at that : it should regard itself rather as a negotiating body . . . [and] as statesmen whose duty it was to seek an *agreed* solution after consultation with both parties."[58] However, the terms of reference of the commission were unambiguous, and they precluded any negotiating functions.[59] In fact the commission refused to consider as relevant any evidence not directly related to the technical aspects of partition, and they rejected the evidence of American anti-partitionists as being irrelevant to their brief.[60]

Weizmann had already commented on the calibre of the commission and his desire that it play the role of an intermediary between Jew and Arab. This, perhaps, is more indicative of his growing feeling of impending disaster than of his faith in the ability of the commission. For whatever the competence of the commission it was an independent body; it had no ties with the distrusted Palestine administration. And it was required to advise, not act on behalf of, the government. Hence, it might serve as a counter-weight to the anti-partitionist forces in the foreign office. Obviously it was a slender hope, but the times were such that even faint chances were given a run.

When Weizmann next met MacDonald he found him in a far less responsive mood.[61] MacDonald was still for partition, and believed the cabinet was too, although the prime minister had some misgivings. But he had received reports that partition held great dangers. Its repercussions would be felt throughout the whole of the Moslem world including India, and that trouble in Palestine would be an additional inducement to Great Britain's enemies in Europe to start some active aggression, the outcome of which might be war. He tested Weizmann's reaction to the so-called Samuel plan : a five-to-ten-year interval during which the Jewish population would not rise above 40 per cent, some immigration into TransJordan, and a promise to review the position at the end of the period.[62]

Weizmann replied that the idea was not new, but "he personally could not put his hand upon it". If Britain persisted, or only flirted with the idea, "it would put half a million Jews who had come to Palestine on a British promise into a death trap . . . [and would] make the task of the moderate Zionists impossible [and] give power to the extremists". Weizmann was convinced that such a compromise would not appease the Arabs. They "would push on all fronts, [it] would mean a permanent minority and a prolongation of the agony". To Weizmann's question whether the government had "really paved the way with the Arabs" about this scheme, Mac-Donald gave the none too reassuring answer, "not sufficiently". It was most unlikely that the implication of this remark eluded Weizmann. This was a perturbing hint of future policy; and Weizmann found it necessary to convey to MacDonald a detailed account of his objections.[63]

The inference of these exchanges was thoroughly disturbing. For it was quite apparent that pending Arab-Jewish agreement on partition—a highly improbable occurrence—the government was considering a solution injurious to Zionist interests. Elliot tried to play down MacDonald's insinuations : "[It was] characteristic of Malcolm's technique. Test all the possibilities in order to come to a clear conclusion." He advised : do nothing except continue the talks with MacDonald.[64]

Weizmann clearly believed that MacDonald was not merely flying a diplomatic kite, and considered implementing his "apocalyptic programme", namely to mobilise world Jewry by calling a conference in America in October under the auspices of Léon Blum, Einstein, and himself :

> Chaim says he cannot leave the destinies of the Jewish people in the hands of Mr. Woodhead and co. . . . nor even in the hands of Malcolm MacDonald. I told Walter on the phone, by Chaim's request . . . [he was] impressed and alarmed. Chaim is right. He gains initiative this way.[65]

But in reality there was little Weizmann could do. He had received disquieting hints, nothing more. MacDonald told him he could leave on his holidays with a quiet mind for there was nothing further to discuss until the commission reported.[66]

On 6 August MacDonald paid an unexpected visit to Palestine, arriving at 8 a.m. and departing the following afternoon. His visit in the main was connected with security problems. July had witnessed an acute upsurge in terrorism.[67] But security and political questions were cut from the same cloth. There could be no imple-

mentation of any political solution while violence reigned and
British authority challenged. Hence the primary need was to maintain order and security. However, MacDonald also exploited his
visit to Jerusalem in order to gauge the administration's opinion to
a political settlement on the lines of his latest overtures to Weizmann. Here he discovered utter confusion. Neither the high commissioner nor his senior officials had any clear, unified conception
of what to do. There were almost as many solutions as there were
officials; or as MacDonald put it: "people's views are at sixes and
sevens regarding this problem at the present time".[68] He himself
still favoured some form of partition if the scheme "could be made
practicable" as the best solution for the next twenty years or so.

"Things . . . about Palestine," reflected Weizmann, "are in a very
bad state and I don't expect the commission to produce any satisfactory solution. What will be the end of all I don't know."[69] In
this humour he faced the commission for the last time. He went
through the usual motions, but his evidence totally lacked conviction or hope: "It was perhaps too late, at this stage, to try and
influence the commission, but he felt obliged to make this statement
as a record before the bar of history." As he left the session Sir John
Woodhead asked: "Then you think we are wrong?" Weizmann
said: "I do." Woodhead replied: "Time alone will tell."[70] If previously they had had their suspicions, now it was patently plain
that the Zionists could expect nothing from the Woodhead commission.

MacDonald's ideas began to crystallise.[71] If the commission made
an offer that the Jews could not accept then "partition went by the
board". Two alternatives remained: either a temporary arrangement between Jews, Arabs and British, on which he did not place
high hopes; or a bi-lateral Jewish-British arrangement. MacDonald
did not expand on the details of the latter alternative. When Sir J.
Shuckburgh saw Weizmann the same day he reintroduced an idea
previously brought up by the Palestine administration: "suppose
they were to create the 'germ' of a Jewish state and an Arab state
and leave the rest of the country under the mandate?"[72] Weizmann
replied that he would like to hear more of this idea. The next day
he wrote to Sir Charles Tegart: "such a proposal might open some
vista of possibilities, but it all turns on what we should be able to
do in the mandated territory".[73] Once again the suggestion turned
on details: the rate of immigration and the scope for land purchases.

Some days later Elliot made available to Mrs. Dugdale a cabinet

M

memorandum[74] on the subject.[75] Elliot termed the proposal "a Tel Aviv concentration camp". Mrs. Dugdale wrote :

> Obvious from it . . . the Peel plan will be reduced—that no frontier will be forced upon the Jews . . . Chaim confronted with the hideous decision of advising acceptance or rejection . . . the alternative to acceptance being most likely a continuance of the mandate with all its restrictions on immigration . . . a permanent minority status . . .[76]

Shuckburgh continued the discussion with Weizmann on 9 September.[77] In the event of the commission's report being a non-starter the obvious alternative was a return to the mandate "with agreement for say five years . . . [with] a limited and agreed immigration—possibly on an ascending scale". Weizmann indicated that an immigration of 50,000 per annum in the existing international situation "represented a bare minimum". Shuckburgh developed the "germ" idea "where economic and other development—including immigration—would proceed without hindrance". In the rest of the country Jewish activities would not be barred, but would be "carefully watched and to some extent restricted". Shuckburgh emphasised that no decision had yet been reached. As soon as the Woodhead report reached the colonial office there would be full consultation. Meanwhile, he was "only exploring all avenues". To both schemes Weizmann was non-committal and fell back on his stock answer : "Everything depends on details, measure of autonomy, financial arrangements, etc."

The "germ idea" or a bilateral Anglo-Zionist arrangement excluded any Arab involvement. This was totally unrealistic. The Arabs had been engaged in active conflict with the British and the Zionists for the past two years. They were not likely to acquiesce passively in the face of an arrangement calculated to damage their interests. The international situation, in Europe and the Far East, demanded that Britain cut her military commitments in the Near East, not invite further involvement. Hence the British were left with no real choice but to develop MacDonald's first alternative of a temporary agreement between Arabs, Jews, and British, with the latter acting the role of an honest broker. In the given context of the period this meant resurrection of the mandate in an emasculated form unacceptable to the Zionists. Weizmann had long foreseen this development. From this stemmed his belief in partition. Now partition seemed a lost cause and Weizmann was faced with the prospect of fighting a rearguard action with little room for manœuvre.

September 1938 was the month of Munich. The effect of the Czech crisis on Zionist affairs was considerable. Indeed it is impossible to understand the meanderings of British policy towards Palestine without consideration of those events.[78] On 24 September, when the Godesburg talks had already broken down and it appeared as though Europe was on the brink of war, MacDonald drew up an emergency programme for Palestine. It involved the abandonment of partition; the absolute suspension of immigration; the continuation of British rule in Palestine "as far as possible in accordance with the terms of the Mandate"; and the postponement of the whole question of future policy into an indefinite future.[79] The Czech crisis passed; but the shadow of war remained. And the MacDonald programme, abrupt and unpolished, bearing all the hallmarks of being decided upon in an atmosphere of panic, remained on record for future reference and refinement.

British policy now begins to emerge with greater clarity. On 13th and 14th September MacDonald conducted conversations with Weizmann.[80] He feared that the commission would propose something "unacceptable" for the Jews. And although he personally still favoured partition, recently several facts had impressed him,

. . . namely: (a) the danger of including a substantial Arab minority in the Jewish state, particularly when that state will be surrounded by powerful neighbours in sympathy with the minority's national aspirations (he naturally quoted the case of the Sudeten Germans); (b) the dangerous position created in the Near East (and even as far East as India) by the support which the Arabs get—both moral and material—from their sympathisers, and from Italy and Germany; (c) lastly, he had been studying the MacMahon correspondence, and thought that there might, in fact, be a conflict of policies.

The second talk opened with the ritual condemnation of the Palestine administration. MacDonald qualified his comments by adding that "the Jews were not entirely free from blame; they were rather aggressive". Weizmann took offence at this remark "coming from a man like 'B' ". Not, one suspects, because Weizmann was unaware of the tenacity of the Zionists when in pursuit of their claims and the hostility this often aroused; but rather because a reference to Jewish aggressiveness from an old friend like Mac-Donald indicated a definite change in atmosphere.

After a rambling, indeterminate discussion on the character of Arab nationalism, MacDonald turned to the crucial point :

> his objective was to see a great Jewish community growing up in Palestine in the next twenty years; this was important from the humanitarian and from the British point of view. The problem was only that of how to attain it. What he was saying now was entirely non-committal and exploratory . . . What about the revival of the mandate and the principle of adsorptive capacity—but, of course, applied cautiously?

He suggested the idea of a graduated rate of immigration, gradually increasing as time went on, "thus allowing an interval for passion to cool down".

MacDonald then made an extraordinary proposal : "even if we disagreed with the government's immigration policy, we could still, even after acquiescing in it formally, continue publicly to denounce the British government on this score". This was obviously intended as a face-saving formula for the Zionists, and in particular for Weizmann who would have to carry the burden of the new policy to his movement. Weizmann rejected the suggestion : "I was not a politician, and that for me denouncing the government was a very difficult and dangerous proceeding."

As to the crux of the policy, Weizmann argued, "could the present administration be trusted to apply any policy in a manner really corresponding to the wishes of H.M.G.?" If MacDonald remained in office for another five years there might be a point in discussing this programme. But political fortunes are fickle, and the attitude of Ormsby Gore and Eden had not been encouraging.

> . . . I was afraid that this proposal . . . was merely another attempt to follow the line of least resistance. And the establishment of an immigration policy with an eye on what is likely to tranquillise the Arabs, even if only as a temporary measure, is, as experience has taught us, a very dangerous procedure.

On the evening of the 19th the final round in this series of talks took place. Mrs. Dugdale recorded :

> Chaim told us the gist of the conversation . . . They are going to sell the Jews also—give up partition, for fear of Arabs, the

Germans, the Italians . . . B.G.'s first reaction—and mine—was that the Jews will fight, physically, rather than go back to the mandate . . . Chaim said nothing much.[81]

The two Zionist leaders reported to their executive on 21 September.[82] Ben Gurion commenced with a report of the last discussion. MacDonald had said that in the year since the publication of the Peel report "the whole of the Moslem world had been aroused . . . In the event of war they could not even be sure that the Arabs, and Moslems generally, would not side with Britain's enemies. They must look for another solution." It was apparent "that in his [MacDonald's] view there could be no question of a Jewish state". MacDonald continued that it was necessary to remove Arab fears. The Jews had set too hard a pace and now they would have to "go slow". The Zionist leaders concluded that partition had been definitely dropped, and that government policy might be summarised as being in favour of a formal restoration of the mandate and the principle of abortive capacity coupled in practice with severe restrictions on immigration and an attempt to reach agreement with the Arabs.

The discussion that followed these disclosures was bitter. The most militant reaction by far came from Weizmann. He insisted that "there would be no Jewish state unless we ourselves made it". MacDonald was engaged in an act of betrayal "and the 400,000 Jews in Palestine would find themselves in a death trap". For him co-operation with the British had always been "the Rock of Gibraltar", but if this was to be the government's policy "we would have to build up our own forces, and ultimately rely on our own strength!" Co-operation had come to an end, and "he saw no use in seeing B. again".

Ben Gurion, together with most of the other participants in the discussion, was far more restrained. He did not advocate a break with MacDonald :

> we should ask for formal preliminary conversations with regard to the main lines of a partition scheme. It might be that a contingency would arise in which we would have to break with Great Britain and oppose her with all the means at our disposal, but we should endeavour to avoid this as long as possible. It would be a terrible blow to the Jews of Europe, who had hitherto felt that there was one great power which was friendly-disposed towards them.

Weizmann's rancour can only be explained in personal terms. For him this was not merely a political setback; it signalled the collapse of his political philosophy. After airing his opinion Weizmann left the meeting. Now his policy was one of "uncompromising hostility . . . to work silently . . . towards arming and preparation . . . [that] would enable Jewry to pursue its own policy in the Middle East".[83]

It was now obvious that MacDonald gave no credence to the Woodhead commission's ability to produce a feasible and acceptable partition plan. For the moment he was paying lip service to the government's adherence to partition. Initially an attempt would be made to attain a tripartite agreement, though no one placed any hope upon that occurrence. Failing agreement the mandate would be continued, but on terms unacceptable to the Zionists. This policy had been maturing since July 1938. By September, with the worsening position in Palestine and Europe, it had become more definite and explicit. While the details of the new policy had yet to be finalised, the principles involved were known to all concerned parties.

At the beginning of October Weizmann decided to mobilise support in America.[84] The Americans responded with good effect. By 15 October the State Department had received about 65,000 telegrams "and they are still coming in. Only on one previous occasion", the memorandum continued, "has the Western Union handled a larger number on one subject."[85] On 12 October Hull instructed Kennedy, the American ambassador in London, to seek an interview with Halifax and inform him "in an unofficial and personal way" that the State Department was under pressure against "alleged alteration of the mandate to curtail immigration".[86] Halifax was unavailable and Kennedy passed on the message to Sir A. Cadogan. Cadogan confirmed that there would be no statement until after the Woodhead commission had submitted its report; and Mac-Donald told the American ambassador "that they had not come to any decision as to policy".[87] On 15 October *The Times* carried an official communiqué from the State Department: "this country 'can decline to recognise the validity of the application to American interests of any modification of Palestine and other Mandates unless such modification has been assented to by the Government of the U.S.' ".

Some days later MacDonald attempted to pacify the mounting concern emanating from the United States by announcing that he had no intention of recommending a stoppage of immigration. He believed that this would "be looked upon rather favourably by the Jewish people".[88] MacDonald had had second thoughts over this question. For on 28 September, he had informed Weizmann that he intended to announce a stoppage.[89] It seems that American pressure fashioned MacDonald's conciliatory gesture. Certainly immigration was not brought to a standstill, although it continued to operate under some restrictions.

In early October Sir Harold MacMichael arrived in London for consultations with the government. He confirmed the government in their intention to reinterpret the mandate and tendered advice to that effect. Oh his return to Palestine he remarked to an American official :

> Sir Harold intimated that partition was no longer a practicable solution but he was . . . emphatic in condemning the form of the present Palestine Mandate . . . he said it was a mistake ever to have separated Palestine from Syria . . . he considers a drastic limitation of immigration . . . essential to any lasting settlement. British circles generally tend to the view that the Arabs can not be brought to discuss the basis of a permanent settlement unless such limitation be enforced at least as an interim measure.[90]

On 17 October MacDonald arranged a meeting between Halifax and Weizmann at Kettner's restaurant, Soho.[91] Halifax denied the rumours concerning restrictions in immigration : "Where do you get this from? Dismiss it from your mind. You have enough to drive you insane." After Halifax left, MacDonald told Weizmann that he had informed the Arabs that the proposed conference agenda[92] could not include questions implying a crystallisation of the National Home. Weizmann retorted that the conference itself implied an abandonment of the Balfour declaration. MacDonald disagreed. The cabinet were in favour of a conference and he could not balk cabinet wishes.[93] He intended to announce the decision to hold a conference on 2 November. By way of encouragement he remarked that the report was not so bad. "That," Weizmann retorted, "means one black eye instead of two."

Weizmann had misgivings on two main issues.[94] He made it clear that the conference must not involve any infringement "of the international character of the mandate". In this way he argued against the tendency to draw in outside Arab rulers as "arbiters" in the Palestine question at the expense of the League of Nations and the United States. Furthermore, he insisted that Britain be a real party to the discussions and not act as an umpire between disputing factions. Britain was bound to enter the conference bound by "definite obligations . . . entailed under the Balfour declaration and the mandate", and they "involve certain fundamentals". These, Weizmann listed as : the establishment of law and order before the conference began, "without this . . . political negotiation is impossible"; no minority status for the Jews in Palestine; and, that immigration continue according to the principle of economic absorptive capacity "generously interpreted". There was nothing new in all this; and it is most unlikely that MacDonald acceded to any of these specific requests.

On 18 October Elliot confided to Mrs. Dugdale the latest government developments.[95] MacDonald wanted to announce the convening of a tripartite conference simultaneously with the publication of the commission's report. If no agreement was reached then the government would impose its own policy. Elliot indicated that the government was toying with a zonal solution.[96] Mrs. Dugdale thought : "We must let H.M.G. impose this . . . short term policy . . . In my view we must take anything we can get."[97] Ben Gurion too did not reject the idea out of hand, but stipulated that everything must depend "on size . . . [on] what arrangements were made for the Jews in other zones, . . . autonomy in Jewish zone".[98]

The Zionists agreed that the zone conception held out possibilities given two conditions : that immigration be unrestricted and the plan only temporary.[99] Weizmann then informed the gathering of an offer from Lord Lloyd[100] proposing an informal conference with Nuri Sa'id with Lloyd acting as "honest broker". Lloyd had been conducting a series of conversations with Ben Gurion and Weizmann throughout October. He told Ben Gurion, "I shall arrange further meetings with Arabs. They trust me."[101] The Zionists tended to believe that this method promised brighter prospects than a formal conference. But they decided to consult MacDonald before arriving at a definite conclusion. Nothing further was heard of this idea. On 19 October a cabinet committee on Palestine was formed; it convened for the first time on the 24th,[102] and recommended that the conference be held.

Towards the end of the month MacDonald again saw Weizmann and Ben Gurion.[103] He denied that the government, as reported in the press, had agreed to cede to the Arabs their maximum demands.[104] But partition had been dropped and the government would now fall back on a "conservatively applied mandate". He reaffirmed the possibility of zonal divisions and the government's determination to impose a solution if no settlement was agreed upon. MacDonald threw in a third possibility: a solution within the framework of an Arab confederation. Weizmann stated that there existed two negative conditions for the acceptance of any scheme: no minority status, and no stoppage of immigration. Again Weizmann defined the latter in terms of an immigration of 50,000 per annum. Even though Weizmann had poured cold water upon the idea of confederation, the concept was to emerge with greater force during a later stage in the negotiations.

The Woodhead report was introduced to the House on 9 November. Its most pertinent conclusion stated: "If we were to adhere strictly to our terms of reference we would have no alternative but to report that we are unable to recommend boundaries for . . . self-supporting Arab and Jewish states."[105] However, the commission produced three alternative plans, A, B, and C. Plan C was considered the "best partition plan we have been able to devise". But this was qualified by serious reservations by two of the four commissioners. In any case Plan C reduced the Peel boundaries to a rump Jewish state of approximately 400 square miles, consisting of the coastal plain from Tel Aviv to Zichron Ya'akov. No Zionist could accept these proposals. At the same time the government issued a statement of policy ratifying that partition was impracticable, proposing a conference to regard "future policy", and promising to continue in their responsibility to find a solution.[106]

Weizmann vented his indignation at the commission's findings on MacDonald.[107] The report was nothing but a "piece of bare-faced cynicism . . . who had given a British official . . . a disgruntled civil servant, and another civil servant the right to revise the mandate and judge the future of the Jewish people in Palestine". MacDonald tried to pacify the storm, but to no effect. Weizmann warned against tampering with the mandate or the National Home. This could only be done "over our dead bodies. The limit had been reached." The inference was that the Zionists would not participate in any conference unless the government confirmed its intention to honour its obligations towards the National Home.[108] MacDonald pleaded for no intemperate conclusions. He could ill afford to alienate Weizmann for without his co-operation it would be impossible to make any headway at all.

The House, when it debated Palestine, heaped general criticism

on the government's indecision and lack of defined policy.[109]
Churchill expounded : "The Court is august, the judges are incor-
ruptible, their private virtues are beyond dispute, but the case is
urgent and all they have been able to do in three whole years of
classic incapacity is to paulter, and maunder and jibber on the
Bench." He put forward his own ten-year plan involving a fixed
immigration of 20,000–25,000 per annum, which he envisaged as
not altering the ratio of Jew to Arab. But he had no constructive
solution to offer if the conflicting sides failed to heed his good
offices : "[then] a need to find other policies of upholding the mandate without incurring heavy military responsibilities". The government drew scant comfort from that remark. Wedgwood detected
the prospect "of another appeasement" and a "retreat before force".
But Earl Winterton, winding up for the government, endeavoured
to reassure the critics : "If, as a result of the conference, an agreement is reached, the House will be asked to approve. The Balfour
declaration and Jewish National Home policy still stands." The
Marquess of Dufferin, summing up the debate in the Lords, also
confirmed that the government "enter these discussions . . . bound
by the obligations of the Balfour declaration and of the Mandate".[110]

Weizmann had achieved his "ministerial statement" placing the
onus of responsibility on the government for maintaining the mandatory policy. But a more realistic evaluation of the situation on
the eve of the conference came from Jerusalem.

In British circles the initial reaction [to the Woodhead report
and government statement] was . . . of intense disillusionment,
bordering on disgust . . . that their government has again evaded
obvious fundamental issues and failed to announce a clear cut
policy. They can see no hope for permanent peace unless Jewish
immigration is stopped or at least drastically curtailed and the
onus placed squarely on the Jews for the building up of an atmosphere of confidence . . .

Among better informed and more thoughtful officials . . . the
view is emerging that a majority of the British Cabinet led by the
Prime Minister and Foreign Secretary, while strongly favouring
frank adoption of a strongly pro-Arab policy and convinced that
no Jewish-Arab agreement can be reached through the projec-
ted London conversations, have compromised on the latter point
with . . . the Secretaries of War [Hore Belisha] and Colonies
[M. MacDonald] . . . the ultimate result it is thought will be the

same, i.e., after failure of the . . . conversations a declaration of policy by the Arab rulers under which Palestine will for a period be administered by Great Britain under a basically modified or re-interpreted mandate.[111]

Weizmann formulated the new Zionist policy at a meeting of the Zionist General Council held at the Anglo-Palestine Club, London.

Partition has been killed by the new commission . . . it is no longer a matter of practical politics . . . the struggle . . . before them was a struggle of their rights under the Balfour declaration and mandate . . . especially their right to immigration, subject only to economic capacity, without any political limitations—avowed or hidden.[112]

NOTES

1   D.D., 9 Dec. 1937.
2   D.D., 21 and 23 Nov. 1937.
3   D.D., 23 Nov. 1937.
4   *Ibid.*
5   See Eden's memorandum, 19 Nov. 1937, C.P.281(37), CAB.24/273.
6   D.D., 23 Nov. 1937.
7   See, A memorandum by Ormsby Gore, 1 Dec. 1937, C.P.289(37), CAB. 24/273.
8   D.D., 23 Nov. 1937.
9   Melchett to Weizmann, 7 Dec. 1937, W.A.
10 See above, p. 107.
11 D.D., 23, 27 and 29 Nov. 1937.
12 D.D., 9 Dec. 1937; also cabinet minutes for 8 Dec. 1937, CAB.23/90.
13 D.D., 9 Dec. 1937.
14 Weizmann to Ormsby Gore, 10 Dec. 1937, W.A.
15 Weizmann to Shuckburgh, 31 Dec. 1937, W.A.
16 *Ibid.*
17 Weizmann to Wise and Lipsky, 21 Dec. 1937, W.A.
18 Cmd. 5479, pp. 366–7.
19 Cmd. 5634, *Policy on Palestine. A Despatch of 23 December, 1937* . . . (Jan. 1938).
20 Amery to Weizmann, 11 Jan. 1938, W.A.
21 Cazalet to Ormsby Gore, 16 Jan. 1938, W.A.
22 Ormsby Gore to Weizmann, 14 Jan. 1938, W.A.
23 Weizmann to Ormsby Gore, 20 Jan. 1938, W.A.
24 D.D., 11 Feb. 1938.
25 *Jewish Chronicle*, 4 Feb. 1938.
26 Cazalet to Weizmann, 2 Feb. 1938, W.A.
27 A report from Beirut by E. Epstein (later Elath), 7 Feb. 1938, W.A.
28 Minutes of an interview between Ormsby Gore and Weizmann, 25 Feb 1938, W.A.

29 Weizmann to Lord Hartington, 9 March 1938, W.A.
30 Minutes of the meeting of 19 Feb. 1938, W.A. Those present were: Weizmann, Ben Gurion, Brodetsky, Goldmann and Lourie.
31 In fact the F.O. memorandum was circulated in Nov. 1937, four months after the publication of the Peel report.
32 This idea reappeared in a report by the U.S. minister in Prague; "Dr. B. Azkin . . . claimed to have learned on good authority that in the Halifax-Hitler conversations Hitler had faulted Britain with temporising too much with the Jews in Palestine . . . Halifax had passed this on to Sir J. Simon and Sir S. Hoare and their associates . . . with the result that the British have since been inclined to take a course less favourable to the Jews," Carr to Hull, 7 Feb. 1938 *F.R.U.S.*, 1938, ii, pp. 896–7.
    There is nothing to this effect in the published German documents of the Hitler-Halifax discussions, *G.D.*, Series D, i, Nos. 31 and 33.
    Professor Azkin was unable to pinpoint the source of his information after so many years had elapsed, but suggests that it might have come from the Polish embassy or Czech legation in London (A private communication).
33 See also notes of an interview between Ormsby Gore and Weizmann, 25 Feb. 1938, W.A. As Weizmann explained it, the plan envisaged a Jewish state consisting of the coastal plain from Tel Aviv to Zichron Ya'akov, plus the Emek and Degania, and possibly the Hulah valley.
34 Weizmann to Tweedsmuir, 22 Feb. 1938, W.A. He requested Tweedsmuir to use his good offices in securing an interview with Halifax.
35 Notes of an interview between Ormsby Gore and Weizmann, 25 Feb. 1938, W.A.
36 W. A. Smart: Oriental Counsellor at Cairo Embassy, 1929–45, Kt. 1942.
37 His wife was the sister of George Antonius, the noted Palestine publicist, and his father-in-law owned the one strongly pro-Palestine Arab newspaper in Egypt, the *Muqattam*.
38 D.D., 7 Feb. 1938. Weizmann returned to this theme just before the publication of the May white paper. See his memorandum, 25 April 1939, W.A.
39 See, for example, a report from Lampson to Eden, 16 Nov. 1937, CAB. 24/273, C.P.28(37), annex III; also his letter to Sir L. Oliphant, 6 Dec. 1938, CAB.24/281, C.P.293(38); and his telegrams of 6 Feb. and 23 March 1939, F.O.371/23231/6/2218, and F.O. 371/23222/6/978.
40 See D.D. 6 Feb. 1938.
41 Mrs. Dugdale to ?, 1 March 1938, C.Z.A., S25/969. The recipient of this letter is not marked.
42 *Ibid.*
43 Hartington to Weizmann, 2 and 4 March 1938, C.Z.A., Z4/17275; Tweedsmuir to Weizmann, 5 March 1938, W.A.
44 D.D., 10 March 1938.
45 See F.O.371/28162/1/1, where Rendel wrote "its necessary to keep our eyes open and do all we can to prevent the C.O. from carrying out their threats" (of pressing partition); See also D.D., 8 and 9 March 1938.
46 Minutes of an interview between Weizmann and Chamberlain, 10 March 1938, W.A.; also D.D., 10 March 1938.
47 See above, pp. 107–8.
48 The Woodhead commission was the technical body instructed to propose

frontiers for the Jewish and Arab states. It arrived in Jerusalem on 27 April.
The commissioners were: Sir J. Woodhead, chairman; Sir A. Russell;
Mr. A. P. Waterfield; Mr. T. Reid; and Mr. S. E. V. Luke, secretary.

49 Weizmann to Mrs. Dugdale, 7 May 1938, W.A.
50 *Ibid.*
51 Minutes of an interview between Haining and Weizmann, 18 May 1938,
    W.A.
52 Weizmann to Mrs. Dugdale, 7 May 1938, W.A.; see also, CAB.24/278,
    C.P.193(38) where MacMichael explained in greater detail his scheme.
53 D.D., 16 May 1938: also Weizmann to Mrs. Dugdale, 17 May 1938, W.A.
54 See P.D., Commons, vol. 337, c. 82–3, 14 June 1938. MacDonald gave
    details of the British action in the course of his speech on the colonial office
    vote.
55 See C.P.190(38), CAB.24/278; and Weizmann's minutes of the interview,
    22 June 1938, W.A. Weizmann also told Mrs. Dugdale, "that the new
    combination of MacMichael, Haining and Tegart [Sir Charles Tegart was
    in Palestine to advise on police organisation] should open a new era . . ."
    D.D., 9 June 1938.
56 These derogatory remarks about the Palestine administration were not
    included in MacDonald's report of the meeting. See CAB.24/278, C.P.
    190(38), Appendix 1.
57 *Ibid.*
58 See Weizmann's report to the Political Advisory Committee, 30 June 1938,
    W.A.; and an interview between MacDonald and Weizmann, 18 July
    1938, W.A.
59 Cmd. 5634, pp. 3–4.
60 See, Weizmann's report to the Political Advisory Committee, 30 June
    1938, W.A.
61 See CAB.24/278, C.P.190(38). Appendix 1; also minutes of an interview
    between MacDonald and Weizmann, 4 July 1938, W.A.
62 For further details of the Samuel plan see his speech in the Lords on 20
    July 1937, vol. 106, c. 641–3.
63 Weizmann to MacDonald, 12 July 1938, W.A.
64 Notes of a conversation between Elliot and Weizmann, 5 July 1938, W.A.
65 D.D., 15 July 1938
66 Note of an interview between MacDonald and Weizmann, 18 July 1938,
    W.A.
67 See MacDonald's statements in the House on 8, 11, 12 and 27 July 1938.
    P.D., Commons, vol. 338, c. 795–6, 1113, and 3091.
68 See his report to the cabinet on his visit, 24 Aug. 1938, CAB.24/278, C.P.
    193(38).
69 Weizmann to Mrs. A. Paterson, 23 August 1938, W.A.
70 Notes of Weizmann's final appearance before the Woodhead commission,
    30 August 1938, W.A.
71 Minutes of an interview between MacDonald and Weizmann, 1 Sept. 1938,
    W.A.
72 Notes of an interview between Shuckburgh and Weizmann, 1 Sept. 1938,
    W.A. See above p. 160 for the Palestine administration exposition of scheme.
73 Weizmann to Tegart, 2 Sept. 1938, W.A.

74   Obviously, C.P.193(38); see below, p. 163, ff. 68.
75   D.D., 6 Sept. 1938.
76   *Ibid.*
77   Notes of an interview between Shuckburgh and Weizmann, 9 Sept. 1938
     W.A.
78   The best general description of the interaction between the Czech crisis and
     Zionist affairs may be found in N. A. Rose, *Baffy: The Diaries of Blanche
     Dugdale*, (Vallentine, Mitchell, London, 1973).
79   See, a secret despatch from MacDonald to Sir H. MacMichael, 24 Sept.
     1938, P.R.O., F.O. 371/2186/1/5603.
80   Summary notes of two conversations with "B" (MacDonald), 13 and 14
     Sept. 1938, W.A. And for subsequent quotations.
81   D.D., 19 Sept. 1938.
82   Summary notes of the meeting of the executive, 21 Sept. 1938, 10.30 a.m.
     W.A. And for subsequent quotations. Those present: Weizmann, Ben Gurion,
     Brodetsky, Berl Locker; Mrs. Dugdale, Namier and A. Lourie.
83   D.D., 21 Sept. 1938.
84   Weizmann to Goldman, Wise, and Lipsky, tel. 6 Oct. 1938, W.A.
85   Memorandum by Alling, acting chief of division of Near Eastern affairs,
     15 Oct. 1938, *F.R.U.S.*, 1938, ii, p. 960. Apparently this was during
     Roosevelt's clash with Congress on the Supreme Court question in Feb.
     1937.
86   Hull to Kennedy, 12 Oct. 1938, *ibid.*, p. 952.
87   Kennedy to Hull, 13 Oct. 1938, *ibid.*, p. 953.
88   Kennedy to Hull, 24 Oct. 1938, *ibid.*, p. 964.
89   D.D., 28 Sept. 1938.
90   Wadsworth to Hull, 25 Oct. 1938, *F.R.U.S.*, 1938, ii, pp. 965–6.
91   Notes of a meeting between Weizmann, Halifax, and MacDonald, 17 Oct.
     1938, W.A.
92   The idea of a round table conference had first been mentioned during the
     conversations held in early July. MacDonald now returned to this suggestion
     in greater detail. See the notes of his meeting with Weizmann, 13 Oct. 1938,
     W.A.
93   There is at present, despite the general relaxation of the fifty-year rule, no
     way of checking what the cabinet thought during these months. For some
     obscure reason the cabinet conclusions appertaining to Palestine affairs for
     19 Oct., 2nd, 9th, 16th, 22nd, and 30 Nov. 1938, are still kept under lock
     and key.
94   See his detailed letter to MacDonald, 17 Oct. 1938, W.A.
95   D.D., 18 Oct. 1938.
96   Weizmann reported on this alternative to his Political Advisory Committee
     on 1 Nov. 1938, W.A.
97   D.D., 18 Oct. 1938.
98   D.D., 21 Oct. 1938.
99   D.D., 24 Oct. 1938. They had met for tea that day at Weizmann's house
     where they discussed this issue.
100 Lord Lloyd (1874–1941): High commissioner for Egypt and Sudan, 1925–9.
101 M. Pearlman, *Ben Gurion Looks Back* (London 1965), pp. 85–8, 92–3.
102 D.D., 18 and 25 Oct. 1938. Its members were Chamberlain, Halifax,
     MacDonald, Zetland, Hoare, Simon and Elliot.

103 See Weizmann's report to the Political Advisory Committee, 1 Nov. 1938, W.A.
104 See, for example, *Daily Herald*, 17 Oct. 1938; *Daily Telegraph*, 19 Oct. 1938; and *Jewish Chronicle*, 21 and 28 Oct. 1938.
105 Cmd. 5854, p. 243.
106 Cmd. 5893. *A Statement of Policy by His Majesty's Government*, (Nov. 1938).
107 Notes of an interview between MacDonald and Weizmann, 9 Nov. 1938, W.A.
108 See also, D.D., 8 Nov. 1938, "For the first time an official document suggests doing away with the Balfour declaration . . . Chaim says he cannot possibly enter into a conference now, unless another ministerial statement disavows the worst parts of the Report."
109 See, P.D., Commons, vol. 341, c. 1987–2107, 24 Nov. 1938.
110 P.D., Lords, vol. III, c. 463, 8 Dec. 1938.
111 Wadsworth to Hull, 12 Nov. 1938, *F.R.U.S.*, 1938, ii, p. 985.
112 Notes of speech at the opening of the Zionist General Council, 10 Nov. 1938, W.A.; see also, *Jewish Chronicle*, 18 Nov. 1938.

8

The Conference at St. James's Palace

"The tide runs strong against us. We feel it in all sorts of ways."[1] With this feeling of presentiment the Zionists entered the preparatory stages to the pledged conference.

By early December the Zionists had heard from reliable sources that the government's post-conference solution included a prohibition of land sales.[2] Their attitude towards immigration had also stiffened. A particularly delicate and emotional problem was that of allowing 10,000 German and Austrian children into Palestine. This question assumed special significance after the pogrom in Germany on the night of 9–10 November. The British refusal to accede to the Zionist demand greatly exacerbated Anglo-Zionist relations. After the government had turned down the proposal to absorb the children in Palestine the fate of the conference appeared to hang in the balance : "Chaim . . . is absolutely prepared to make this a test case for going into the conference . . . [he] is all up on his toes."[3] He told MacDonald : "We shall fight you from here to San Francisco, and when I say fight I mean *fight*." MacDonald asked : "Do you mean I am to go to the House on Friday and announce that you will not come to the conference?" Weizmann answered : "We shall have saved you the trouble."[4] This question came before the cabinet on 14 December.[5] MacDonald then admitted that the children could be absorbed in Palestine "without causing injury to anyone's interest". But the balance of opinion was against it. The Palestine administration and British officials throughout the Near East argued that to admit the children would inflame an already volatile atmosphere and endanger the forthcoming conference. Halifax, at a later date, was quite blunt about the conference's purpose : it was "to ensure that the Arab states would be friendly towards us", but he could not for the present say "how far we should go in order to meet their views".[6] Chamberlain and MacDonald brushed aside Weizmann's threat of non-co-operation : the Jews had no option but

N

to attend. Eventually it was decided to allow the children into England, no doubt on humanitarian grounds, but also to sap Zionist opposition.

MacDonald hinted that in the rising tide of anti-Zionist feeling he still acted as a moderate factor.[7] "Thus the administration had wanted to end immigration and land sales, but he had not accepted this." He admitted the government's attitude was "quite irreconcilable" with that of two months ago. But "things had now to be looked at on a larger plane". The Zionists voiced concern at the invitation extended to the Arab countries to participate in the conference.[8] MacDonald agreed that the Jewish position would be difficult, but they would be making a great mistake if they boycotted the conference. Namier concluded :

> B. full of vague talks on coming to an understanding with the Arabs. No indication of how this was to be done . . . [he is] prepared to promise everything for the future, to admit everything for the past, and to give nothing for the present.

Namier remained convinced that there was nothing to be gained by going to conference. But Weizmann's former belligerency softened. By 16 December he had decided not to break on the issue of the children.[9]

In Palestine the *Yishuv* was engaged in stormy discussions regarding participation in the conference.[10] Many Palestinian Jews believed that the government was bent on burying the mandate and sacrificing European Jewry, hence there was little point and less honour in attending their own funeral. After a bitter debate and much soul-searching the *Yishuv* decided in favour. It may well be that the decision to enter into the discussions was guided by the internecine strife between the Nashashibis and Husainis as to the composition of the Palestine delegation. Weizmann believed this might yet sabotage the conference : "Had a long happy talk with Chaim . . . The political situation regarding Palestine is more hopeful than before Christmas. MacDonald's conference does not look like materialising—the Arabs cannot agree among themselves even to form a delegation."[11] Indeed the chief concern of MacDonald before the conference opened was in getting the Palestinians to agree among themselves to a single delegation. He was unable to report the achievement of this aim until 15 February, eight days after the conference had opened.[12]

In mid-January 1939 the chiefs of staff issued a powerful memorandum stressing that "if our future policy in relation to Palestine is such that it cannot be accepted by the Arab states as equitable, and is not a clear earnest of our intentions to maintain their friendship, those states who are already shaken in their belief in our good intentions will at last become alienated". It was clearly inferred, if not stated explicitly, that as "our hold on the Middle East is an essential in our present scheme of Imperial Defence" it was absolutely vital to reach an agreement favourable to the demands of the Arab states.[13] On 18 January MacDonald circulated a memorandum for the cabinet committee on Palestine outlining the general policy lines to be adopted at the conference.[14]

> No Jewish state—no Arab state—no stoppage of Jewish immigration, but a ten year proviso that it shall not exceed 40% at most or even less . . . restriction of land sales . . . no real zoning—an Advisory Council on basis of parity . . . I told Walter I did not think there was a chance of the minority quota being acceptable . . . He did not think . . . there was a chance of getting that altered . . . MacDonald referred to the spiritual argument of Zionism. Neville . . . could not understand what was meant—but Halifax saw the point. Inskip swallows whole the military arguments for placating the Arabs . . . takes the line that as the Jews are dependent on Britain they must take what they are given . . . Walter hinted that if the Jews do not agree to terms, immigration may be stopped altogether.[15]

This was an accurate enough summary of the MacDonald memorandum.

Perhaps two other points should be mentioned. MacDonald put forward two plans, A and B, to satisfy the most controversial question of all, immigration. In plan A the level of Jewish immigration would be regulated over a ten-year period so that it would not exceed 40 per cent, or, if the Arabs proved obdurate, 35 per cent of the total population. Both these figures were well above the average yearly rate of immigration from 1920 to 1933, though well below those for 1934–5, and would have meant, if the 40 per cent estimate had been kept, a rise of 11 per cent in the Jewish population, again well in keeping with the previous average. At the end of the ten-year period the future of immigration policy would be the subject for discussion between the concerned parties. According to plan B, the details would remain the same except that at the end of the period there could be no more Jewish immigration unless the Arabs agreed. In fact, an Arab veto. MacDonald was under no illusion that eventually "we are almost certain to have to move to proposal B" which, for the Arabs, would set a limit "beyond which the Jewish National Home cannot expand without their consent". He was equally under no illusion that the Jews would find this proposal "quite unacceptable". But, if there was to be deadlock, MacDonald would break it by going "a long way to meet the Arab representatives", though he rejected a total surrender to their maximum demands of a complete and immediate suspension of immigration and the cessation of land sales.

The other point that emerges is MacDonald's intention to satisfy moderate Arab opinion : "Our main aim during the London discussions should be to reach agreement, or expressed or tacit, with the Arab delegations . . . and [hence] to make concessions to them, perhaps considerable concessions." He rationalised this conclusion by explaining that "in the long run it is the wisest policy from the point of view of the Jews themselves".

Nevertheless, there still appeared some room for manœuvre. The Jews would certainly not accept permanent minority status or severe restrictions in land sales. But the constitutional proposal of parity was a Zionist conception; it resurrected the promise given by Malcolm MacDonald's father to Weizmann in July 1931. They could hardly reject it out of hand. No doubt MacDonald counted on it as a fulcrum to lever the required concessions in immigration and land sales. This *quid pro quo* aspect of British policy reached its consummation during the latter stages of the conference.

On 5 February Weizmann welcomed the Jewish delegates to the conference at the first meeting of the Palestine Discussion Conference Committee, known as the Panel.[16] He met them in an atmosphere of uncertainty. Since the beginning of the new year war rumours were everywhere.[17] A foreign official had recently told Weizmann that war was inevitable and "could come from anywhere".[18] Did these *canards* have their effect upon the Zionists? "We all feel that war is so likely in a few weeks that it is hard to take plans seriously".[19] Weizmann spoke to his colleagues plainly. Owing to the imminence of war the loyalty, or at least the neutrality, of the Arab countries was considered essential by the government. There were only "gradations" in government policy, and none were geared to meet Jewish needs. Some spoke of putting the Jews "into cold storage for a few years until things became easier"; others of calling a full stop now and leaving future policy for the future; while others wished to placate the Arabs "by reducing the irritant to its minimum".

Weizmann defined the Jewish objectives as : "large-scale immigration . . . government assistance for the resettlement of refugees . . . development and organisation of the Jewish defence forces in Palestine". Immigration was the crucial question. "Any concession . . . would mean they were consciously giving up so and so many thousands of Jewish lives." None the less if an understanding with the Arabs was feasible he envisaged the possibility of compromise. He asked the delegates not to forget "the historic debt of gratitude" owed by the Jews to Britain. "The cornerstone of their policy throughout had been co-operation with the government. They should like to continue, but limits were set to co-operation."

Two days later the conference was formally opened by Neville Chamberlain at St. James's Palace. At the second meeting Weizmann put the Jewish case.[20] In the main he rephrased his evidence before the Royal Commission. He told his audience what he had said to Sir Miles Lampson : "You cannot stop an organic growth; you cannot stop a plant from growing; you cannot stop the sun from turning round; it is a natural process. Only Joshua succeeded in doing it, and I am afraid I cannot attempt it."

He continued :

> I believe that you have become great because your work and your policy has been inspired by the Book which we have produced in Palestine. This is the secret of why the Balfour declaration came as a natural expression of British conscience in a time of great trial for the British nation. It is written in the stars that you should be the sponsors just as it is written . . . that Palestine will be a Jewish National Home.

His statement was well received. Both MacDonald and Halifax offered congratulations "on a moving and logical speech". Here was the crux. Emotion and logic were no longer of sufficient weight to counteract the lessons of the Arab rebellion.

This was made quite plain when MacDonald presented the Arab case to the Jews.[21] The whole situation was anomalous. As there was no direct contact between the conflicting parties the government took upon itself the role of spokesman for the Arab case. This placed the conference in a peculiar light. It required considerable semantic skill to differentiate between the Arab and the government case. MacDonald was unable to meet this requirement. The

Jews drew the conclusion that, "the colonial secretary . . ., although clothing them in the form of arguments as advanced by the Arabs, conveyed the impression that in reality he was speaking the government's own mind".[22]

MacDonald's exposition was an able one. He revived an old fable concerning the ignorance of British ministers of conditions prevailing in Palestine at the time of the Balfour declaration and the mandate, and entered into a new controversy regarding the precise, or rather imprecise, meaning of the phrase Jewish National Home. He hinted that the principle of economic absorptive capacity was not inherent in the mandate, nor could it be considered as inviolate. But the main burden of his speech was on safeguarding the "natural rights" of the Arabs and not denying them self-governing institutions. He insisted that the government could not impose a solution on the Arabs by force : "He would reject this whole-heartedly on moral and political grounds . . . The Arabs outside Palestine would not sit still." The one method remaining was by consent. He did not particularise how this was to be achieved.

On 15 February, MacDonald, following the lines of his own memorandum of 18 January, specified the government proposals, on immigration in particular, and on land sales and constitutional measures in general.[23] Weizmann replied that these suggestions were "inconceivable" and "untenable". Ben Gurion launched into a long tirade :

> They would not consider a minority status in a foreign state. They could not consider Palestine as a bondage [Galuth] . . . He was a law abiding Jew, but there was something which was higher than the law. He could not recognise a law by which the Mufti would have the right to exclude the Jews from Palestine.

There was no question of the Jews accepting these suggestions as a basis for discussion. But it was a mark of the Jewish position that Weizmann appeared "relieved that the proposals were not worse".[24]

On the same day Wedgwood wrote a memorandum setting out a plan of civil resistance to the government's intentions. In it a tripartite federal solution was assumed.

> To get this firmness is essential. Firmness can only be shown by threat of force. Will only be believed if you show no confidence in the government. There must be no "I shall not be able to get the Jews to accept", but "I shall not accept and I shall do

my best to upset . . .". Remember Mirabeau in the Convention
. . . "You may pass this law, but I swear I will never obey it".[25]

The gist of Wedgwood's advice was not to ask for justice but to
show a display of strength.

Wedgwood had long been of the opinion that only militant
action would force the government's hand. His memorandum was
the sequel to a remarkable letter sent to the Jewish Former Army
Officers Association, Tel Aviv. In it he advised, *inter alia* : "the
occupation of land and refusal to leave except by force of law;
going to prison; refusal to pay taxes; refusal to plead in the courts
or recognise their jurisdiction; attending demonstrations which
have been banned; distributing illegal literature; assisting illegal
immigration; [and] picketing and boycotting the disloyal".[26] Weizmann felt unable to accede to his supporter's bellicose wishes :
"Chaim . . . flung it [the memorandum] aside scornfully, and would
make no use of it, indeed, hardly reading it."[27]

The Jews officially rejected MacDonald's proposals on 17 February.[28] The Arab veto was totally unacceptable; but Weizmann
devoted equal time in criticising the land proposals. The Jews hoped
to evade these restrictions by reviving the suggestion for a development scheme.[29] Weizmann argued that after three years of disturbances poverty was one of the main causes of unrest in Palestine :
"remove that and people are less likely to make trouble". This proposal was studiously ignored throughout the conference.

MacDonald elaborated on his immigration proposals during an
informal conversation with Ben Gurion.[30] He outlined plans A and
B : either an immigration of 40 per cent extended over a period of
ten years with an Arab veto at the end; or, an immigration of not
more than 35 per cent without a veto. There was a brief exchange
over the time factor. Ben Gruion wanted to shorten it to five years.
MacDonald refused : "The longer the period the better satisfied the
Arab states will be and this after all is the most important thing."
Ben Gurion would not agree to any arrangement "which involves
or implies a denial of our fundamental rights", or countenances any
idea "that our return to Palestine is dependent upon Arab consent".
The deadlock persisted.

But Ben Gurion did propose three alternative solutions. First, a
Jewish state within a semitic federation. This, he said, would be the
ideal solution and will one day materialise. Secondly, partition,
more or less on the lines of the Peel recommendations. Both these

ideas were ruled out as not being in the realm of present day practical politics, though MacDonald had touched upon them favourably in his memorandum as presenting solutions in the long run. And, thirdly, a temporary arrangement, fixing in advance the rate of immigration for the coming five years with no veto at the end.

The Jews were clearly prepared for concessions.[31] Possibly Ben Gurion saw a glimmer of light in the 35 per cent proposal, for his last suggestion was an implicit abandonment of the principle of economic absorptive capacity, hitherto the bedrock of their immigration policy. But they were not prepared to let others bar the door; and that was how the veto appeared to them.

However, even this glimmer faded at the next session.[32] MacDonald refined his immigration proposals to one of 35-40 per cent over a period of ten years with a veto. Regarding land he suggested a tripartite division consisting of prohibited, restricted, and unrestricted zones. The land and immigration proposals had not yet been put to the Arabs, but they had already rejected constitutional parity. These proposals were again rejected by the Jews as forming "no basis for discussion".

The general impression of these parleys is one of an unbridgeable gap separating Jewish and government interests. This was reflected by sections of the Jewish delegation being in favour of breaking off the talks.[33] The question resolved itself into one of tactics. Shertok favoured informing the government that there was no basis for further discussion and leaving the next move to them, thereby avoiding a spectacular walk-out.[34] After the meeting of the 20th no further date was arranged to continue the talks. Mrs. Dugdale commented : "the conference does seem to be dying on our side".[35] But Weizmann, for the moment, was unwilling to break, and his view appeared decisive.

The pro-Zionist lobby in the United States was considered an important asset on the Jewish side. If properly organised, American public opinion sympathetic to the Zionists was both considerable and influential. Without question the United States government could not ignore a mass demonstration of public feeling favourable to the Zionists. During the autumn of 1938, "the agitation . . . when we were rumoured to be contemplating a complete stoppage of Jewish immigration was the most sustained and embarrassing agitation that the President has had to face since his first few months of office".[36] Nevertheless, it is apparent that the Jews consistently overrated the effects of a pro-Zionist agitation upon the actions of the

American government; or rather they underrated the spoiling action taken by the government to contain that agitation.

The government was obviously as wary of American opinion as the Zionists were aware of its potentialities, and had long come to the conclusion that "If it comes to war, the sympathy and support of the United States will be more important in the long run than any support that the Arab countries will give us."[37] To this extent they were obliged to insure their Palestine policy with the Americans. This they did, apparently with a marked degree of success. On 1 March Chamberlain told his cabinet "that Roosevelt would not interfere against anything H.M.G. chose to do".[38] Some days later Elliot informed Mrs. Dugdale that Roosevelt had sent another message intimating that he would stand by the government although "he expected some anti-British demonstrations if this policy goes through".[39]

Whether Roosevelt's message reflected his own opinion or that of the state department is not quite clear. When the government finally published its statement of policy in May, Roosevelt's instinctive reaction differed considerably from that of his officials. But at this stage of the negotiations, before the details of any policy had been strictly defined and agreed upon, such differences were without much meaning. In any event the messages from the United States were most encouraging, and the government could continue with the conference without fear of being pulled back from Washington.

On 23 and 24 February, at informal gatherings between the Jews and representatives of the Arab states, MacDonald put forward more detailed constitutional proposals involving the termination of the mandate and the establishment of an independent Palestine state in treaty relations with Great Britain at some future date. For the interim period an executive council with the participation of three Arabs and two Jews, and an advisory council based on proportional representation would be set up. Parity had been ruled out. The government, MacDonald disclosed, was also thinking in terms of an agreed five-year immigration plan. To prepare the ground for this overall settlement a round table conference would be convened in the autumn.[40] These proposals were a considerable retreat from MacDonald's original ideas,[41] and no doubt were a result of the Arabs', particularly the Palestinians', intransigence and MacDonald's declared readiness to go a long way towards meeting their demands. At any rate, both the general trend and the details of the government's policy were now clear. The Arab delegations, though not the Palestinians, accepted the general tenor of MacDonald's suggestions; the Jews rejected them categorically : "anything symbolising or leading up to permanent minority status for Jews in Palestine would not be accepted".[42]

The weekend of 24–26 February was, in many respects, the watershed of the conference. Weizmann recalled that

> On Saturday . . . I received a letter from the colonial office, addressed to me obviously by a clerical error—it was apparently meant only for members of the Arab delegation. There, in clear terms, was the outline of what was afterwards to be the white paper, submitted for Arab approval; an Arab state of Palestine in five years; a limited Jewish immigration during these five years, and none thereafter without Arab consent . . . to see the actual terms, in black and white, already prepared and communicated to the Arabs while "negotiations" were proceeding was utterly baffling.[43]

This account is somewhat tendentious and misleading.

On the afternoon of Saturday, 25 February, Weizmann, Ben Gurion and Shertok met MacDonald at the latter's invitation.[44] The main purpose of the meeting was to survey in greater detail the constitutional proposals made two days ago. No great headway was made. Weizmann said that the "underlying principles of the mandate and the Balfour declaration must be embodied in any new constitutional changes". MacDonald thought the Jews were taking a "lop-sided view", and envisaged the constitutional settlement as being spread over ten years.

Weizmann pressed him on immigration. And here, for the first time, MacDonald spoke in actual figures and not percentages. The figures he had in mind were 10,000 per annum for the next five years, plus 10,000 refugee children in the first year. However much the Jews expected to make concessions the stark reality of these figures must have come as a violent shock. Certainly it appears to have been the crucial factor in their decision to break the conference. The following Sunday, Mrs. Dugdale recorded : "Went to Zionist Organisation before lunch . . . heard Jews had decided to break, after hearing from Malcolm . . . yesterday what H.M.G.'s terms were . . . It is a complete sellout."[45] The rest of the day was spent in preparing a draft statement to be read by Weizmann on Monday, 27 February.

On the same Sunday the government despatched to the Jewish Agency minutes of the meeting of 24 February.[46] Accompanying the minutes was a second document (the letter referred to by Weizmann in his account) which, according to Lord Reading, "embodied precise proposals", but "omitted references to the continued existence of the National Home after the independent state had come into being".[47] The second document was a summary of the constitutional proposals that had been mooted throughout the conference, particularly at the meeting of the 24th. In this sense they could have come as no surprise to Weizmann or the Jewish Agency executive.

But two new factors had emerged. First, the exact nature of the immigration proposals. And secondly, the document had also been sent to the Arab delegation and a garbled version had subsequently appeared in the Palestine press which resulted in victory demonstrations amongst the local Arab population.[48] This, it was all too readily assumed, in order to force the government's hand.

At MacDonald's instance an immediate meeting was arranged to repair the deteriorating situation.[49] They convened on the evening of Sunday, 26 February, at Weizmann's home. MacDonald explained :

> He himself had gone through those minutes [of the 24th], made some alterations and said to the official concerned : "When you send this out, make it clear in a covering letter that this is only a summary of what has taken place at that particular meeting." But somebody had misunderstood the instructions and taken them to mean that the minutes of the meeting should be accompanied by a summary of the proposals.[50]

He continued that as far as he knew the only minutes intended for circulation were those of the meeting of the 24th. What had happened was an error; in any case the second document did not represent "any definite proposals".

Lord Reading thereupon offered two suggestions. That the government publish a statement repudiating the reports in the Arab press. And, that it address a letter to the Jewish delegation saying that the proposals were not definitive, that the whole question still remained flexible, and that fundamental principles, such as the continued existence of the National Home, would be incorporated in the new constitution. MacDonald accepted the first suggestion; but to the second "neither assented nor dissented".[51]

While the Panel was still debating these events, MacDonald telephoned Weizmann requesting him not to break off contact with the government. "Chaim answered with reserve",[52] but, after some differences of opinion, the Panel decided on submitting a prepared statement to the government to the effect that "the suggestions put forward by H.M.G. on 24 February form no basis for further discussion", and that they required a letter from the government confirming that the situation still remained fluid.[53]

It seems evident that the Jewish Agency executive had decided on breaking the conference after the meeting with MacDonald on 25 February. But tactically they could not simply stage a walk-out. They had to satisfy the non-Zionist members of the Panel that all conceivable solutions had been tried and found wanting. And, if possible, to place the onus of responsibility on breaking the conference upon the government. In this sense a clerk's error in the colonial office came as a blessing in disguise, and one which the Zionists exploited to good effect.

An important sequel of these developments was that MacDonald became totally *persona non grata* with the Zionists. As was perhaps inevitable his relations with the Zionists began to languish upon his assumption of office as colonial secretary. But their fruitful period of collaboration was difficult to cast off. Hence, even at the last Panel meeting an opinion had been voiced that MacDonald had committed a "grave blunder", but that his actions could not yet be regarded as "machiavellian".[54] Others, possibly the majority, took a stronger view. "Walter and I had a rather heated talk . . . I said that if H.M.G. brought tomorrow not only new proposals, but a new man to talk about them, the Jews might go on. MacDonald had earned nothing but their contempt, disgust and hatred . . . they would not believe his word."[55]

This lamentable state of personal relationships engendered an endemic suspicion of government policy which placed normal diplomatic intercourse at a high premium. This is not to say that the Zionists had no ground for suspicion. They were only too aware of the lessons to be drawn from the Munich settlement.[56] And this, coupled with the tragic position in which European Jewry found itself during this period, created a highly charged, emotional atmosphere not conducive to patient bargaining or giving the benefit of the doubt. It was an unfortunate, but inevitable consequence of the international situation.

Informal discussions dragged on until early March.[57] There was little to show for them. Throughout, the Zionists were on the defensive. Although MacDonald floated the idea of a federal solution and Weizmann was prepared to "consider cantonisation, with a view to a federal state" (a concession some of his chief advisers thought "dangerous"[58]), the main argument turned on safeguards for the *Yishuv* in an independent Palestine. MacDonald made it clear that the transitional period would not be terminated unless "genuine Arab-Jewish co-operation" was attained and the necessary safeguards agreed upon. But, he added, there was "little prospect of agreement at present".[59] In a sense this argument was self-defeating, for if "genuine Arab-Jewish co-operation" was attained there would be little need for the necessary safeguards; but if not, no safeguards could be sufficient.

One other important factor emerged. The idea of a round table conference had been dropped. The Jews were never keen on this prospect; now, apparently, the Arabs had vetoed the suggestion. This was of some consequence. It meant that the government could no longer fall back on delaying tactics, on gentle hints regarding the nature of the settlement. Now it would have to itemise the restrictions it intended.

It was Elliot who tersely summarised the government's aim : "they work towards terminating the mandate . . . they will restrict land and immigration . . . they will not give the Arabs an independent state nor in any way relax control".[60] In other words, British policy was bent on promising a Palestinian state but imposing such conditions as to make its eventual establishment an object for the indefinite future.

Weizmann illustrated the Jewish quandary : "The framework might be acceptable, but not the contents. If they could not get an appreciable number of Jews into Palestine or acquire land there, then the discussion would become useless."[61] It was generally felt that the government was playing for time. The question remained how could the Jews retire gracefully from the conference? A resolution was passed dissolving the Panel and placing full authority in the hands of the Jewish Agency executive. It was also decided to send a letter to the government pointing out that no proposals had yet been received which were essentially different from those contained in the minutes of the meeting of 24 February. The letter would set out the two possibilities open for discussion : continuation of the mandate, or an independent state with the consent of both parties.[62] The executive would then make a decision with regard to dissolution contingent upon the government's reply.[63]

On the morning of 8 March the cabinet decided that restricted immigration, from 75,000–100,000, would continue for another five years; henceforth it would be subject to an Arab veto. As a *quid pro quo* the establishment of a Palestinian state was made dependent upon Jewish consent. Thus, it was hoped, agreement would be prized by giving both sides the power to deny to each other that which they most desired. The one dissenting voice was Elliot's, who wished to qualify the veto on immigration by a system of cantonisation with each side having a clear majority in its own area thereby limiting Jewish immigration into its own canton at the end of the five-year period. MacDonald agreed that the proposed statement of policy might include some indication of cantonisation (as indeed it did), but added : "the plain fact was that the Jews had made no attempt to co-operate with the Arabs in the last twenty years; but now they would have to do so".[64]

On 10 March Weizmann flew to Paris to seek an interview with W. Bullitt, the American ambassador in Paris. He pleaded for a period of respite : "Weizmann . . . asked for nothing but delay and stated that Chamberlain had said to him recently that within 6 months the world situation might have changed to such an extent that the whole problem could be reconsidered.[65] This appeal had some effect. But the Americans waited until the conference officially wound up before they acted.

Two more informal discussions were held.[66] Both sides did not budge one iota from their established positions. Ben Gurion argued that there could be no independent state in which the Jews "are a minority or hold minority status. They could not trust paper safeguards." While MacDonald would not relinquish the Arab veto on immigration : "[it was] one of the conditions which might lead to peace and co-operation".[67] And although MacDonald persisted that the constitutional suggestions "were . . . open for discussion", the veto on immigration and its consequences blocked any reasonable compromise. At the conclusion of the last meeting MacDonald announced that he would present the government's definitive proposals on 15 March.

Given the existing circumstances there was little the Gentile Zionists could do during the actual course of negotiations to sway the government from their present policy. However, even before the conference began, Weizmann had requested Smuts to come to Europe where he felt his "presence would be invaluable".[68] Smuts would not commit himself and indeed was not in Europe during the conference, but Weizmann kept him fully informed of developments.[69] Smuts was, as usual, full of sympathy and kind words. But apart from lecturing the government on their obligations under the mandate his influence was nominal. Moral strictures were not likely to outweigh the exigencies of administrative necessity.

Nor was the parliamentary pro-Palestine committee more effective. Headed by Amery, a delegation was received by the prime minister on 13 March, and presented him with a memorandum setting out British declarations of policy concerning the future of Palestine. They asked that these be adhered to in the final settlement. Chamberlain was non-committal, though he left the deputation with the impression that the government remained undecided in its final attitude.[70]

Weizmann vented his anger upon MacDonald. He accused the minister of treachery: "he had betrayed them . . . and created theories to justify the betrayal . . . Everything had been prejudged . . . three months ago . . . [he] never mentioned that an independent state was in his mind . . . [his] strategic arguments were so much bunk."[71] Weizmann reproached him for expressing anti-Jewish remarks,[72] and insisted on seeing the prime minister alone, a reflection of MacDonald's personal standing with the Zionists. He refused to co-operate further with MacDonald, or to attend the final conference on 15 March.[73]

When he met Chamberlain he found the prime minister in a very depressed mood. Chamberlain did not blame Weizmann for his mood of resentment. He invoked the pro-Zionist traditions of the Chamberlain family and stressed that he would have liked to have handed Palestine over to the Jews. (He had told his cabinet that he would have liked to have done better for the Jews who might be considered to have been roughly treated after great expectations of previous years.[74] He would help in every way, "but his advisers had made out an unanswerable case".[75]

The dying stages of the St. James's conference were accompanied by the collapse of the Munich settlement. It can be assumed with reasonable certainty that the events in Prague confirmed the government in its resolve to shed all secondary obligations. And as the international situation deteriorated with the German occupation of Memel, the Italian invasion of Albania, and the Polish crisis, the government, even had it wanted to, found itself unable to abandon its chosen path.

The final session of the conference was held on 15 March.[76] Neither Weizmann nor Ben Gurion was present. MacDonald informed the Jews of the government's proposals; the Jews neither asked questions nor provoked any discussion. The proposals were as anticipated. Although, as Shertok explained, "the definitive form contained certain new negative points".[77] The scheme provided for the establishment of a Palestinian state in treaty relations with Great Britain after a transitionary period of ten years, with the possibility of a federal solution. The constitution would be worked out by a National Assembly and would have to include safeguards for the National Home and British interests. Eventual independence would depend upon the degree of co-operation reached between the two communities. In any event the government would not relinquish its authority until it was satisfied on this score.

On immigration a total of 75,000 would be allowed within the next five years at a rate of 10,000 per annum and 25,000 refugees. But the degree of immigration would depend on the absorptive capacity of the country, and it would be up to the Jews to make out a convincing case. After the said period there would be no further immigration without Arab consent. Land sales were to include prohibited, regulated, and free land sales zones.

The additional negative points that Shertok mentioned included the drawing up of the constitution by a National Assembly, where an Arab majority was taken for granted. Further, that the Arabs and the government would have to be consulted and convinced of the Zionist case for immigration : hence even the 10,000 per annum was not guaranteed. And lastly the negative equality nature of the British proposals : to deny each side that which it most covets and thereby to put pressure on both sides to reach a compromise was condemned as illusionary : "It . . . could satisfy neither party and would fail to create good will."[78]

MacDonald knew the Jews would be unable to accept these proposals.[79] However, they were final, and although he would be prepared to discuss details if agreement were possible, the main principles remained inviolate.

The conference had taken an unprecedented time in dying. The MacDonald proposals brought the death agonies to a rapid conclusion.

> The Jewish Delegation, having carefully considered the proposals communicated to them by His Majesty's Government on March 15, 1939, regret that they are unable to accept them as a basis for agreement, and decide, accordingly, to dissolve.

Weizmann terminated the proceedings :

> All that was happening was an episode, one more turn in the ups and downs that their people had known. They had had wonderful hopes and these had been partly shattered. They would build them afresh. They had waited for thousands of years, and they would plod along another five years.[80]

On 17 March Weizmann informed MacDonald of their decision.[81] MacDonald acknowledged his letter "with regret".[82]

The Zionists now saw it as their duty to press for a delay in any official statement. They contrived to build up pressure from the United States and parliament to that effect. On 19 March, Sumner Welles wrote to Kennedy : "Please take an early occasion informally to offer the suggestion in the right quarter that in view of the international crisis [the Germans had occupied Prague on 15 March] . . . a short delay in the timing of publication might be of advantage."[83] Kennedy replied : "I saw MacDonald and Halifax about the Palestine matter. It will be held up in accordance with your suggestion and you will be notified before they put anything into effect."[84]

In London, Cazalet privately urged on Halifax delay.[85] Elliot believed the cabinet might be impressed if they were aware that the Jews and Arabs were engaged in serious negotiations. The Zionists readily gave this assurance.[86] Weizmann wrote to Chamberlain pleading for a stay of grace :

> In times so deeply disturbed, could we not avoid adding to the turmoil. For such would be the result of putting forward a policy which . . . satisfies no one. If the announcement of the decision is postponed, I do not mean to leave the time unused. Every effort [will be] made . . . and contact used to explore the possibilities of Jewish-Arab agreement or *rapprochement* . . . cannot promise any success . . . [but] suggest that lapse of time may open possibilities in this direction . . .[87]

It is curious that Elliot, the Zionists' main source of government policy, did not believe there would be any postponement. And this was true even after the Americans had received their assurance from Halifax and MacDonald.[88] It may well be that by this time Elliot was regarded by his colleagues as being too heavily tainted with Zionism to be trusted with inside information. At a later date Elliot himself reached this conclusion. "He [Elliot] thinks his own

o

value to us is now at an end. He will not be consulted any more and will not form part of the inner ring which settles things."[89]

MacDonald was well aware of Elliot's connections. This would tend to increase his reluctance to confide in Elliot information of this kind. At any rate, two days after Kennedy received satisfaction Elliot was still ignorant of the decision to postpone the statement. Possibly, MacDonald was deliberately excluding Elliot from information in order to avoid leakages and hence keep the pressure on the Zionists to reach agreement with the government. As Elliot was still a member of the cabinet committee on Palestine it is hardly conceivable that he lacked the opportunity to discuss Palestine matters with MacDonald, or *vice versa*.

A meeting of some twenty-four M.P.s who supported the government, but were sympathetic to the National Home, was held on 20 March.[90] Their inclination was to demand that the whips be removed in the forthcoming debate to allow for a free vote. Cazalet hinted that there would be a number of members who would go into the opposition lobby. He later expanded on this theme :

> I have already told the Chief Whip that I, for one, would vote against the government if their proposals are anything like as reported in the press. I think about twenty other M.P.'s would probably do the same and may be another twenty abstain.[91]

The government whips were, apparently, not enamoured with this idea and advised postponement. Mrs. Dugdale was able to note : ". . . the House of Commons work has been done well".[92] Two days earlier MacDonald had postponed consideration of the draft white paper;[93] it was not to be published until 17 May.

The reasons for this delay, however, were only partially a result of Zionist agitation. Paradoxically, for a few brief weeks the Zionists rode on the crest of international events. In the United States, for example, State Department officials were pressing for postponement because American-Jewish demonstrations might effect the discussion on the amendment of the Neutrality Laws,[94] while throughout March, April, and early May, the British cabinet was preoccupied digesting the results of Hitler's and Mussolini's latest moves, and anticipating their next ones.[95]

There was another important factor. The government throughout this whole period was engaged in discussions with the Arab states seeking to extract from them a declaration of general approval of the government's policy.[96] It was believed that this would soften up Palestinian opposition, and quite obviously would have been a major coup for the government had it succeeded. But it took time and patience. Eventually, the talks collapsed owing to the extremity of the Arabs' demands, particularly on constitutional questions.[97] But until that happened some six weeks had elapsed.

NOTES

1 D.D., 1 Dec. 1938.
2 D.D., 1 and 2 Dec. 1938.
3 D.D., 11 Dec. 1938.
4 D.D., 12 Dec. 1938.
5 See Cabinet minutes, CAB.23/96.
6 Cabinet minutes for 21 Dec. 1938, *ibid*.
7 Notes of an interview between MacDonald, Weizmann, and Namier, 14 Dec. 1938, W.A.
8 On 7 Dec. MacDonald informed the House that invitations had been sent to and accepted by Egypt, Iraq, Saudi Arabia, and TransJordan. An invitation had also been sent to the Yemen, P.D., Commons, vol. 342, c. 1149–50.
9 D.D., 16 Dec. 1938.
10 Bauer, p. 22.
11 D.D., 10 Jan. 1939.
12 See Cabinet minutes, CAB.23/97.
13 See, CAB.24/282, C.P.7(39). A report of the chiefs of staff subcommittee, 16 Jan. 1939.
14 See CAB.24/282, C.P.4(39). The cabinet accepted his recommendations as set out in the paper on 1 Feb. 1939, see CAB.23/97.
15 D.D., 27 Jan. 1939.
16 Minutes of the Panel, 5 Feb. 1939, W.A. The Panel, which included representatives of the Jewish Agency, *Agudath Yisrael* (the religious group), and Anglo-Jewry (known as "the Lords"), acted purely in an advisory capacity. The main political decisions were taken by the Jewish Agency executive which met more frequently than the more unwieldy Panel. However, they reported in full to the Panel and co-opted members for the actual negotiations from time to time.
17 See, for example, Johnson (U.S. chargé in the U.K.) to Hull, *F.R.U.S.*, 1939, i, pp. 2–6.
18 From a report given at a meeting of the Zionist executive, 18 Jan. 1939, W.A.
19 D.D., 27 Jan. 1939.
20 Minutes of the second session, 8 Feb. 1939. Copies of the official government minutes of the conference may be found in C.Z.A., S25/7632, 7633, where I inspected them.
21 Official minutes of the third session, 10 Feb. 1939.

22 Minutes of the Panel meeting of 12 Feb. 1939, W.A. Weizmann, Ben Gurion, Shertok and Brodetsky all expressed this sentiment.
23 Official minutes of the sixth meeting, 15 Feb. 1939; also, Notes on the meeting of 15 Feb. 1939, W.A.
24 D.D., 15 Feb. 1939.
25 Wedgwood's memorandum for Weizmann, 15 Feb. 1939, W.A.
26 Wedgwood to the Association, 30 May 1938, C.Z.A., J1/200. For further examples of Wedgwood's belligerent mood, see, P.D., Commons, vol. 337, c. 142–3, 14 June 1938; vol. 347, c. 1992–2001, 22 May 1939; also his letter to the *Manchester Guardian*, 21 March 1939.
27 A note by Rabbi Stephen Wise, 16 Feb. 1939, W.A.
28 Official minutes of the seventh session, 17 Feb. 1939.
29 Raised in a meeting with Chamberlain and MacDonald, 16 Feb. 1939, W.A.
30 Notes of the meeting, 18 Feb. 1939, W.A.
31 MacDonald told the cabinet that the 'Jews had showed willingness to make considerable concessions, e.g. over immigration, see cabinet minutes for 22 Feb. 1939, CAB.23/97. Rabbi Wise and Mr. R. Szold told Kennedy that they were 'prepared to make concessions both as regards land purchases and immigration'. Kennedy to Hull, 22 Feb. 1939, *F.R.U.S.*, 1939, iv, p. 715.
32 Official minutes of the eighth session, 20 Feb. 1939.
33 D.D., 19 Feb. 1939.
34 D.D., 20 Feb. 1939.
35 D.D., 21 Feb. 1939.
36 Remarks made by Kennedy to MacDonald, CAB.24/282, C.P.4(39).
37 *Ibid.*
38 D.D., 4 March 1939.
39 D.D., 8 March 1939.
40 See cabinet minutes for 2 March 1939, CAB.23/97; and CAB.24/284, C.P.56(39); also minutes of the Panel, 24 Feb. 1939, W.A.
41 See below, pp. 181–2.
42 Minutes of the Panel, 24 Feb. 1939, W.A.
43 Weizmann, p. 499.
44 Minutes of an interview between Weizmann, Ben Gurion, and MacDonald, 25 Feb. 1939, W.A.
45 D.D., 26 Feb. 1939.
46 Minutes of the Panel, 27 Feb. 1939, W.A. The general sequence of events for that weekend is constructed from these minutes.
47 *Ibid.*
48 See, *Manchester Guardian*, 27 Feb. 1939; and cabinet conclusions for 2 March 1939, CAB.23/97.
49 Minutes of the Panel, 27 Feb. 1939, *op. cit.*
50 *Ibid.*
51 *Ibid.*
52 D.D., 27 Feb. 1939.
53 Minutes of the Panel, 27 Feb. 1939, *op. cit.*
54 This view was expressed by Simon Marks.
55 D.D., 27 Feb. 1939.
56 See, for example, D.D., 13 Jan. 1939; and, Minutes of the Panel, 7 March 1939, W.A.

57 These may be followed in: official minutes of 9th session, 27 Feb. 1939; of an informal meeting on 28 Feb. 1939, W.A.; of the Panel, 2 and 7 March 1939, W.A.; of 2nd and 3rd informal meetings, 3 and 6 March 1939, C.Z.A., S25/7635; and D.D. for this period.

58 D.D., 6 March 1939.

59 Minutes of 3rd informal meeting, 6 March 1939.

60 D.D., 4 March 1939.

61 Minutes of the Panel, 7 March 1939, W.A.

62 See Weizmann to M. MacDonald, 8 March 1939, W.A.

63 Minutes of the Panel, 7 March 1939, *op. cit.* Although there was a decision to dissolve the Panel, and in fact members of the Palestine and American delegation left for home, a rump Panel continued in session and had one more official meeting on 16 March.

64 See cabinet minutes for 8 March 1939, CAB.23/97; also D.D., 8 March 1939.

65 Bullitt to Hull, 10 March 1939, *F.R.U.S.*, 1939, iv, p. 731.

66 Minutes of the fourth and fifth informal meetings, 11 and 12 March 1939, C.Z.A., S25/7635.

67 *Ibid.*

68 Minutes of a telephone conversation between Smuts and Weizmann, 14 Oct. 1938, W.A.

69 Smuts telephoned Weizmann on 7 March 1939, W.D., W.A. The following day Weizmann cabled him a long despatch reporting on the dismal state the conference had reached, Weizmann to Smuts, tel. 8 March 1939, W.A.

70 D.D., 13 March 1939. Also, *The Times* and *Manchester Guardian*, 14 March 1939; and, *The Zionist Review*, 16 March 1939. The deputation consisted of: Amery, V. Cazalet, Wedgwood, T. Williams and R. D. Denman.

71 D.D., 14 March 1939; see also, Weizmann's report to a meeting of the Jewish Agency executive, 15 March 1939, W.A. He had met MacDonald on 14 March.

72 MacDonald was reported as having told the Arabs "that it was in the nature of the Jews to ask for too much", D.D., 10 March 1939.

73 Weizmann's report to the Jewish Agency executive, 15 March 1939, *op. cit.*

74 See cabinet minutes for 8 March 1939, CAB.23/97.

75 Weizmann's report to a meeting of Jewish Agency executive, 15 March 1939, *op. cit.*

76 Official minutes of the final session, 15 March 1939, C.Z.A., S25/7633; and, Minutes of the Panel, 16 March 1939, W.A.

77 Minutes of the Panel, 16 March 1939, W.A.

78 *Ibid.*

79 Official minutes of the final session, 15 March 1939, C.Z.A., S25/7633; also, Minutes of the Panel, 16 March 1939, W.A.

80 Minutes of the Panel, 16 March 1939, W.A.

81 Weizmann to MacDonald, 17 March 1939, W.A.

82 MacDonald to Weizmann, 17 March 1939, W.A.

83 Welles to Kennedy, 19 March 1939, *F.R.U.S.*, 1939, iv, p. 737.

84 Kennedy to Hull, 20 March 1939, *ibid.*, pp. 737–8.

85 D.D., 18 March 1939.

86 D.D., 19 March 1939. Weizmann did, in fact, continue his informal contacts

with the Arabs. Immediately after the termination of the conference he arrived in Cairo and met, through the auspices of Aly Maher, a number of leading Egyptians, including the premier, Muhammad Mahmud, Weizmann, p. 502; and *Manchester Guardian*, 12 April 1939.

87 Weizmann to Chamberlain, 24 March 1939, W.A.
88 D.D., 20 and 22 March 1939.
89 Mrs. Dugdale to Shertok, 5 June 1939, C.Z.A., S25/969.
90 Cazalet to Capt. H. D. Margesson (government chief whip), 21 March 1939, C.Z.A., Z4/17309.
91 Cazalet to Lt.-Col. Moore-Brabazon, 31 March 1939, W.A.
92 D.D., 24 March 1939.
93 See cabinet minutes for 22 March 1939, CAB.23/98.
94 See cabinet minutes for 22 March 1939, CAB.23/98.
95 See cabinet minutes for this period, CAB.23/98 and 99.
96 *Ibid.*
97 See cabinet minutes for 3 and 10 May 1939, CAB.23/99.

9

The May White Paper

When the Zionists learned of the government's decision to postpone the statement they set themselves two main objectives : to delay the statement for as long a period as possible; and to mobilise opinion against government policy.

They were engaged until the beginning of May in the most feverish activity designed to bring about the realisation of these objectives.[1] Possibly the most powerful attempt to revise the policy came from Elliot.[2] He argued that "our recent proposed solutions . . . embody concessions made after a terrorist campaign aimed not only at the Jews but at British officials" and "will tend to be taken in present circumstances as a concession not from strength but from weakness". Such a concession could only have adverse effects in Palestine "when we are taking up in general a position of resistance to aggression, and aggression conducted for the most part precisely by this technique". Together with this, the destruction of Albania by Italy, and "the new close grouping of Great Britain and Turkey" present a situation "very different from that in which we previously considered this problem". He also touched upon the Jewish position and "of the immense damage to our position at home and abroad which would result if Great Britain found herself involved in hostilities great or small, against the Jews at this time". He therefore suggested that "it is not possible . . . to proceed further with the consideration of far-reaching constitutional changes . . . and that we should meanwhile work in practice towards a federal solution".[3]

Elliot's memorandum came before the cabinet on 1 May.[4] It found no echo of support in the discussion.[5] He fought a lone battle, and the cabinet decided that no change could be made in the policy.

After the failure of Elliot's intervention, the situation appeared so desperate that Weizmann decided to return to England to attempt one, final appeal.[6] Sinclair wrote to him : "The outlook is one of almost unrelieved gloom. There is not even the ray of light

from the United States which has comforted us in recent crises."[7]
He urged Weizmann's return : "Your authority on the Jewish problem with public opinion in this country is incomparable. Those who
are unfriendly will listen to you as to nobody else; while those who
are friendly can be stirred to action by you as by nobody else." On
the evening of 10 May Weizmann arrived at Croydon airport.[8]

The following evening he saw the prime minister and MacDonald
at the House of Commons.[9] Weizmann described the state of affairs
in Palestine.

> In the past twenty years a Jewish nation had grown up in that
> country which represented a distinctive civilisation. This the
> government was now out to suppress. There was more moral and
> intellectual strength to the square milometer in the Jewish part of
> Palestine than in any other country in the world. What the
> Arabs were after was their very blood. They wanted their lives,
> their houses, their gardens—and they would set about getting
> them as soon as they were given the chance. They had been
> promised by Hitler the £90 million which the Jews had invested
> in Palestine. The tragedy of it would be that the law would be
> on their side, and British bayonets would be there to help them
> achieve their purpose.

Chamberlain was "considerably startled" by this outburst and
inquired whether Weizmann was not overstating his case. Weizmann stood his ground, adding "that his mother was already preparing his *trousseau* for the Seychelles".

Weizmann continued that the forthcoming white paper would
kill any chance of Arab-Jewish collaboration. He brushed aside the
strategic arguments calling for appeasement of the Mufti, invoking
the opinion of General Haining who "thought very little of the
military value of the Arab states". Only when the political manipu-
lations of the cabal at Cairo were mentioned did Chamberlain react.
He sharply reprimanded Weizmann : "the policy they had decided
upon was not the policy of Sir Miles Lampson, it was their own".
For the most part Chamberlain remained impassive. "He expressed
his deep regret and sympathy with the Jews, but said he could not
see his way to change the decision which had been reached."

MacDonald had contributed very little to this conversation. As it
terminated he asked Weizmann whether they were still on speaking
terms, and suggested they meet for dinner. Weizmann replied that
he had not come to London to indulge in dinner parties. Mac-

Donald insisted; and invited Weizmann to his country house, Hyde Hall, in Essex, for tea that Saturday. Weizmann, feeling embarrassed at MacDonald's persistent overtures in the presence of the prime minister, finally acquiesced.[10]

Whatever remained of their personal relationship was surely destroyed as a result of this tea-party. It left Weizmann "shattered".[11] He related that "it was the worst afternoon of his life, that he had never spoken so rudely and so straight to any man and that it left a bitter taste in his mouth . . . he must have left MacDonald a bitter enemy for life, but . . . as it turned out he was always that".[12]

> Mr. MacDonald opened by saying that the Arabs were very much disgruntled. So were the Egyptians. Dr. Weizmann said that it was small wonder . . ., seeing that they had only got 90% of what they wanted . . . MacDonald suggested that even 50% would be an over-estimate . . . The Egyptians felt distinctly let down . . . Sir Miles was furious.

There was then an uneasy pause. Weizmann broke it, saying that he had nothing to tell MacDonald except that "every thing he had done, and the way in which he had done it, had aroused their uncompromising hostility". MacDonald still attempted to justify his policy. He told Weizmann that in fifty years' time the Jews would dominate the whole Middle East, but only after Palestine had been put on a proper basis.

> Mr. MacDonald said that the Jews had made many mistakes . . . Dr. Weizmann replied : "Oh, yes, certainly we have made mistakes; our chief mistake is that we exist at all." Mr. MacDonald said that they had instilled fear into the Arabs. Dr. Weizmann said that Hitler was saying precisely the same thing; he was teaching German children to fear the Jews.
>
> The conversation reached its crisis when Dr. Weizmann in analysing the government's new policy, said that at least in Hitler one found the virtue of an absolutely frank brutality, whereas Mr. MacDonald was covering up his betrayal of the Jews under a semblance of legality. He added that Mr. MacDonald was handing over the Jews to their assassin. Mr. MacDonald showed great indignation and said it was no use to talk to him like that. He said he knew the Jews had been calling him a hypocrite and a coward. Dr. Weizmann replied : "I have never called you a coward."

Weizmann swept on. He challenged the government to bring the matter to the Hague Court. He pitied the prime minister, "the innocent victim of specious advisers". He claimed the Jewish Agency was being spied upon, "their letters . . . opened and their telephone tapped".

It was a savage attack. Nor, judging from this report, did MacDonald make a spirited defence of his policy. He remarked that "the Arabs did have a moral case", and that eventually "they would . . . have to come before the bar of British public opinion". But Weizmann, apart from his unshakable conviction in the righteousness of his cause, was obviously enmeshed in a wave of passionate, emotional indignation. Such a combination was sufficient to sweep away any opposition.

The interview was symptomatic of another development. This was not a discussion between two diplomats, but rather a long, one-sided harangue from Weizmann. There was no element of give and take; no indication of compromise. Indeed it is difficult to comprehend MacDonald's motive in inviting Weizmann at all.[13] Above all else the meeting personified the absolute collapse in relations between the government and the Jewish Agency.

The centre of activity now moved perceptibly towards the imminent parliamentary debates. The opposition had requested a two-day debate. The Zionists were determined to sustain the pressure throughout the debate : "If we can keep it up all that time, we may wear Malcolm down. The great thing is to break his nerve before and during."[14] Mrs. Dugdale in particular was more than usually active in organising the mechanics of the debate.[15] Both Amery and Tom Williams were opposed to referring the matter to a select committee of the House where, Amery believed, "the balance . . . would be unfavourable".[16] Mrs. Dugdale summed up their parliamentary tactics.

> MacDonald would not have many efficient or well informed people to help him. He expected a bad time in the Commons and they should see that he got it. They should ask from the government as many things as they could, because every refusal . . . made its position more difficult.[17]

Mrs. Dugdale also urged Elliot to break with the government : "[I] implored him once again not to carry the sin of MacDonald on his soul . . . let him cut loose now from the consequences of a policy which he hates and knows to be wrong."[18] An ex-cabinet minister would have been a powerful reinforcement to the ranks of the government's opponents, and would have severely embarrassed the government. But Elliot remained a member of the cabinet. However, when the House divided after the debate Elliot and Hore-Belisha conspicuously absented themselves from the division. Many back-benchers were reported to be indignant over this breach of cabinet solidarity because they "had strained their consciences to vote with H.M.G.".[19]

A copy of the white paper was forwarded to the State Department before publication. The American officials saw "the final British decisions . . . as reasonable a compromise between Jewish and Arab aspirations as it is practicable to attempt to effect at this time".[20] The president had some doubts concerning the legality of the white paper.

> I have read with interest and a good deal of dismay the decisions of the British government regarding . . . Palestine . . . I do not believe that the British are wholly correct in saying that the framers of the Palestine Mandate "could not have intended that Palestine should be converted into a Jewish state against the will of the Arab population of the country."
>
> My recollection is . . . it nevertheless did intend to convert Palestine into a Jewish Home which might very possibly become preponderantly Jewish within a comparatively short time . . . that was the impression given to the whole world at the time . . . Frankly, I do not see how the Bristish Government reads into the original Mandate or into the White Paper of 1922 any policy that would limit . . . immigration . . . Before we do anything formal about this please talk with me.[21]

Roosevelt's scepticism was not expressed by any United States pressure on the government to alter or amend their policy. During the St. James's conference the Americans had indicated clearly that they would stand by the British; there is nothing to suggest that they changed their opinion. Indeed in London Kennedy was playing down the consequences of anti-British agitation resulting from the publication of the white paper. American Jewry, he confided to MacDonald, were already unpopular, and although they might be able to work up some agitation it would not last long.[22] There was some concern that the Jews might upset the forthcoming visit of the King and Queen to North America. Once again Kennedy set British

fears at rest, and the visit did in fact pass off without any disturb-
ance.[23]

The white paper[24] appeared on the evening of 17 May. The
government's proposals were identical with those it made on 15
March. *The Times* commented, "They are not a very hopeful background . . . Either the Arabs are to be swamped or the Jewish
National Home is to exist . . . on sufferance." And went on to suggest
concentrating on a "possible federal solution".[25] The *Manchester
Guardian* summed up its feelings in a leader entitled : "A Disastrous
Policy".[26] On the whole the statement of policy did not receive a
good press.

On 19 May Mrs. Dugdale went to the colonial office to see
MacDonald.

> He was alone . . . he smoked, which he seldom does . . . thanked
> me for coming, said : "Say anything you like" . . . I then made the
> point about the consequences of trying to keep out the illegals . . .
> he answered that the whole thing was fraught with difficuties . . .
> I said my next point was more difficult . . . He again said : "Say
> what you like" and spoke of my courage in coming. I mentioned
> then how he had broken the love and loyalty of the Jews . . .
> ruined the fair name of Britain—and I referred to his father,
> and how he had once helped him to repair a far lesser injustice.
> At this point he leaned his arm on the table, hid his face and
> gave out sounds like groans, and said : "I have thought of all
> that". I said . . . without Jewish co-operation he could not enforce
> the law . . . he could still do something . . . by accepting
> the Conservative [dissidents] amendment to take it to the League
> . . . He did not answer.[27]

At the same time the Zionists were trying to swamp the press, in
particular *The Times*, with letters that would appear concurrently
with the debate in parliament.[28] This, it was hoped, would provide
a favourable backcloth to the debates. On 22 May, the day the
debate opened in the Commons, a letter appeared in *The Times*
over the signatures of the surviving members of the Peel commission.[29] The ex-commissioners wrote : "a unitary state coupled with
the cessation of immigration . . . does not eliminate the fear of
domination; it only transfers it from Arab minds to Jewish". They
placed the full weight of their authority behind "the possibility of a
federal solution" which, they considered, provided the best chance
of "a just solution".

The government did not put up a distinguished performance during the debate.[30] MacDonald asked the House to approve the government's new policy. T. Williams moved the amendment: "The command paper is inconsistent with the letter and spirit of the mandate . . . the House is of the opinion that parliament should not be committed pending an examination of the proposals by the Permanent Mandates Commission." The highlight of the first day was Amery's contribution. Logical and persuasive, he warned the government : "I shall most certainly give my vote to the Opposition Amendment tomorrow. I would be ashamed to take any other course."

On the second day Churchill invited Weizmann to lunch : "he was now determined to speak, having been roused to anger by yesterday's debate".[31] Churchill's was the most impressive speech of the entire debate. Perhaps it gained in stature because he preceded Inskip who, winding up for the government, made a contribution full of hesitancy and subject to innumerable interruptions. Weizmann wrote to Churchill : "Your magnificent speech may yet destroy this policy. Words fail to express my thanks."[32]

The House divided on a three-line whip and the government emerged, somewhat shakily, with a majority of only eighty-nine. This could only be classified as a nominal victory for their usual majority was around 250.[33] Neither the debate nor the division could have caused the government much satisfaction.

When the Lords debated the new policy a curious incident occurred which indicated either that the government spokesmen were not adequately briefed, or that there had been an attempt to deceive the Zionists. Lord Dufferin interrupted Samuel's speech to say that there was no Jewish veto on the establishment of the Palestinian state.[34] Of course, MacDonald had spoken in terms of co-operation between the two communities as being a *sine qua non* to the establishment of a state. The word veto had not been used, only implied. But this was certainly how the Zionists interpreted Mac-Donald's *quid pro quo* policy,[35] and they were given no reason to doubt that this was how they were intended to interpret it. The question must be asked : who spoke for the government? Mac-Donald or Dufferin? Or were the channels of communication between the Lords and the Commons so faulty as to allow such a wide discrepancy between two government spokesmen on the same topic? Another explanation comes to mind. Dufferin might have been guilty only of a slip of the tongue. Such accidents occur and are fully comprehensible. But again this argument loses much of its credibility when it is remembered that he deliberately intervened in the debate to make his point. Whatever the explanation the authority of the government was not enhanced, and the incident could only be expected to add to the doubts, already quite widespread, as to the probity of the government's policy.

However much the Zionists railed against the white paper its provisions could not have taken them by surprise. They had been aware of British intentions to abandon partition and reach a *modus vivendi* with the Arabs since July 1938, and in September of the same year MacDonald clearly outlined to them the shape of future British policy.[36] Moreover, it is even possible to detect in the Peel report a precursor of certain aspects of the white paper policy. For example, the palliatives which the commission recommended included zonal restrictions, prohibition of land purchases and "a political high level" of immigration.[37]

For all that, the white paper came as a traumatic shock to the Zionists. The provisions that rankled most deeply were those concerning immigration. This was not just a question of crippling the development of the National Home, however iniquitous and unacceptable this was in Zionist eyes. Of far greater import was the fate of European Jewry. As Ben Gurion said :

> There was no need to talk about protection for the Jews in Palestine, who were well able to look after themselves. The safeguard of the *Yishuv* was its own existence, and if there was anything . . ., it was not the fate of the *Yishuv* but that of the Jews who were not yet in Palestine.[38]

The failure of the Evian conference[39] to provide a solution to the refugee problem accentuated the importance of Palestine as a refuge for Jewish persecution. At the same time harrowing scenes involving illegal immigrant ships, the "death-ships", were being enacted off the shores of Palestine. None of these tales lost their dramatic impact when recounted in Tel Aviv or London. The Zionist leaders were living under an intolerable emotional strain. The Jewish world they had known in Europe was disintegrating and, as it must have appeared to them, their ability to effectively render help was being made conditional upon callous administrative and political dictates. The Zionists in a sense were overpowered by the moral rightness of their case; and, it is true to add, many Gentiles shared that indignation. Hence, although their political acumen recognised the necessity for some compromise,[40] their emotional entanglement in the tragedy in Europe allowed no great deviation from their allotted path.

The Zionists hoped that the present crisis was only a transient phase in their relations with the government. The white paper was viewed as a temporary aberration in British policy brought about by administrative necessity; when that necessity disappeared so too would the white paper policy. After the publication of the document Weizmann told a Jewish audience at the Kingsway Hall,

> there were a great many Englishmen who were equally unhappy, grieved and distressed by this sort of mental and moral aberration of the British government . . . this . . . would pass and . . . the Jewish National Home would flourish and be a source of pride not only to the Jews but also to the British people.[41]

The British too were placed in an acute dilemma. It would be idle to suggest that the government was unaware of, or even indifferent to, the Jewish refugee problem. But they had to fit their Palestine policy within the wider spectrum of British political, military and strategic needs. And, to contemporaries, these often acquired nightmarish proportions. The Zionists might argue, as indeed they did, that the British exaggerated and over-estimated the Arab threat to their security.[42] But these strictures remained purely academic until put to the test; when the test finally arrived and war broke out, it became even more academic to alter the policy. This was an inherent weakness in the Zionist case.

Was the May white paper a "turning point" in Anglo-Zionist relations, as it has so often been described? If one has to use such inexact expressions, then the answer is surely no. The Zionists knew quite well what the government intended, and they fully comprehended the motives pushing the government forward. Hence their readiness for compromise. They knew, as did the government, that in the event of war immigration would in any case be restricted; they were confident, rightly as it turned out, that they could evade the restrictions on land sales; while the prospect of a Palestinian state ten years in the future and dependent for its establishment upon Arab-Jewish co-operation, seemed a sufficiently remote possibility as to exclude it from the realms of political reality. Of course, for many different reasons they were unable to acquiesce in the government's policy. And the violent manner and expression of their rejection reflected the position of European Jewry on the eve of the holocaust. But they hoped, and with every justification, that when the international crisis had passed and the Axis powers brought to their knees, they would resume their traditional relationship with the British government based upon the mandate and the MacDonald letter. If it is necessary to talk in terms of "turning points", it would be far more profitable to see one in the Labour government's refusal to rescind the white paper at the end of the war, rather than in the actual formulation of that policy by Chamberlain's government on the eve of war.

There is another point worth remembering. The British, throughout this period, found themselves baffled by a phenomenon hitherto absent from their political lexicon, or at least unfamiliar to them in its present form : the phenomenon of extra-European nationalism. This was true not only in Palestine but throughout the Empire. From Egypt to India the government grappled, ineffectively, with this problem. It took on the form of the *hydra* of Greek mythology. The more conferences or consultations or negotiations, the more intractable the problem appeared. There was indeed an unbridgeable gap between the demands of the nationalists on the one hand, and the principles upon which the Empire was founded on the other. And, without question, the government never really grasped the fundamental motivating forces which inspired the growth of this movement. In Palestine, for reasons enunciated enough throughout this work, the question was infinitely more complicated. Faced with these almost insurmountable problems, government policy was bound to appear erratic and to vacillate from one posture to another.

Now that the white paper had been formally acknowledged by parliament the government had to submit the new policy for approval before the permanent mandates commission. The Zionists intended to use the commission as a wedge to dislodge the government from its position. The cabinet had considered, somewhat apprehensively, the possibility of the new policy being brought before the Hague Court and League Council as a result of the permanent mandates commission's, which was "much under the influence of Zionist opinion", intervention.[43] Lord Dufferin had made a significant aside during the debate in the Lords to the effect that if the mandates commission opposed the white paper, "we would immediately ask the Council to alter the mandate".[44] This disclosure opened up new horizons for the Zionists.

Weizmann pointed out that changing the mandate was "a long and tedious business", and, moreover, "cannot be done without the consent of the United States. Should the government embark on this adventure then America can really save the situation and the whole thing fought out again."[45] But first the commission had to oppose the government's policy.

Weizmann was on excellent terms with at least two of its members, the chairman, M. Orts, and the vice-chairman, Professor Rappard. Of the former he wrote : "In him . . . we found a sympathetic and critical appreciation of our efforts, and a deep understanding of the bearing of the Jewish problem on the National Home." Of the latter : "He was a man of the greatest intellectual capacity, with a deep understanding of the Jewish problem in all its bearings and as deep a sympathy with our hopes and endeavours."[46] The Commission began its deliberations on 10 June. The previous day Weizmann wrote to Rappard :

> I trust to God that justice will be done . . . I feel sure that the . . . commission will hold the scales of justice in honour . . . it is the only body still left in this distracted world which has courage and is capable of an independent judgment, and "spiritual values" don't for them recede before administrative necessity.[47]

In early July the commission terminated its session. In its report to the Council of the League of Nations, the commission unanimously declared that "the policy set out in the white paper was not in accordance with the interpretation which, in agreement with the Mandatory Power and the Council, the commission had placed upon the Palestine Mandate". But there did emerge a difference of opinion. Three members, Great Britain, France, and Portugal thought that existing circumstances might justify the white paper provided the Council ratified it. The remaining four, Belgium, Holland, Norway and Switzerland found the white paper absolutely contrary to the terms of the mandate.[48] This, quite obviously, was not the decision the Zionists had hoped for. An element of doubt remained. Moreover, the two great powers on the commission were acting in concert and had provided a loophole through which the white paper could slip when the Council next met in September. Mrs. Dugdale commented :

P

Heard to my great dismay that the . . . commission failed to get a unanimous report, owing to Hankey [Sir Maurice Hankey had put the British case before the commission], and so have decided . . . to refer the matter to the League Council in September. This throws our plans for a Parliamentary debate into the melting pot, and it is hard to decide what to do.[49]

She wrote to Weizmann of the commission having failed to justify "our hopes".[50]

But the Zionists also placed great expectations on circumventing the white paper by opting for a federal solution. The white paper did not explicitly exclude such a possibility.[51]

As we have seen the idea of a federal solution has emerged many times in this narrative, and it continued to find some powerful protagonists. In a leader on 18 May *The Times* advised parliament "to concentrate on a possible federal solution as envisaged in the white paper"; it repeated this suggestion on 24 May. Geoffrey Dawson, the editor, told Weizmann that he thought "the policy was folly, and that federalism seemed the only real solution".[52]

The four surviving members of the Peel commission publicly endorsed the policy of *The Times*, hinting at "extending the federal plan beyond the artificial frontiers created only twenty years ago".[53] Lord Lugard expressed similar opinions.[54]

MacDonald himself was not impervious to the federal solution in principle.[55] He wrote to Lugard : "I entirely agree with your view that the best hope of an ultimate solution lies in some form of federation either within Palestine or within a larger area."[56] As usual the acceptance of the principle turned on the degree of agreement over details. Weizmann noted,

In my letter of the 10th . . . [I] used a rather specific proposal, *viz.* : the setting up of an administration for Palestine based on a federal arrangement with full Jewish control over immigration, and federal institutions based on parity, always allowing for growth of the Jewish National Home.[57]

Shertok emphasised the basic requirements of any federal scheme : "(1) . . . the Jewish section . . . must contain . . . a fair margin for territorial expansion (2) . . . the Jews must have full control of their own immigration."[58]

The Zionists' main collaborator in this venture was Professor

Coupland, Beit professor of history of the British Empire at Oxford. Ever since the Peel commission Coupland had remained on close terms with Weizmann. He was a firm advocate of partition, indeed it is evident that he devised the scheme. Now that partition had been pushed aside he devoted his considerable ingenuity and experience to devising a federal scheme acceptable to the Zionists. Nor was he adopting a completely new approach. He was, in fact, reviving his transitional federal proposal of January 1937.[59]

Weizmann drove down to Coupland's home at Oxford on the evening of 20 June. The following morning Lord Lothian joined them. During the course of the discussions the broad outline of a federal scheme was adopted, and the method by which it should be brought to the notice of the government.[60]

> I believe Professor Coupland intends to commit his views in greater detail in the course of next week, trying to make some concrete and constructive proposals along federal lines—i.e. something not unlike partition on an improved Peel line, but without sovereignty to begin with—taking into account the possibility of a future federation including Syria and Trans-Jordan as well as Palestine. He will try to enlist the support of an influential British committee for his scheme, consisting, besides himself and the surviving members of the Royal Commission, of people like Lord Lugard, Lord Hailey, Lord Lothian (he would be willing to support such an idea, but without publicly identifying himself with it on account of his position as an Ambassador to the U.S.), the Archbishop of Canterbury, Mr. Geoffrey Dawson, Lord Willington, and others of similar standing.[61]

For Rappard's benefit Weizmann gave the impression that in all these negotiations he was acting as "a private observer", while the initiative remained in Coupland's hands. He continued that it was by no means certain that the scheme would receive the approval of the Jewish Agency : "Partition without independence would be a bitter pill for Zionists!" But Weizmann was confident that in the existing circumstances this was the right path to take. "It seems to me to be the first ray of light which has pierced the fog of the white paper policy."

Weizmann's confidence in the scheme was reinforced by the unease which he knew existed within government circles over the present stalemate. Halifax had told Coupland that "he was not the architect of the white paper policy, and that he inclined to think that . . . Coupland's letter to *The Times* might offer a way out of the impasse".[62] Weizmann was equally impressed with what Sir Joseph Ball, then director of the Conservative Research Department, had told him. They had met on 20 June at Sir Joseph's request.

> Sir Joseph was clearly unhappy about the Palestine debates . . . and only too anxious to find some constructive way out of the difficulty. He is not at all concerned with foreign policy; his interest lies in the smooth functioning of the party machine in the election which may take place in October or November this year, and in the further debates which may follow the mandate commission's announcement of its decision.[63]

The federal scheme was to be used when it became evident that the white paper policy had collapsed.[64] There seemed little need for immediate urgency. Coupland informed Weizmann that he intended drafting "a possible letter to *The Times* for use if parliament discusses Palestine again before August".[65] Until then they would await the outcome of the mandate commission's deliberations, and see to what degree the new policy was carried out in Palestine, or ignored. Weizmann had given a clear warning on this pitfall : "for any scheme to have a prospect of success it is essential that every care should be taken to ensure that no *fait accompli* should meanwhile be created by the Palestine administration on the basis of the new policy".[66]

The Zionists' plan for another parliamentary debate on Palestine was scotched as a result of the mandate commission's findings. Mrs. Dugdale and Amery agreed "that the atmosphere and the time are most unfavourable for trying to raise our affairs in Parliament".[67] As a substitute for keeping Zionist activities in the public eye Amery suggested,

> [a] carefully managed leakage of facts about the . . . mandates commission—so that when their minutes are published in August the newspapers may report them. Our object should be to rouse interest and curiosity, and to hint that the result is by no means a triumph for Malcolm.[68]

On 12 July the government announced the cancellation of the immigration quota for the period October 1939–March 1940, owing to the large influx of illegal immigrants who had entered Palestine.[69] By the following afternoon the opposition had decided to raise the issue on the occasion of the colonial office vote on 20 July.[70] The Zionists had achieved their parliamentary debate. But had the Palestine administration accomplished their *fait accompli*? Apparently Weizmann thought so. He spoke "about the 'sinister purpose' behind all this".[71]

The Zionists asked the Labour party not to press their claims for a debate; but to no avail. Mrs. Dugdale noticed : "I am not surprised from their Party point of view, but consider it very unfortunate from ours. How can Walter and others abstain from a Vote on Supply. So we have to work hard to make the debate itself as good as possible."[72] Mrs. Dugdale and Shertok addressed "[a] good meeting" of the pro-Palestine parliamentary committee on 19 July. About thirty members were present, "many of them conservatives. They will mostly abstain and (we hope) be in the House and remain seated."[73] The Zionists were reasonably pleased with the debate.[74] Shertok cabled Weizmann :

> Debate changed nothing but served express growing unrest regarding White paper policy marked further undermining of its authority. Balance opinions expressed even more pronouncedly on our side than last occasion . . . Government very bitterly attacked MacDonald defended policy singlehanded.[75]

The day the announcement on immigration had been made, Elliot informed Mrs. Dugdale that the decision had been taken without prior consultation with the cabinet.[76] The records now reveal that it was only on 19 July that MacDonald explained to the cabinet the decision and the reasons for it.[77] In consequence it was decided to reconstitute the cabinet committee on Palestine, and the cabinet issued a directive to MacDonald instructing him to prepare a memorandum indicating how he intended to implement his policy.[78] If MacDonald had cancelled the immigration quota solely on the advice of his officials without taking more authoritative political soundings, there was clearly a need to resurrect a political framework to supervise and restrain him. The cabinet could not allow this haphazard method of being provoked into parliamentary debates on such ill-chosen ground to continue. Certainly, they could ill afford a repetition of the debate over the white paper which, in effect, amounted to a vote of non-confidence in the government. Mrs. Dugdale noted : "all indications point to growing realisation on the part of the cabinet that he [MacDonald] is getting himself and them into a mess".[79]

On 3 August MacDonald circulated two documents preparatory to the cabinet committee meeting due the following day. "But neither of them met the point of where this policy is leading."[80] Elliot wrote of the committee meeting :

> . . . federalism has now come so far forward as the final goal, as to monopolise the picture even to the extent of blotting out the proposed constitutional arrangements. For the rest, nothing likely to cause clashes is to be expected in the immediate future, and if your friends keep their heads all may yet be well.[81]

The picture of events since 17 May was not one of unrelieved gloom. The House had by no measure ratified whole-heartedly the new policy. MacDonald had encountered difficulties, even opposition, within the cabinet. And the campaign for federalism appeared to be winning many new adherents. These promising developments, however, were overshadowed by the approach of war.

From 16 to 25 August the twenty-first Zionist Congress met at Geneva in "an atmosphere of unreality and irrelevance".[82] Weizmann bade farewell to the delegates.

> We shall meet again [prolonged applause]. We shall meet again in common labour for our land and people. Our people is deathless, our land eternal.
> There are some things which cannot fail to come to pass, things without which the world cannot be imagined. The remnant shall work on, fight on, live on until the dawn of better days.
> Towards that dawn I greet you. May we meet again in peace [prolonged applause].[83]

Weizmann, after embracing "Ussishkin and Ben Gurion as if he would never let them go",[84] left the auditorium to a standing ovation.

International developments overtook the Anglo-Zionist dispute. On 19 August Weizmann wrote to Chamberlain :

> In this hour of supreme crisis, the consciouness that the Jews have a contribution to make to the defence of sacred values impels me to write this letter. I wish to confirm in the most explicit manner, the declarations which I and my colleagues have made during the last months, and especially in the last week : that the Jews "stand by Great Britain and will fight on the side of the democracies".

. . . and therefore would place ourselves in matters big and small, under the co-ordinating direction of His Majesty's Government. The Jewish Agency is ready to enter into immediate arrangements for utilising Jewish manpower, technical abilities, resources, etc.

The Jewish Agency has recently had difficulties in the political field with the mandatory power. We would like these difficulties to give way before the greater and more pressing necessities of the time.[85]

On 2 September Chamberlain replied, somewhat stiffly :

I should like to express my warm appreciation of the contents of your letter . . . and of the spirit which prompted it. It is true that differences of opinion exist . . . but I gladly accept the assurances contained in your letter. I note with pleasure that in this time of supreme emergency when these things which we hold dear are at stake, Britain can rely on the whole-hearted co-operation of the Jewish Agency. You will not expect me to say more at this stage than that your public-spirited assurances are welcome and will be kept in mind.[86]

A temporary truce had been called. Mr. A. Eban has accurately defined Weizmann's objective at this time. "His aim was to put the White Paper into refrigeration and create conditions in which it would appear after the victory as a grotesque and unseemly anachronism."[87]

NOTES

1 See, for example, Tom William's letter, 5 April 1939, C.Z.A., S25/7642; the D.D. for this period; Weizmann's telegram to Blum and Brandeis, 18 and 19 April 1939, W.A.; London Zionist Executive to Ben Gurion, tel., 21 April 1939, W.A.; and Weizmann's letters and telegrams to Amery, T. Williams, Churchill, Sinclair and Chamberlain, 25 April–4 May 1939, W.A.

2 See his memorandum of 28 April 1939, CAB.24/285, C.P.100(39).

3 This was a pet theme of Elliot's. He had first aired the idea in November 1937 as a result of the foreign office attack on partition.

4 See cabinet minutes for 1 May 1939, CAB.23/99.

5 Hore Belisha accepted the deductive reasoning behind the memorandum; but was unable to accept its conclusions.

6 D.D., 8 May 1939.

7 Sinclair to Weizmann, 9 May 1939, W.A.

8   W.D., 10 May 1939, W.A. This was an appointments diary only, and contained no extra comments.

9   Notes of a conversation with the prime minister, 11 May 1939, W.A.

10 Notes of a conversation between Weizmann and Mrs. A. Paterson on the MacDonald-Weizmann meeting, 13 May 1939, W.A.

11 D.D., 14 May 1939.

12 Notes of a conversation between Weizmann and Mrs. A. Paterson, 13 May 1939, *op. cit.* The following account is based on these notes.

13 Weizmann asked himself the same question, Weizmann to Mrs. A. Paterson, 13 May 1939, W.A.

14 D.D., 15 May 1939.

15 D.D., 14, 15, 16 and 17 May 1939.

16 D.D., 15 May 1939.

17 Mrs. Dugdale's report to the London executive, 16 May 1939, W.A.

18 D.D., 16 May 1939.

19 D.D., 25 May 1939.

20 Memorandum by Murrey (chief of the Near Eastern division) to Hull 15 May 1939, *F.R.U.S.*, 1939, iv, p. 756.

21 Roosevelt to Hull, 17 May 1939, *F.R.U.S.*, 1939, iv, pp. 757–8.

22 See MacDonald's report to the cabinet on their conversation, 10 May 1939, CAB.23/99.

23 See J. Wheeler Bennet, *King George VI* (London, 1958), pp. 371 ff., 381–92.

24 Cmd. 6019, *Palestine: A Statement of Policy* (May 1939).

25 *The Times*, 18 May 1939.

26 The *Manchester Guardian*, 18 May 1939.

27 D.D., 19 May 1939.

28 See, Weizmann to Professor Coupland, 17 May 1939, W.A. Weizmann requested that Coupland "help us by getting Sir Arthur Salter—Sir Horace Rumbold to write to *The Times* . . . and Sir Edward Grigg''; also, Weizmann to Admiral [sic] King-Hall, 17 May 1939, W.A.; and, Weizmann to Lord Lugard, 17 May 1939, W.A.

29 *The Times*, 22 May 1939: signed by Sir H. Rumbold, Sir W. Carter, Sir H. Morris and Professor R. Coupland.

30 P.D., Commons, vol. 347, c. 1937–2056, 22 May 1939; and c. 2129–90, 23 May 1939.

31 D.D., 23 May 1939.

32 Weizmann to Churchill, tel. 23 May 1939, W.A. Mrs. Dugdale concurred with this judgment and believed it "must have accounted for a good many of the enormous number of abstentions', D.D., 23 May 1939.

33 It is interesting to note that the government majority in this debate was only eight more than in the debate over the Norwegian campaign in May 1940; a vote that led to the fall of the Chamberlain government.

34 P.D., Lords, vol. 113, c. 105, 23 May 1939.

35 See below, p. 194. This is not to argue that the Zionists accepted MacDonald's thesis.

36 See below, pp. 161–62, 165–67.

37 See, Cmd. 5479, pp. 366–7.

38 Minutes of the Panel, 24 Feb. 1939, W.A.

39 The Evian conference was convened on the initiative of the United States

on 6 July 1938, to provide solutions for the European refugee problem. Thirty-two countries participated. The conference became the occasion for sophistry, not decisions. Only the Dominican Republic made a generous gesture: it offered to take in 100,000 Jews from Germany and Austria. But no striking public decisions were taken at Evian, and it is generally agreed that the conference terminated in a welter of speechifying.

40 See, for example, Weizmann's willingness to "accept the stoppage of immigration for a year at longest", D.D., 2 Feb. 1937. He later told the Panel: "Had the government only said that they could not retain the mandate, but gave the Jews assurance that the fundamental principles of the mandate would be embodied in the new form of government; or even that they recognised the principle of absorptive capacity, but asked the Jews to go slow for two or three years in view of the situation; but the government said nothing of the kind. The government representatives were always talking of the Arabs agreeing to this or that figure of immigration", 7 March 1939, W.A. Ben Gurion told the Panel: "[We] ought to be ready to make concessions to the Arabs on the basis of give and take provided the Arabs were prepared to recognise the special status of the Jews in Palestine", 24 Feb. 1939, W.A.

41 *Jewish Chronicle*, 26 May 1939.

42 See, for example, official minutes of the fifth session of the conference, 14 Feb. 1939, C.Z.A., S25/7632.

43 See cabinet minutes for 17 and 23 May 1939, CAB.23/99.

44 P.D., Lords, vol. 113, c. 89, 23 May 1949.

45 Weizmann to Dr. S. Goldmann (president of the Zionist Organisation of America), 30 May 1939, W.A.

46 Weizmann, p. 463-4.

47 Weizmann to Rappard, 9 June 1939, W.A.

48 See *The Times*, 18 Aug. 1939; and *ESCO*, ii, p. 927.

49 D.D., 3 July 1939.

50 Mrs. Dugdale to Weizmann, 6 July 1939, W.A. The commission also managed to disappoint the government. See cabinet minutes for 28 June and 19 July 1939, CAB.23/100.

51 See Cmd. 6019, pp. 5-6.

52 Contained in Weizmann to Rappard, 26 June 1939, W.A. Weizmann had met Dawson on the 24th.

53 *The Times*, 22 May 1939.

54 *The Times*, 23 May 1939.

55 MacDonald to Weizmann, 15 March 1939, W.A.

56 Contained in Lugard to Weizmann, 23 June 1939, W.A.

57 Weizmann to MacDonald, 24 March 1939, W.A.

58 Shertok to Amery, 22 May 1939, C.Z.A., Z4/17125.

59 See below, p. 127-28.

60 W.D., 20 and 21 June 1939, W.A.; Weizmann to Lugard, 22 June 1939, W.A.; and D.D., 23 June 1939.

61 Weizmann to Rappard, 26 June 1939, W.A. And for subsequent quotations.

62 *Ibid.* Although Halifax was not the architect of the policy, he had given MacDonald his fullest support, and sometimes had gone well beyond his brief (see the cabinet records for Dec. 1938, CAB.23/98, and Jan.–May

1939, CAB.23/97, 99). Possibly the reaction to the white paper had taken him aback and he now began to have second thoughts.

63 *Ibid.*; also W.D., 20 June 1939.
64 D.D., 23 June 1939.
65 Coupland to Weizmann, 24 June 1939, W.A.
66 Weizmann to Rappard, 26 June 1939, W.A.
67 Mrs. Dugdale to Weizmann, 6 July 1939, W.A.; also D.D., 6 July 1939.
68 Mrs. Dugdale to Weizmann, 6 July 1939, W.A.
69 P.D., Commons, vol. 349, c. 2276, 12 July 1939.
70 D.D., 13 July 1939.
71 Mrs. Dugdale to Weizmann, 15 July 1939, W.A.
72 D.D., 17 July 1939.
73 D.D., 19 July 1939.
74 D.D., 20 July 1939.
75 Shertok to Weizmann, tel. 21 July 1939, C.Z.A., Z4/17060.
76 D.D., 13 July 1939.
77 See cabinet minutes for 19 July 1939, CAB.23/100.
78 D.D., 20 and 23 July 1939.
79 D.D., 23 July 1939.
80 D.D., 3 Aug. 1939.
81 D.D., 10 Aug. 1939.
82 Weizmann, p. 508.
83 Weisgal and Carmichael, pp. 245–6.
84 D.D., 24 Aug. 1939.
85 Weizmann to Chamberlain, 29 Aug. 1939, W.A. Quoted in Weisgal and Carmichael, p. 253.
86 Chamberlain to Weizmann, 2 Sept. 1939, W.A.
87 Weisgal and Carmichael, p. 253.

10

Some Conclusions

There can be little doubt that the inter-war years witnessed a steady decline in the influence of Gentile Zionism. The Balfour declaration saw its flowering; the crisis of 1929–31 gave it a brief ascendancy; while the May white paper of 1939 personified its nadir. But while Gentile Zionism as a factor of political substance lost ground, the Gentile Zionist continued to flourish.

Without question the most outstanding example during this period was Mrs. E. C. Blanche Dugdale. Of all those sympathisers with Zionism only Mrs. Dugdale completely identified herself with the movement. She alone among the Gentiles was admitted into the inner circle of Weizmann's advisers, participated in Zionist policy-making bodies, and devoted her day-to-day activities to the cause.[1] For Weizmann "she had become the truest and most intimate of all his Gentile friends".[2] Her diaries constitute an invaluable source to Zionist activity throughout this period, and an illuminating insight into the mind of a Gentile Zionist.

While Mrs. Dugdale remained the classic example of a Gentile Zionist, there were many others who gave of their best. Amery, Churchill, Lloyd George, Sir Archibald Sinclair, Wedgwood, Kenworthy, Victor Cazalet, John Buchan, Ormsby Gore and many others all contributed in no small measure to whatever successes Zionism achieved. But it must not be forgotten that for them Zionism was only one of many problems that they devoted their time and energy to. Often it became a topic of immense importance in their lives, but not, with very few exceptions, to the exclusion of all else.

Of course they did not act in a vacuum. Their greatest achievements came when British and Zionist interests coincided. Or, when a susceptible government showed a particularly heavy hand in dealing with the Zionists, as was evident during the crisis of 1929–31. Then, although genuinely sympathetic towards Zionism, not all the protestors acted solely out of love for Zion. The smell of party strife was in the air. And the opposition did not hesitate to harry an insecure, minority government exploiting the Passfield white paper as a convenient, if honourable, hobby horse. But for inter-party squabbles to intrude in this manner was the exception rather than the rule.

The debate over partition offers the most striking example of the way the Zionists would often overstate their case and then, as a result, find themselves being outpaced by their Gentile supporters. From the outset the Weizmann group came down strongly in favour of the principle of partition. For them the discussion turned on details. And their insistence on emphasising, often in an exaggerated manner, the negative aspects of the Peel proposals confirmed the opinion of many Gentile Zionists that there was little of value in the scheme as such. There was in any case a natural tendency on the part of Gentile Zionists to reject partition. Instinctively they saw in it a repudiation of past obligations, a concession to violence, an abandonment of the dream of a Jewish National Home thriving under British patronage. The Zionist propaganda machine did little to help assuage these feelings. Self-restraint was not a virtue deeply rooted in Zionist diplomatic practice.

Partition was in many ways the crucial issue of this period. It could not have escaped the notice of the government that the Zionist parliamentary lobby was almost one hundred per cent against the proposal (Amery being the most conspicuous exception). There is no way of judging whether Gentile support for partition would have swayed the government during its moments of indecision. The evidence suggests that this would have been most unlikely. But certainly articulate Gentile opposition to the scheme must have encouraged the government in its final decision to discard partition. If, ultimately, the debate on partition went against them, the Zionists must assume their share of the responsibility.

There was also a Zionist tendency to exaggerate the importance of their own contacts. For example, during 1938-9 the Zionists set great store on the influence American public opinion would bring to bear upon the government. After the publication of the May white paper Weizmann ventured the opinion that "America can really save the situation". This was a totally unrealistic and illusionary evaluation of Washington's influence at Whitehall. There was certainly no question of deliberately antagonising the Americans, but equally overt American interference in British foreign policy often aroused much resentment in London. No doubt the feeling existed that as the United States stood aside from the general pattern of European affairs she should make her reservations concerning the correctness or otherwise of British policy with the utmost caution and modesty. An examination of the published American documents on Palestine leaves the impression that the Americans too appreciated the ambivalence of their position. Directives issued to the American ambassador in London invariably stressed the necessity of adopting an unofficial, personal approach to the British government. In the final analysis the Americans bowed before British policy whatever the number of protests that poured into the State Department.

It is evident that as the 1930s drew to a close, the ability of the Gentile Zionist to effectively aid the Zionists lessened. During the crisis of 1929–31 it was possible to isolate the Palestine question and deal with it, more or less, on its own merits. This offered the Gentile Zionist more scope for activity, more room for manœuvre. After 1935 it was no longer possible to criticise the government's Palestine policy without bringing into question its whole conception of Near East affairs. And as Britain's international position deteriorated it became increasingly difficult for the run-of-mill politician to rock the boat. Either you opposed the government, including its Palestine policy; or you supported it, and left moral misgivings to take care of themselves. Hence the Zionists were thrown back increasingly upon their own resources. The latter years of the 1930s witnessed a curious paradox : as the Zionists' need for help grew so the ability of the Gentile Zionists to offer them sustenance diminished.

The personal standing of Weizmann was also a factor in the lessening of Zionist influence in government circles. During his long sojourn in England he had assimilated from the English characteristics which were to hold him in good stead throughout his political life : pragmatism, balance, poise, political style, a dislike of rhetoric and tub-thumping, a distrust of ideological entrenchment and programme making, characteristics which were sadly lacking in the Zionist movement. He spoke in a language and manner comprehensible to his listeners.

He had early come to the conclusion that there was no other choice but England as the mandatory power. Hence, whatever other motives Weizmann attributed to Anglo-Zionist relations, their relationship at its lowest common denominator was one of Hobson's choice. He said :

Whatever revolutionary methods I adopt in getting the Jews into Palestine, I can't do it without the support of Great Britain. And if I want British support, I've got to win the confidence of the British government. I've got to take the ruling class at its face value. I've got to put the best interpretation on everything it says. Because, if I don't, where am I?[3]

His attitude towards the English Gentile underwent no radical change despite the bitter disappointments which the mandate brought. In 1911 he proclaimed :

The English Gentiles are the best Gentiles in the world. England has helped small nations to gain their independence. We should try and get Gentile support for Zionism.[4]

In 1947, at the height of the Palestine disturbances and when Anglo-Zionist relations had plummeted to their nadir, he wrote to a friend :

It is axiomatic for me that we can do nothing . . . unless we re-establish confidence between the Movement and the British Government and . . . people. This confidence has been shattered . . . the British are, to great extent, responsible for it. The White Paper [of May 1939] was a disaster—our tactics were disastrous. It is a grave mistake to believe that what we have lost in England we will recover in America or even . . . in France.[5]

What was Weizmann's appeal to the English? In part, paradoxically, it was his unadorned Jewishness. Weizmann never forgot the background from which he sprang. Quite the contrary, he was its supreme embodiment, and this was one reason why he was such an attractive personality in their eyes.

The attraction of Weizmann for the British was precisely that he was the most Jewish Jew we had met. He impressed us because he was not Western, *because* he was not assimilated, *because* he was utterly proud to be a Russian Jew from the Pale, *because* he had no feeling of double loyalty, *because* he knew only one patriotism, the love of a country that did not yet exist.[6]

The appeal of Weizmann to the Gentiles was that he cut through a Gordian knot of their own invention : the dilemma between pandering to age-old, anti-semitic prejudice, or acknowledging the liberal tendencies of the day. He was the "most Jewish Jew" they had met. But his Zionism dispersed their own contradictions and freed their relationship from the restrictions and undertones of prejudice they felt, unconsciously or otherwise, when in the continuous company of the assimilated Jew. As well as providing a solution for the Jewish problem, Weizmann contributed towards settling a Gentile quandary.

It was to Weizmann's credit that he related British needs to Jewish hopes, convincing many British statesmen of an identity of interests between the British Empire and a Jewish National Home in Palestine. But this alone would not have been sufficient to rouse British statesmen into advocating Zionism. Underlying all their activity was the feeling that in doing something for the Jews they were righting ancient wrongs, repaying in some small measure the enormous debt owed by the Gentile world for the suffering inflicted upon the Jewish people over the centuries. Nurtured on the scriptures, strengthened by a deeply felt bond with the Old Testament, they acted and felt as though they were fulfilling an historical mission. This dichotomy in Gentile Zionist motivation was essential for the conscription of his services. It was Weizmann's great asset, perhaps his greatest, that he personified through the strength of his own personality these twin aspects of Zionism : The Return and the vested interest, the spiritual and the practical.

By the end of the 1930s he was still the undisputed leader, and in the field of Anglo-Zionist relations towered head and shoulders above any of his contemporaries or rivals. But his position had altered considerably since his heyday at the time of the Balfour declaration and the ratification of the mandate. Stricter limitations were imposed on his individualistic style of diplomacy. He had now to look over his shoulder more often and with more consideration at the reactions of American and Palestinian Jewries. No longer could he take for granted that they would follow his lead.

In Palestine in particular he was made aware of this fact. By the latter years of the 1930s the *Yishuv* had developed into a national community in its own right. It gave birth to its own political institutions and leaders representing the most dynamic facet of contemporary Jewish life. Weizmann, in a strange way, stood apart from this development. He lived in Palestine but was not an intrinsic part of its organic growth. Unlike Ben Gurion he did not have the benefits of an organised party, or a powerful organisation such as the *Histadruth*,[7] at his finger-tips. One suspects that this feature of political life, its grass-roots aspect, did not really attract him. He was more at ease, more familiar, and more effective in the cloistered atmosphere of diplomatic bargaining than in the hurly-burly setting of vote catching.

Weizmann was in no sense of the word a party man. He generally stood aloof from Zionist inter-party squabbles. But he was dependent upon party support in order to push through his policies in Congress. More often than not he succeeded, and formed an easy, working alliance with the labour groups of the Zionist movement. But the impression remains that his reliance upon the political support of these groups caused him much anxiety and inhibited his usual political style.

Ultimately Weizmann was captive to the permanent international crisis of the 1930s, and in particular to the Jewish situation in Europe. The appalling position in which European Jewry found itself dominated the thoughts and actions of the whole Zionist movement. The key to Zionist militancy in Palestine lies in the tragic plight of the Jewish communities of Berlin, Warsaw and Bucharest. Weizmann was in the position where he believed that one unnecessary concession might entail the extinction of Jewish communities he knew and had grown up in. His personal correspondence for this period clearly reveals the strain this responsibility imposed upon his diplomacy. It overshadowed all other considerations; it gave an added bite to his dealings with the government. In consequence he lost the degree of flexibility which had distinguished so much of his diplomacy at an earlier period.

Were Weizmann's methods now outdated? Had his relationship with Britain evolved into an infatuation which sapped his critical faculties? Did his desire to preserve the British connexion make him easy prey for government dictates? None of these explanations, so often assumed, can stand serious analysis. Apart from certain fringe elements within the movement Weizmann's diplomacy was accepted in its broad outlines by the mainstream of Zionist thought. Indeed, on some occasions the "moderate" Weizmann had to be restrained from not breaking with the government by more "extreme" elements. Although he was often the subject of criticism, neither his methods nor his policy were seriously challenged. There was, in fact, no viable alternative to Weizmannism.

It was often said, by Weizmann among others, that the failure of Zionist diplomacy during this period lay in the inability of British ministers to grasp the true implications of Zionism. They were not, the Zionists contended, of the same calibre as those ministers who issued the Balfour declaration. "My other trouble," Weizmann complained, "is that I find myself dealing with Pharaohs who 'know not Egypt' . . . their standards and outlook . . . differ widely from those that animated Balfour."

It is true that in the war cabinet of 1917 three of the five members—Lloyd George, Milner and Smuts—were Zionist sympathisers. While Balfour occupied high office as foreign secretary, and Sir Mark Sykes and Amery had been appointed to the influential posts of assistant secretaries to the cabinet. During the 1930s the Zionists could rely on no equivalent team equally susceptible to their logic. But this argument should not be taken too far. The Zionists still had a voice in the cabinet. Ormsby Gore and Malcolm MacDonald (his appointment as colonial secretary, even as late as May 1938, was greeted with sighs of relief by the Zionists) were both well known for their Zionist affiliations, and both held the office of colonial secretary. Walter Elliot, a close friend of Mrs. Dugdale, acted in unison with the Zionists and was consistently feeding them information from cabinet sessions and placing Zionist views before the cabinet. While of Halifax Weizmann remarked, "he felt for the first time there might be something of the quality of understanding that A.J.B. used to display". If Weizmann did not have the same easy access to ministers as in previous times, he certainly did not find all doors barred before him and continually made his presence and opinions strongly felt, even if the atmosphere was markedly cooler than Weizmann would have liked. It was not so much the men as the circumstances which had changed.

NOTES

1   For a full account of her activities, see N. A. Rose, *Baffy: The Diaries of Blanche Dugdale* (Vallentine, Mitchell, London, 1972).
2   Weisgal and Carmichael, pp. 327-8.
3   R. Crossman, *A Nation Reborn* (London, 1960), p. 37.
4   M. Weisgal and J. Carmichael, ed., *Chaim Weizmann: A Biography by Several Hands* (New York, 1963), p. 92.
5   L. Stein, *Weizmann and England* (London, 1964), p. 29.
6   Crossman, p. 41.
7   *The Histadruth:* The General Federation of Jewish Labour in Palestine. This organisation was more than just a trades union. It engaged, *inter alia*, in public health and educational activities, organised a vast co-operative construction company, and indulged in marketing and consumer work.

Bibliography

This is not an exhaustive bibliography on the Palestine mandate or Anglo-Zionist relations. It incorporates only those sources that I have used in the preparation of this study, or found useful in providing background material for it. More comprehensive bibliographies may be found in:
ESCO, Palestine: A Study of Jewish, Arab and British Policies (Yale University Press, 1947), pp. 1238–80. And J. C. Hurewitz, *The Struggle for Palestine* (New York, 1950), pp. 363–88.

I. *Primary Unpublished Sources*
   The Weizmann Archives, Rehovot, Israel.
   The Central Zionist Archives, Jerusalem, Israel.
   The Public Record Office, London.
   The Passfield Papers, The London School of Economics and Political Science.

II. *Primary Published Sources*
   (a) *Documents on German Foreign Policy, 1918–1945, Series D, Volume V* (H.M.S.O.).
       Documents on British Foreign Policy, 1918–1939.
       First Series, iv and viii (H.M.S.O.).
       Third Series, iii and v (H.M.S.O.).
       Foreign Relations of the United States, 1936, iii,
       Foreign Relations of the United States, 1937, ii.
       Foreign Relations of the United States, 1938, ii,
       Foreign Relations of the United States, 1939, iv.
   (b) *Hansard*, 5th series. Parliamentary Debates, Lords and Commons.
   (c) Command Papers:
       Cmd. 1500. *The Final Draft of the Mandate* (Aug. 1921).
       Cmd. 1499. *An Interim Report on the Civil Administration of Palestine, 1 July 1920–30 June 1921*. The Samuel Report.
       Cmd. 1540. *The Haycroft Report into the Disturbances of May 1921, with Correspondence* (Oct. 1921).
       Cmd. 1700. *Correspondence with the Palestine Arab Delegation and the Zionist Organisation. And a Statement of British Policy on Palestine* (June 1922). The Churchill White Paper.
       Cmd. 1889. *Papers relating to Elections for the Legislative Council* (June 1923).
       Cmd. 1989. *Correspondence with the High Commissioner on the proposed formation of an Arab Agency* (Oct.–Nov. 1923).

Cmd. 3229. *A Memorandum by the Colonial Secretary on the Wailing Wall* (Nov. 1928).

Cmd. 3530. *The Shaw Report on the Disturbances of August 1929* (March 1930).

Cmd. 3582. *A Statement of Policy with regard to Palestine* (May 1930).

Cmd. 3686. *The Hope Simpson Report on Immigration, Land Settlement and Development* (Oct. 1930).

Cmd. 3687. *Appendix to above report containing maps.*

Cmd. 3692. *A Statement of Policy.* (Oct. 1930). The Passfield White Paper.

Cmd. 5119. *The Proposed New Constitution for Palestine* (March 1936).

Cmd. 5479. *The Report of the Palestine Royal Commission* (July 1937). The Peel Report.

Cmd. 5513. *Palestine: A Statement of Policy by His Majesty's Government* (July 1937).

Cmd. 5634. *Policy on Palestine. A Despatch of 23 December, 1937, from the Secretary of State for the Colonies to the High Commissioner for Palestine* (Jan. 1938). Contains the terms of reference for the Partition commission.

Cmd. 5726. *The Anglo-Italian Agreement, 16 April 1938.*

Cmd. 5854. *The Palestine Partition Report* (Oct. 1938). The Woodhead Report.

Cmd. 5893. *A Statement of Policy by His Majesty's Government* (Nov. 1938).

Cmd. 5957. *The Text of the Correspondence between Sir Henry MacMahon and the Sherif Hussein of Mecca. July 1915–March 1916* (March 1939).

Cmd. 5964. *Statements Made on Behalf of His Majesty's Government during the year 1918 in Regard to the Future Status of Certain Parts of the Ottoman Empire* (March 1939).

Cmd. 5974. *Report on a Committee Set Up to Consider Certain Correspondence between Sir Henry MacMahon and the Sherif of Mecca in 1915 and 1916* (March 1939).

Cmd. 6019. *Palestine: A Statement of Policy* (May 1939). The May White Papers.

(d) *The Palestine Government*
Annual Blue Books, 1925–38.
The Official Gazette, fortnightly, 1919–47.

(e) *Newspapers and Periodicals*
The Press Cutting Library at Chatham House.
The *Jewish Chronicle.*
The *Zionist Review.*
The *New Judaea.*

III. *Secondary Sources: Books and Articles.*
Abdullah. *Memoirs* (London, 1950).
Amery, L. S. *My Political Life* (London, 1953).
Antonius, G. *The Arab Awakening* (London, 1938).
Ashbee, C. *A Palestine Notebook, 1918–1923* (London, 1923).
Arlosoroff, C. "The 9th Dominion. Shall Palestine become an Integral Part of the British Empire?" *The New Palestine* (5 April 1929).
Balfour, A. J. *Speeches on Zionism* (London, 1928).
Barbour, N. *Nisi Dominus. A Survey of the Palestine Controversy* (London, 1946).

Bauer, Y. *Diplomat'ya Umachteret BaMedinyut HaTsionit* (*Diplomacy and Underground in Zionist Policy*) (Jerusalem, 1966).

—— "From Co-operation to Resistance: The Haganah 1938–1946", *Middle Eastern Studies* (April 1966).

Ben Gurion, D. *The Peel Report and the Jewish State* (London, 1938).

Barzilai, D. "On the Genesis of the Balfour Declaration", *Zion*, No. 3–4, (Jerusalem, 1968).

Bentwich, N. *My Seventy Seven Years* (London, 1962).

—— *Mandate Memories* (London, 1965).

—— and Kisch, M. *Brigadier Frederick Kisch* (London, 1966).

Bowle, J. *Viscount Samuel* (London, 1957).

Bowman, H. *Middle East Window* (London, 1942).

Bullard, Sir R. *The Camels Must Go* (London, 1961).

Bullock, A. *The Life and Times of Ernest Bevin, 1881–1940*, i (London, 1960).

Cohen, A. *Yisrael VeHaOlam HaAravi* (Israel and the Arab World) (Tel Aviv, 1964).

Cohen, I. *The Zionist Movement* (London, 1945).

Crossman, R. *A Nation Reborn* (London, 1960).

Cust, A. "Cantonization: A Plan for Palestine," *Journal of Royal Central Asian Society* (April 1936).

Duff, D. V. *Sword for Hire* (London, 1937).

—— *May The Winds Blow* (London, 1948).

Dugdale, B. *Arthur James Balfour*, i and ii (New York, 1937).

—— *The Balfour Declaration: Origins and Background* (Jewish Agency, London, 1940).

Edelman, M. *Ben Gurion: A Political Biography* (London, 1964).

Elath, E. *Memories of Sir Wyndham Deedes* (London, 1958).

ESCO Foundation. *Palestine: A Study of Jewish, Arab and British Policies*, i and ii (Yale University Press, 1947).

Goodman, P. *Chaim Weizmann* (London, 1945).

Graves, P. *Palestine: The Land of Three Faiths* (London, 1923).

Gwynn, Maj. Gen. Sir C. W. *Imperial Policing* (London, 1939).

Hamilton, M.A. *Arthur Henderson* (London, 1938).

Hancock, W. K. and Cowing, M. M. *The History of the Second World War, Civil Series. The British War Economy* (London, 1949).

Hanna, P. *British Policy in Palestine* (Washington, 1942).

Hart, Sir B. Liddell. *Memoirs*, ii (London, 1965).

Hirszowicz, L. *The Third Reich and the Arab East* (London, 1966).

Hurewitz, J. C. *The Struggle for Palestine* (New York, 1950).

—— *Diplomacy in the Near and Middle East* (Princeton, 1956).

Hyamson, A. M. *Palestine Under the Mandate* (London, 1950).

—— *British Projects for the Restoration of the Jews* (London, 1917).

Jeffries, J. M. N. *Palestine: The Reality* (London, 1939).

Jewish Agency. *Documents Relating to Palestine* (London, 1945).

—— *Memoranda on the Development of the Jewish National Home, 1930–38* (inclusive).

—— *Jewish Case Against the May White Paper* (London, 1939).

—— *Palestine: The Disturbances of 1936: Statistical Tables* (London, 1936).

—— *Memorandum Submitted to the Royal Commission* (London, 1936).

—— *Documents Relating to the Balfour Declaration and Mandate* (London, 1939).

Jewish Dominion of Palestine League. *A Memorandum submitted to the Anglo-American Committee of Enquiry on Palestine* (London, 1946).

Kedourie, E. *England and the Middle East: The Destruction of the Ottoman Empire* (London, 1956).

—— "Cairo and Khartoum on the Arab Question", *Historical Journal*, vii, No. 2 (1964).

Kisch, Col. F. H. *Palestine Diary* (London, 1938).

Leslie, S. *Mark Sykes: His Life and Letters* (London, 1923).

Levin, S. *Youth in Revolt* (London, 1939).

Luke, H. *Cities and Men* (London, 1956).

Locker, B. *BeChavlei Kiyum VeT'kuma (Jewish Survival and Revival)* (Jerusalem, 1963).

Lloyd George, D. *The Truth About the Peace Treaties*, ii (London, 1938).

Machover, J. M. *Governing Palestine: The Case Against a Parliament* (London, 1936).

Manuel, F. *The Realities of American-Palestine Relations* (Washington, 1949).

Minney, R. J. *The Private Papers of Hore Belisha* (London, 1960).

Monroe, E. *Britain's Moment in the Middle East, 1914–1956* (London, 1963).

Marlowe, J. *Arab Nationalism and British Imperialism* (London, 1961).

—— *Rebellion in Palestine* (London, 1946).

—— *The Seat of Pilate: An Account of the Palestine Mandate* (London, 1959).

Meinertzhagen, Col. R. *Middle East Diary, 1917–56* (London, 1959).

Namier, Sir L. B. *Conflicts* (London, 1942).

—— *Historical Survey of the Discussions leading up to the Prime Minister's letter of February 13, 1931, to Dr. Weizmann* (London, 1931).

Parkinson, C. *The Colonial Office From Within, 1909–1945* (London, 1945).

Pearlman, M. *Ben Gurion Looks Back* (London, 1965).

Playfair, Maj. Gen. I. S. O. *History of the Second World War. Military Series. The Mediterranean and the Middle East*, i (London, 1956).

Rendel, Sir C. W. *The Sword and the Olive* (London, 1957).

Rose, N. A. *Baffy: The Diaries of Blanche Dugdale 1936–47* (Vallentine, Mitchell, London, 1972)

—— "The Arab Rulers and Palestine, 1936: The British Reaction," *Journal of Modern History* (June 1972).

Royal Institute of International Affairs. *Great Britain and Palestine. Information Papers*, No. 20. Third Edition (1915–45), (London, 1946).

—— *Survey of International Affairs, 1930, 1934, 1936, 1937, 1938*.

Sacher, H. *Zionist Portraits and Other Essays* (London, 1959).

Samuel, Viscount. *Memoirs* (London, 1945).

Samuel, Horace. *Beneath the Whitewash* (London, 1930).

—— *Unholy Memories of the Holy Land* (London, 1930).

Schechtman, J. B. *Fighter and Prophet. The Vladimir Jacotinsky Story. The Last Years* (London, 1961).

Sidebotham, H. *Great Britain and Palestine* (London, 1937).

Schmidt, H. "The Nazi Party in Palestine and the Levant", *International Affairs* (1952).

Simson, H. J. *British Rule and Rebellion* (London, 1937).

Slotski, Y. *Toldot HaHaganah (History of the Haganah)*, ii (Tel Aviv, 1964).

Smith, J. A. *John Buchan* (London, 1965).

Stein, L. *The Balfour Declaration* (London, 1961).

—— *Weizmann and England* (London, 1964).

—— *Memorandum on the Disturbances of August 1929* (Jewish Agency, London, 1929).

—— *Memorandum on the Shaw Commission Report* (Jewish Agency, London, 1930).

—— *The Palestine White Paper of October, 1930* (Jewish Agency, London, 1930).

—— *Promises and Afterthoughts* (London, 1939, Jewish Agency).

Storrs, R. *Orientations* (London, 1937).

Sykes, C. *Two Studies in Virtue* (London, 1953).

—— *Orde Wingate* (London, 1959).

—— *Crossroads to Israel* (London, 1965).

Verité, M. "The Balfour Declaration and Its Makers," *Middle Eastern Studies* (Jan. 1970).

—— "The idea of the Restoration of the Jews in English Protestant Thought, 1790–1840," *Zion*, No. 3–4 (Jerusalem, 1968).

Wauchope, Sir A. G. *Impressions of Palestine* (London, 1932).

Wedgwood, C. V. *The Last of the Radicals* (London, 1951).

Wedgwood, J. C. *The Seventh Dominion* (London, 1928).

—— *American Addresses* (New York, 1926).

Weisgal, M. (editor) *Chaim Weizmann: Statesman and Scientist* (New York, 1944).

—— and Carmichael .J. *Chaim Weizmann: A Biography by Several Hands* (New York, 1963).

Weizmann, C. *Trial and Error* (London, 1950).

—— "Palestine's Role in the Solution of the Jewish Problem," *Foreign Affairs*, (Jan. 1942).

Weizmann, V. *The Impossible Takes Longer* (London, 1967).

Young, K. *Balfour* (London, 1963).

Zeine, Z. N. *The Struggle for Arab Independence* (Beirut, 1960).

Index

Abyssinia, 97; repercussions of war against, 102–5
Alanbrooke, Lord, 97
America, *see* United States
Amery, L. S., 4, 5, 15, 17, 25, 44, 45; attitude towards Dominion scheme, 78–9; 90, 123, 129, 130, 131; favours partition, 132–3; follows Weizmann's line, 139; 154, 193, 204; threatens to vote with Opposition, 207; suggestions of, 214; 221; conspicuous exception of, 222; 227
Andrews, L. Y., murdered, 144
Anglo-American Commission of Enquiry, 92
Anglo-Italian Agreement, 107–8, 113; negotiations leading to, 159
Anglo-Jewish conference, 1930–1, 21–6, 49
Anglo-Zionist relations, shattered, 17; 51; sabotaged, 77; grind to an official halt, 80; devastating blow against, 81; 82; better period for, 91; 97; Wingate on, 111; gulf develops, 126; impaired, 141–2; arrangement between, 163; agreement between unrealistic, 164; exacerbated, 179; turning point for, 209; international events overtake, 216; and Hobson's choice, 223
Anti-semitism, 100, 133
Arabs, Palestinian, 3; attitude towards self-government, 43; militant temper of, 55; present memo., 59; 61; position on self-government, 64 n; not taken seriously, 71; 75; hostility of, 84; fears of being swamped, 101; gains of, 104; 106; appeasement of, 110; no guarantee about, 115; critically analysed, 154; 157; minority in Jewish state, 160; conflict with

British and Zionists, 164; as a substantial minority, 165; 166; side with Britain's enemies, 167; attempt to reach agreement with, 167; meetings with Lord Lloyd, 170; reach agreement with, 181; 182; natural rights of, 184; 185; reject parity, 186; accept MacDonald's ideas, 188; 189; veto suggestion, 191; extreme demands of, 197; disgruntled, 203
Arab delegations, deadlock with government, 9; 44, 46, 64, 72; no agreement on composition of, 180; agreement with, 182
Arab Higher Committee, 123, 125, 126; conditions of, 146 n
Arab Kings or Rulers, intervention of, 125–6; opposition of, 151; brought in, 169; informal discussions with, 187
Arab-Zionist relations, 81, 87; to resolve in wider framework, 102; agreement between highly unlikely, 162; co-operation between, 191; serious negotiations between, 195; 202
Arlosoroff, C., 53, 55; searching analysis by, 79; 94 n
Asquith, H. H., 97, 98
Atatürk, contacts with Zionists, 112
Attlee C., 131; shocked at partition, 132

Backstansky, L., 89
Baldwin, S., 10, 17, 19; leadership attacked, 34; 57; 104, 123, 125, 157
Balfour, A. J., 2, 3, 6; and Jewish state, 72; 93 n; and American mandate, 99; 159, 227
Balfour declaration, 4, 18, 19, 45, 54, 71; as foundation stone of British rule, 99; complex motives behind,

99; policy of, 100; 101; as an historic piece of paper, 133; abandonment of, 169; still stands, 172; 177 n; secret behind, 183; 184, 188, 221
Ball, Sir J., 214
Ben Gurion, D., 51, 52, 56, 57, 58; appears before Peel commission, 82; instinctive reaction to partition, 83, 94 n; rift with Weizmann, 130; favours partition, 133; fulminates, 137; reports to executive, 167; converses with Lord Lloyd, 170; long tirade by, 184; proposes solutions, 185; 186, 188, 192, 193, 208, 216; willing to compromise, 218 n; Histadruth at fingertips of, 225
Bevin, E., 37, 38, 39
Bi-Nationalism, 53, 66 n; proponents of oppose partition, 149 n
Blum, L., favours partition, 128; 129, 131, 162
Board of Deputies, 89
Brith Shalom movement, 44, 49, 65 n, 66 n
British Empire, 5, 72, 73, 74, 76, 77, 78, 81, 82, 83, 84, 86, 90, 91, 93 n; and communications of, 97; 98; 100; great danger facing, 107; authority challenged, 133; moral principles of, 141; breach with Moslem world, 153
Brodetsky, Professor S., 85
Brown, E., 152
Buchan, J., 6, 10, 87, 88, 221
Bullit, W., 192

Cabinet sub-committee, 20, 21; and terms of reference of, 22; 23, 49, 50
Cadogan, Sir A., and utter ignorance of Zionism of, 159; 168
Cairo Embassy, as clearing house for anti-partition agitation, 157; presses the Arab case, 157–8; cabal at, 202
Canterbury, Archbishop of, valuable contribution of, 139; 213
Cazalet, V., 129, 131, 132, 154; urges postponement, 195; threatens to vote against government, 196; 221
Cecil, Lord R., 64, 99
Chamberlain, Sir A., 17, 26, 62
Chamberlain, J., 92 n
Chamberlain, N., 102, 106, 107, 108, 109, 137, 140; knows nothing about Palestine, 153; 156, 157, 159, 172, 179, 181; opens conference, 183; 192;

depressed, 193; startled, 202, 210; 216, 217
Chancellor, Sir J., 11, 24; and representative government, 44; 46, 47, 48, 50; relationship with Zionists, 53
Chatfield, Admiral, 107
Churchill, W. L. S., 18, 42, 43, 62; principal guest at dinner-party, 131; emphatically disapproves of partition, 132; polemics of, 133; 139; explains folly of partition, 144; ardour of explained, 148 n; 153; expounds own plan, 172; roused to anger, 207; 221
Ciano, Count, 108
Colonial Office, 2, 3, 10; conspires with Palestine administration, 11, 22; transfer of Middle East from, 23; 24, 25, 26, 27, 41, 49, 51, 144, 215
Conservatives, 8, 18, 19, 45, 62; government of 1922, 99
Conway, Sir M., 5, 76
Coupland, Professor R., 85; proposes federal partition, 127–8; 129; discloses scheme, 130–1; and federal plan, 212–13; 214
Cripps, Sir S., 37; plan of, 126; 128
Cunliffe-Lister, Sir P., 55, 56, 57, 101, 104, 123
Curzon, Lord, 99

Dawson, G., 212, 213
De Bunsen Committee, 98
Deedes, Sir W., 72
Development Schemes, 8, 12; guaranteed loan for, 15; 24, 25, 51, 61; revived, 185
Drummond, see Perth
Duff Cooper, A., 84
Dufferin, Lord, intervenes in debate, 207–8, 210
Dugdale, B. E. C., 2, 17, 25, 45, 57; optimism of, 60; 62; conducts vendetta against Thomas, 63–4; 85, 86, 87, 88, 90; 94 n, 107; on Wingate, 111; 123, 124, 129, 130, 131, 133; sees Peel report, 134; smooths matters over, 137; influences Ormsby Gore, 138; 140, 141, 142, 144, 145, 151, 154; and 'Hindenburg line', 155; confirms suspicions about Cairo embassy, 157; 158, 163, 164, 166, 170, 181, 186, 187, 188, 190, 196; active in organising debates, 204–5; interviews MacDonald, 206; 211–12,

214, 215; as outstanding example, 221, 227

Eban, A., 217
Eden, A., 85, 86, 102, 103, 129, 143, 151, 152; resigns, 156, 166
Egypt, 45; 1936 treaty with Great Britain, 102; 151; 203
Einstein, A., 162
Elliot, W., 5, 6, 19, 63, 85–6, 87, 88, 112, 124, 129, 134, 137, 140, 142, 145, 151, 152; and "Hindenburg line", 155; 162, 163; and Tel Aviv concentration camp, 164; 170, 181, 187, 190; on government's aims, 191; 192; tainted with Zionism, 195–6; powerful attempt by to revise policy, 201; 204–5, 215, 216, 217 n, 227
Evian conference, 208, 218 n

Federalism, 171, 184, 185, 190–1, 194, 201, 206, 212; scheme set out, 213; when to use scheme, 214; monopolises picture, 216; 217 n
Foreign Office, 22; transfer of Middle East to, 23; 26, 108; attacks partition, 151, 156, 157, 159, 161
France, 99, 102; offered two divisions, 109; 110; unwillingness of, 131

Germany, 100, 115, 151, 165; pogrom in, 179; occupies Memel, 193; occupies Prague, 195
Goldman, Dr. N., 105
Graves, P., 29, 85
Great Britain, 9; demonstrations against, 17, 80; decisions of departmentalised, 63; receptive to Zionism, 71; protector of the National Home, 72, 75; attitude towards Dominion scheme, 77–8; 81, 84, 85; position in eastern Mediterranean, 86, 87; misgivings of, 90, 91; and strategy in Near East, 97 passim; reconsiders policy, 99; as guardian of Jewish immigration, 100; dilemma for, 101–2; relations with Egypt, 102; interests demand a peaceful Mediterranean, 102; 103; decline in prestige of, 104; under pressure from Italy, 105–7; military problems of, 109–11; interests of coincidence with Jews, 112; and Turkey, 113; reliance on Arab countries, 114–15; accurate prognosis of, 115; ignores France,

131; weakened international position of, 133; policy of, 139; dissatisfaction of, 140; determination of, 145; change in policy of, 151; reversal of policy, 156; reasons for reversal, 158; considers injurious solution, 162; and agreement with Arabs and Jews, 163; as an honest broker, 164; clarifies policy, 165; 167; consults with MacMichael, 169; obligations of, 170; and zonal solution, 170; indecision of, 172; buries the mandate, 180; and need to placate Arabs, 181; gradations in policy of, 182; as spokesman for Arabs, 183; not impose solution, 184; and unbridgeable gap with Jews, 186; wary of American opinion, 187; insure Palestine policy with U.S., 187; clarifies policy, 187–8; endemic suspicion of, 190; final proposals of, 194; and discussions with Arab states, 196–7; no change in policy of, 201; and collapse of relations with J. A., 204; undistinguished performance of, 207; nominal victory of, 208; acute dilemma for, 209; baffled by extra-European nationalism, 210; uneasy over stalemate, 213; cancels immigration quota, 214; bitterly attacked, 215; Jews fight by side of, 216; 217; 218 n; interests of coincide with Zionists', 221; and difficulties in criticising Palestine policy of, 223; and inability to understand Zionism, 226–7
Grey, Sir E., 98
Grossman, M., 142

Haganah, memo. of, 108, 114; cooperation with, 110; policy of, 111
Hague Court, 204, 210
Haifa, 86, 87, 101; fleet based on, 102; advantages of, 103; as base for light naval forces, 107; 134, 142; garrisoned by 2 million Jews, 145
Hailsham, Lord, 18
Haining, General, 110, 111, 159, 202
Halifax, Lord, 86, 109, 112; advocates administrative necessity, 115; 129; talks with Hitler, 156, 174 n; impresses Weizmann, 159; 168; meets Weizmann, 169; 172; on conference's purpose, 179; 181, 183, 195,

213; supports MacDonald, 219–20; 227
Hall, J., 37–8
Hamilton, Sir H., 5
Hammond, Sir L., 127
Hankey, Sir M., 97, 212
Harlech, *see* Ormsby Gore
Hashomer Hatzair, 66 n
Henderson, A., 4; chairman of Anglo-Jewish conference, 21; 22; tired and overworked, 23; 25, 26, 27, 39, 49
Herzl, T., 71, 92 n
Hexter, Dr. M., 20, 23, 25
Hitler, 100; talks with Halifax, 156; 174 n; 196, 203
Hoare, Sir S., 103
Hope Simpson, Sir J., 8, 9, 11, 12, 14; perturbed at Jewish policy, 15; report of, 15; 16, 17, 48
Hore Belisha, L., 76, 88, 109, 172, 205
Hos, D., 37
Hudson, A. V. M., 89
Hull, C., 168
Husaini faction, 44; 67 n, 180
Husaini, Haj Amin al, 104, 131, 155, 156, 157, 202

Ibn Saud, 151
Immigration, quota, 2, 3, 8; suspension of, 11; 12; release of certificates of, 14, 38; limitation of, 15; unprecedented heights of, 28; 37; temporary suspension of, 43; 45, 46, 50, 57, 125; restrictions in, 60; 101; far-reaching changes in basis of, 125; 126, 129, 130, 134; political restrictions on, 137–8; 153, 154, 163; ascending scale of, 164; abandonment of, 165; cautiously applied, 166; restrictions on, 167; no stoppage of, 169; 170, 171, 172; and refugee children, 179; end of, 180; and MacDonald's plans, A and B, 181–2; as the crucial question, 184; proposals about elaborated, 185; and veto, 186; and five-year plan, 187; actual figures regarding, 188; exact nature of, 189; restrictions and Arab veto decided upon, 191–2; veto on blocks compromise, 192; final terms on, 194; 208; cancellation of quota of, 214; 215
India, and Moslems, 10; 18, 45; Moslems in, 101; 104; shortcomings of army of, 109; 165

Inskip, Sir T., 103, 181
Iraq, 45, 55, 97, 114, 151
Ironside, General, 110
Italy, 97, 99; as major threat to Great Britain in Mediterranean, 102; 103; exploits Arab rebellion, 104–5; 107, 108; and Bari broadcasts, 118 n; 151; relations with Great Britain, 156; 159, 165; occupies Albania, 193; 201

Jabotinsky, V., 52, 76; enthusiastic for Dominion scheme, 77
Janner, B., 38
Jerusalem, 86, 101, 134, 138, 139, 163, 172
Jewish Agency for Palestine, 21, 22; not consulted, 24; 25, 26, 39, 47; meeting of executive of, 56, 156–57; refuses to co-operate, 60; 105, 155, 189; decides to break conference, 190; given full authority, 191; conditions of, 191; 197 n; and collapse in relations with government, 204; 213; co-operates with Great Britain, 217
Jewish Chronicle, 38, 51; supports Dominion scheme, 76; 80; opposes partition, 135
Jewish National Home, conception of, 14; resolution in favour of, 18; 22; 24; consolidation of, 28; 38, 41, 52; three-pronged attack upon, 60; 63; ultimate development of, 71; 75, 78, 79–80; conception of, 81–2; 101, 105, 110, 141; minority status for, 151; liquidation of, 153; crystallisation of, 169; obligations towards, 171; policy towards still stands, 172; precise meaning of, 184; 189, 222

Kennedy, J., 168, 195, 196; sets government's mind at rest, 205–6
Kenworthy, Commander J., 17, 18, 27, 76, 92, 221
Kerr, P., *see* Lothian

Labour, Government of 1929, 5, 6; deadlocks with Arabs, 9; statement of policy of, 12; protests against, 12; 18–19, 45; Government of 1945, 210
Labour party, 8, 18–19, 38, 39, 61, 62, 63, 215
Lampson, Sir M., 104; influenced by Smart, 157; 158, 183, 202, 203
Land, settlement and sales, 3, 8, 12, 14; limitations in, 15; 25, 46; restrictions

in contemplated, 49; 50; restrictions
in, 60, 181, 182, 191; 61, 126, 154,
163; prohibition of, 179, 180; 184,
185; prohibited, restricted and unrestricted zones, 186; final terms on,
194
Laski, Professor H., 16, 20, 39
League of Nations, 3, 27, 78, 81, 82, 83,
84; and sanctions policy, 102; 143,
169, 206, 210, 211
Legislative Council, 24, 41 passim, 51,
53, 54, 55, 56, 57; main features of
scheme, 58; 59; privileges regarding,
61; 62, 64, 184
Liberal, party, 18, 19, 38, 39, 62
Liddel Hart, B., agrees with Haganah
memo., 110; gives warning of, 114
Lloyd, Lord, as an honest broker, 170
Lloyd George, D., 6, 10, 18, 19; and
divided party, 34; and Jewish state,
72; 98; wishes to retain spoils of war,
117 n, 131, 139, 221, 227
Loraine, Sir P., 113
Lothian, Lord, 213
Lourie, A., 90
Lugard, Lord, 212, 213
Luke, H., 9, 29

MacDonald, Malcolm, 11; gives re-
assurances, 12; 13, 14; as the indispensable link, 20; genuinely sympathetic to Zionism, 21; 24, 25; thanked
for consistent work and friendship,
27; 51; as a staunch friend, 57; 58;
and beginning of rift with Zionists',
67 n; 112, 114, 115; replaces Ormsby
Gore, 160; tests Weizmann's reactions, 161–2; and snap visit to
Palestine, 162–3; still favours partition, 163; ideas crystallise, 163–8;
and emergency programme, 165;
and no Jewish state, Jews must go
slow, 167; no faith in Woodhead
commission, 168; pacifies U.S. concern, second thoughts about immigration, 169; denies appeasing Arabs,
170; 171, 172, 179; as a moderate
factor, 180; memo. of, 181; intentions
of, 182; presents Arab case, 183–4;
details his proposals, 184; elaborates
immigration proposals, 185; 186;
retreats from original ideas, 187–8,
189; becomes persona non grata, 190;
191, 192; standing with Zionists, 193;

ends conference, 194; 195; keeps
pressure on Zionists, 196; 197 n; and
anti-Jewish remarks, 199 n; invites
Weizmann to dinner, 202–3; displays
great indignance, 203; cannot defend
policy, 204; 205; sees Mrs. Dugdale,
206; 207, 208; considers federalism,
212; 214; asked how to implement
policy, 215; 216, 227
MacDonald, Ramsay, 3, 6, 7; attitude
to Shaw report, 7; 8, 9, 10, 11; and
impatient with Zionists', 12; 15, 17,
18, 19; tired and overworked, 20; 21,
22, 24, 26; letter of, 27, 50, 101,
210; evaluation of letter, 28; and
Anglo-American relations, 32; 49, 51,
52; telegram of, 56; 57; promise of,
182; 206
MacMahon-Hussein correspondence,
98; MacMahon's explanation of,
116 n; and conflict of policies, 165
MacMichael, Sir H., sympathy of, and
creation of a 'nucleus', 160; 163;
consults with government about
eventual settlement, 169
Magnus, Dr. J. L., 44
Marcus, Major, 18, 39
Marks, S., 123
May White Paper, 28, 91, 115, 187;
outline of, 188; terms of, 194; postponement of consideration of draft of,
196; 201 passim; copy of given to
U.S., 205; published, receives bad
press, 206; as a traumatic shock,
208; as a temporary aberration, 209;
as a "turning-point", 209–10; to be
put into refrigeration, 217; 221, 222
Meinertzhagen, Colonel R., 2
Melchett, 1st Lord, Alfred Mond,
resigns, 17
Melchett, 2nd Lord, Henry Mond, 38,
62; as a guiding-light, 85; 86, 87, 88;
ceases Zionist activity, 89; 145, 152
Morrison, H., 108
Mufti, The, see Husaini, Haj Amin al
Munich, settlement at, 109; effect on
Zionist affairs, 165; lessons to be
drawn from, 190; collapse of, 193
Mussolini, 105, 196

Namier, Professor L. B., 9, 13, 16, 21,
22, 24, 25; strained relations with
Zionists, 36 n; 51, 52, 54, 61, 126;
drafts memo., 129; 131, 137, 140,

142; against participation in conference, 180

Nashashibi faction, 44, 67 n, 180

Noel Baker, P., 39

Norwich, Lord, *see* Duff Cooper

Nuri Sa'id, conversations with Ormsby Gore, and Haj Amin al Husaini, 155; 156, 170

Ormsby Gore, W., 5, 64, 85; extraordinary request of, 87; 88, 89, 107, 124; recommends not to suspend immigration, 125; 129, 133, 134; refuses Weizmann an advance copy of Report, 136–7; difficulties as colonial secretary, 137; 138; gives no specific undertaking, 139; 140, 142; vulnerable position of, and temporary breach with Weizmann, 143; 144, 151; hints at resignation, 152; 153, 154; conversations with Nuri, 155; difficulties in office, 157; leaves office, 160; 166, 221, 227

Orts, M., 211

Ottoman Empire, 97, 98

Oxford, *see* Asquith

Palestine, Administration, Weizmann complains about, 1; 2, 7; conspires with colonial office, 10, 11; and unholy alliance with colonial office, 22; 24, 25, 27; exerts pressure on government, 47; 48, 49, 52, 55; conduct of, 58; endemic suspicion against, 59; crushing indictment of, 75; 77, 83, 84; riots directed against, 101; 134; need to restore authority of, 144; need to escape from, 153; new partition scheme of, 156; as tenthrate, 160; 161; utter confusion in, 163; ritual condemnation of, 165; for curtailing Zionist work, 172–3; 179, 180; prevent *fait accompli* by, 214–15

Palestine Crown Colony Association, 83–4, 90

Palestine, Mandate for, 2, 18, 19, 21, 22; intended to serve Zionist interests, 41; 44, 45, 52, 54, 59, 72, 78, 81; termination of, 82; 83; retention of, 87; 90; and British policy, 91; 100, 101; retreat from, 110; and Peel commission, 124; end of, 129; perseverance in, 133; 153; resurrection

of, 164; and Munich crisis, 165; revival of, 166; formal restoration of, 167; no modification of without U.S. consent, 168; reinterpretation of, 169; international character of, 169; to be conservatively applied, 171; to be modified, 172–3; 180; 184; termination of, 187; 188, 191, 210, 211

Panel, The, meets in atmosphere of uncertainty, 182; rejects proposals, 185; prepared for concessions, 186; and unbridgeable gap with government, 186; informal discussions with, 187; decides to break conference, 188; debates events, 189; dissolves, 190–1; 197 n, 199 n

Parity, 43, 51, 52, 53, 54, 55, 56, 57, 58, 59, 181; as a Zionist conception, 182; rejected, 186; ruled out, 187

Parliamentary pro-Palestine group, set up and purpose of, 5, 59; ineffectiveness of, 193; holds a meeting, 196; a good meeting of, 215

Partition, 82, 84, 85, 86, 87, 89, 90, 91, 106, 107, 108; buried, 114; 123 *passim*; first hint of, 126–7; objections to, 133; given unenthusiastic reception, 139; 142; government undecided about, 143; folly of, 144; *volte face* in policy of, 145; minority opposition to, 149 n; 151 *passim*; only imposed by force, 151; coalition against, 152; 153; new scheme of, 156; goes by the board, 163; abandonment of, 165; preliminary conversations about, 167; dropped, 170; 185, 213; as crucial issue of period, 222

Passfield, Lord, 1, 2, 3, 4, 7, 8; breaks word, 9; and insufficient control over officials, 11; 14, 15, 16, 18, 19; gives ultimatum, 24; rumours about resignation of, 26; and inept handling of crisis, 26; reluctant to meet Weizmann, 29; has mind of German professor, 33; 46, 47, 48, 137

Passfield white paper, 10; adequate discussion of, 16; shatters Anglo-Zionist relations, 17; validity of, 18; roundly condemned, 19; 22–8, 37, 39, 49, 50, 52; repetition of, 60, 81; exploited, 222

Peel Commission, 82, 84, 86, 87, 106,

123 *passim*; begins enquiries, 126; 127; courage of, 129; 130, 131, 132; quandary of, 140; 144; commissioners and terms of reference of, 147 n; proposes partition and kills the mandate, 154; proposes too much, 155; 183; commissioners of promote federalism, 206, 212

Peel Commission, Report of, 72, 82, 87, 107; retreat from, 110; 134, 136; published, 137; 139, 141; alleged unanimity of, 148 n; attacked, 151; 159, 164; as forerunner to May white paper, 208

Percy, Lord E., 61

Perlzweig, Rev. M., 89

Permanent Mandates Commission, 9, 15, 44, 53, 129, 207; to be exploited as wedge against government, 210–11; adjudicates on May white paper, 211–12

Perth, Lord, 108

Plymouth, Earl of, 61

Poland, and international crisis, 193

Rappard, Professor, 129, 211, 213

Reading, Lord, 15, 16, 189

Rendel, Sir G. W., inspires attack against partition, 107–8; as real author of memo., 151

Revisionists, 13, 52; support Dominion scheme, 76; 80, 92

Riots, of 1921, 43; of 1929, 1, 44, *80*; repetition of, 124; of 1933, 101; and rebellion of 1936, 64; and general strike, 82; 104; 123 *passim*; and guerrilla operations, 125; end of strike, 126; 153; lessons to be drawn from, 183

Roosevelt, F. D., 187; doubts concerning May white paper, 205

Rothschild, Sir James de, 5, 131

Round Table Conference, 3, 22, 48, 51, 52, 169, 176 n; to be convened, 187; idea dropped, 191

Royal Commission, *see* Peel

Rutenberg, P., proposals of, 14–15; plan of, 46–7; 48; works of, 129, 134, 138

Saadabad Pact, 114

Sacher, H., 45

St. James's Conference, 115; agenda of, 169; 171, 177–95; watershed of, 188–90; deadlock at, 192; dying stages of, 193; 205

Samuel, Viscount, 5; attitude towards self-government, 43; 44; threatens to resign, 65 n; advocates restoration of Jews in Palestine, 98; authoritative speech of, 139; views of gaining ground, 140; 207

Seventh Dominion League, 71 *passim*; ideas of received by public, 75; inauguration of, 75; aims of, 76; as a Zionist pressure group, 78; attraction of, 80; breaks up, 80; cedes from politics, 81; does not die, 82; 83, 84, 85, 87; adopted by Anglo-Jewry, 98; 90, 91, 92, 100

Shaw, Commission, 2; exceeds terms of reference, 3, 5; 6, 9, 45, 80; And Report, confirms worst expectations, 7; 8, 12; second thoughts about, 29; summary of, 31 n; Zionist rebuttal of, 31

Shertok, M., 58; brings disquieting news, 123; 130, 186, 188, 194; outlines basic requirements of federal scheme, 212; 215

Shiels, Dr. D., 6, 13, 23, 47, 48, 76

Shuckburgh, Sir J., 42, 46, 163; develops "germ" idea, 164

Sidebotham, H., 129

Simon, Sir J., 18, 144

Sinclair, Sir A., 10, 76, 131, 132, 139, 145, 201, 221

Smart, W., links with Palestine nationalists, 157; as *eminence grise*, 158; 174 n

Smuts, Field-Marshal J., explains meaning of Balfour declaration, 4; influence over a British cabinet, 5; 6, 8, 18; dissatisfied with Passfield white paper, 34; asked to come to Europe, 192; expresses sympathy and kind words, 193; 199 n, 227

Snell, Lord, minority report of, 31; 38; motion by, 61

Snowden, P., 15; and Mrs. Snowdon, 89

Special Night Squads, activities and organisation of, 111

Stein, L., 21, 22, 25, 66 n, 85, 142

Swinton, *see* Cunliffe-Lister

Sykes, Sir M., 227

Sykes-Picot Agreement, 98

Syria, 55, 131, 169

Tegart, Sir C., 163
Tel Aviv, 101, 208
Thomas, J. H., 24, 59; no basis in assurances of, 60; would prefer scheme dropped, 61; in dying stages of long career, 63; 64, 123, 124
The Times, 6, 8, 9, 12, 17, 19, 75, 85, 168; promotes federalism, 206; 212, 214
TransJordan, 15, 22, 24, 45
Turkey, 86, 98, 102, 103; as key to eastern Mediterranean security, 111–14; 201
Tweedsmuir, *see* Buchan

Uganda, 92 n
United Nations, 91
United States, 11, 81, 94 n; retreats from overseas commitments, 135; 153; and relations with Great Britain, 156; 162; Zionist activity in, 168; 170; pro-Zionist lobby in, 186–7; encouraging messages from, 187; 192; Zionist pressure in, 195; presses for delay, 196; 202; copy of white paper given to, 205; will stand by British government, 205; can save situation, 211; influence of public opinion in, 222; ambivalent position of 223; Jewry in, 225
Ussishkin, M., 135, 216

Vansittart, Sir R., 23

Wailing Wall, 1; incident at, 28–9
Warburg, F., 10; resignation of, 17
Wauchope, Sir A., and Passfield pledge, 50; 52, 53, 54, 55, 56, 57, 58; blind logic of, 59; breach with, 60; initiative of, 61; threatens to resign, 63; powers of, 67 n; presses for Royal Commission, 123; presses for temporary suspension of immigration, 125; 126; supports partition, 130
Wavell, General A., 111; on Zionism and Wingate, 120 n
Webb, *see* Passfield
Wedgwood, Colonel J., 2; as chairman of parliamentary group, 5; 59; slays Palestine constitution, 62; 64; publishes *Seventh Dominion*, 73; 74, 75, 76, 77, 78, 79, 80, 81, 82, 89, 90, 91, 92, 100; assails Cripps plan, 126; 131, 132, 139; detects another appease-ment, 172; advocates civil resistance, 184–5; 198 n, 221
Weizmann, C., 1; hints at resignation, 3, 7, 11; 4, 5; conception of Zionism, 6; lambasts administration, 7; wary of government intentions, 8; makes out case, 8; indignant, 9; contends situation untenable, 10; on Anglo-Zionist relations, 12; 13; contacts with Passfield, 14; 15; voices objections to Passfield white paper, 16; resigns, 17; 18, 20, 21, 22, 23, 24, 25, 26, 27, 28, 29, 39, 42, 44, 45, 46, 47, 48, 49, 50; comes under heavy attack, 50–1; 52, 53; subtleties of, bitter mood of, 54; 55, 56, 57, 58, 59, 60, 61, 62, 63, 67 n; attitude to Jewish state, 71, 72; 79, 84, 85, 86, 88, 89, 90, 91, 92, 92 n; argues for British protectorate, 99; 101; on effects of Abyssinian war, 104; 105, 106, 107; on Wingate, 111; on role of Turkey, 111–14; opposes Peel commission, 123, 124; 125, 126; sceptical about partition, 127, 128; enthusiastic for partition, 128, 129; considers a halt in immigration, 129; rift with Ben Gurion, 130; 131; puts case for partition, 132; 133, 134; attacks anti-partitionists, pleads for unity, 135; limitations on diplomacy of, 136; refused advance copy of Report, 136–7; impression of Report, 138, 139; key speech at Congress, 140; attacked, 142; breach with Ormsby Gore, relations with Gentile politicians, 143; 144; succumbs to false sense of security, 145; 151; believes in partition, 153; criticises Arab nationalism, 154; commitment to partition, 154–5; diplomatic style of limited, 157; 158; diplomatic exertions of, 159; 160; and Woodhead commission, 159–61, 163; discussions with M. MacDonald, 161–2; and apocalyptic programme, 162; 164; takes offence, 165; 166; militant reaction of, 167; collapse of political philosophy of, 168; meets Halifax, 169; puts forward conditions, 170–1, 172; formulates new Zionist policy, 173, 174 n; threatens non-co-operation, 179; attitude softens, 180; welcomes delegates,

182–3; defines Jewish policy, 183; 184, 185; unwilling to break conference, 186; 188, 189, 190; on Jewish quandary, 191; flies to Paris, 192; vents anger against MacDonald, 193; terminates conference negotiations, 194–5; urges postponement, 195; and Arab contacts, 199–200 n; 201; describes situation in Palestine, 202; relationship with MacDonald destroyed, 203–4; thanks Churchill, 207; 209; and Permanent Mandates Commission, 211; 212; and Coupland, 213; 214, 215; bids farewell, 216–17; aim of, 217; willing to compromise, 218 n; 221; favours partition, 222; an evaluation of, 223–7; political style of, 223; relations with English Gentiles, 223–4; his appeal to the English, 224; solves a Gentile quandry, 225; changed position of, 225–7; relies on party support, 226; captive to international crises, 226; no alternative to, 226; 227

Welles, S., 195

Whitechapel, by election in, 37–9

Williams, T., 139, 204; moves amendment, 207

Wingate, O., 110–11

Winterton, Earl, 172

Wise, Rabbi S., opposes partition, 135; 144

Wood, see Halifax

Woodhead Commission, 91, 95 n, 143–4; Zionists unhappy about, 144; terms of reference of, 151; final decision about, 153; as the Re-Peel commission, 154; 159; uneasiness of, 160; calibre and tasks of, 160–1; 162, 163; report of, 164; unacceptable proposals of, 165; unable to produce report, 168; 170; reports and conclusions of, 171; 174–5 n

Yishuv, 28; opposes self-government, 44; 56, 79, 83, 85, 91; key role of in imperial defence, 108, 110; 180; safeguards for, 191; develops as national entity, 225–6

Zionist Congress, of 1931, 51, 52, 57, 59; of 1935, 59; of 1937, 133, 140–1, 142; of 1939, 216–17

Zionist Federation, 89

Zionists, fear government intentions, 3; scope of contacts of, 6; attack Shaw report, 7; satisfactory position of, 8; 10, 12; deficiency in diplomacy of, 13; 14; and Palestine to remain above party loyalties, 18; 19, 22, 24, 26; and MacDonald letter, 27; bête noire of, 28; complain of indifference to letter, 28; objections to self-government, 41–2; 43; no concessions by, 47; unanimity of, 49; satisfaction of, 53; 55, 56; tactics of, 57; time working in favour of, 57; minor tactical victory for, 58; 59; swamped by problems, 60; no plan of campaign by, 61; 62; come of age and double-dealing, 71, 92 n; 75; setbacks for, 80; 82, 92; argued for British protectorate, caught in cleft stick, 101; contacts with Italians, 105; concerned over Italian talks, 107; 108, 110; Wingate's advice to, 111; contacts with Atatürk, 112–14; 115; hostile to Peel commission, 124; fears about immigration, 125; object to outside intervention, 126; generally accept Weizmann's views, 129; unequal to task, 130; lay down minimum requirements, 133–4; oppose partition, 135; display utter confusion, 137; given another enquiry, 138; did work too well, 140; 141; estranged from government, 143; suspect Woodhead commission, 144; wish to improve scheme, 145; given an impossible hand to play, 156; believe in conspiracy theory, 158; relieved at MacDonald appointment, 160; attitude to Woodhead commission, 160–1; solution injurious to, 162; tenacity of, 165; face-saving formula for, 166; set too hard a pace, 167; active in U.S., 168; on zonal solution, 170; cannot accept proposals, 171; devise new policy, 173; 179; feeling against, 180; 182; reject proposals, 185; prepared for concessions, 186; overrate agitation in U.S., 186–7; informal discussions with, 187; decide to break conference, 188; exploit clerk's error, 190; 194; press for postponement, 195; ride on crest of international events,

196; readiness to compromise, 198 n; objectives of, 201; and collapse in relations with government, 204; put pressure on press, 206; white paper no surprise to, 208; emotional strain of, 208–9; attitude to white paper, 209–10; opt for federalism, 212; plans scotched, 214–15; stand with Great Britain, 216; interests coincide, 221; display little self-restraint, 222; exaggerate importance of own contacts, 222–3; thrown back upon themselves, 223; key to militancy of, 226; still had voice in cabinet, 227

Zionists, Gentile, ix, 2, 44; initiative of, 61; outpace Zionist leadership, 62; 71, 72; motivations of, 73–5; 80, 82; favour continuance of mandate, 84–5; differences with Zionists, 85; 89, 92; instinctive dislike of partition, 126, 130, 133, 139; Weizmann's success with, 143; 144; hostile towards partition, 149 n; can do little, 192; decline in influence of, 221; reject partition, 222; become less effective, 223; dichotomy in motivation of, 225